Finance for Dentists

T0304044

Finance for Dentists

THE ESSENTIAL HANDBOOK

PAUL KENDALL
Founder and former Chairman
National Association of Specialist Dental Accountants
Partner, Dodd & Co Chartered Accountants, Penrith

CRC Press
Taylor & Francis Group
Boca Raton London New York

CRC Press is an imprint of the
Taylor & Francis Group, an **informa** business

CRC Press
Taylor & Francis Group
6000 Broken Sound Parkway NW, Suite 300
Boca Raton, FL 33487-2742

CRC Press is an imprint of Taylor & Francis Group, an Informa business
No claim to original U.S. Government works

Visit the Taylor & Francis Web site at
http://www.taylorandfrancis.com

and the CRC Press Web site at
http://www.crcpress.com

British Library Cataloguing in Publication Data

A catalogue record for this book is available from the British Library.

ISBN-13: 978 184619 359 0

Typeset by Pindar NZ, Auckland, New Zealand
Printed and bound by TJI Digital, Padstow, Cornwall, UK

Contents

About the author

Paul Kendall is a Chartered Accountant in practice, who has been advising dentists on financial and tax issues for more than 25 years. He is the founder and former Chairman of the National Association of Specialist Dental Accountants and is often asked to contribute to dental publications. He is the author of *Dentists: An Industry and Auditing Guide*, which provides details of the specialist financial needs of dentists for the benefit of accountants in practice. He is a partner in Dodd & Co Chartered Accountants, based in Penrith, and deals with dentists and orthodontists in the North of England and Scotland.

Abbreviations

Within this book, for the sake of brevity, a number of abbreviations have been used. These are set out below in the order in which they appear in the book.

NHS	National Health Service
GDC	General Dental Council
DCPs	dental care professionals
NASDA	National Association of Specialist Dental Accountants
ICAEW	Institute of Chartered Accountants in England and Wales
HMRC	HM Revenue & Customs
PAYE	Pay-as-you-earn
UDAs	units of dental activity
BACS	Bankers' Automated Clearing Services
BDA	British Dental Association
ACCA	Association of Chartered Certified Accountants
VAT	Value Added Tax
PCT	primary care trust
VDPs	vocational dental practitioners
CPD	continuing professional development
NVQ	national vocational qualification
DDRB	Doctors and Dentists Pay Review Body
CGT	Capital Gains Tax
PDS	personal dental services
GDS	general dental services
PCOs	primary care organisations
BUPA	British Union Provident Association
DoH	Department of Health
SHA	strategic health authority
LHB	local health board
LHCC	local healthcare cooperative

HSSB	health and social service board
CoTs	courses of treatment
LDC	local dental committee
DPB	Dental Practice Board
GDPs	general dental practitioners
SIPP	self-invested personal pension
IFA	independent financial adviser
RICS	The Royal Institute of Chartered Surveyors
NHSPS	NHS Pension Scheme
NICs	National Insurance contributions
ESI	Employment Status Indicator
CARE	career average revalued earnings
AP	additional pension
MPAVCs	money purchase additional voluntary contributions

CHAPTER 1

Introduction

Most dentists starting out in practice know very little about finance and can often miss out on extra profits and tax savings as a result of that lack of knowledge. The reason for this is that the majority of dental schools will only provide a brief introduction to dental finances to their students, with the content of that introduction not being enough to provide them with sufficient knowledge of the accounting, taxation and pension issues pertinent to their profession. As a result they can become reliant upon accountants and financial advisers to run their businesses which can increase their costs, but also can result in the appointment of advisers with little specialist knowledge of the profession, with all the problems that can arise as a consequence of that appointment.

THE AIM OF THE BOOK

The aim of this book is to provide dentists, whether in practice or planning to start up a practice, with sufficient knowledge to take an active role in their own finances. It also aims to give them an insight into the level of knowledge that they would expect to receive from a specialist financial adviser to the dental profession.

WHAT TOPICS WILL BE COVERED?

This book provides a comprehensive analysis of dental finance with detailed appendices that will provide useful reference material for the dentist in practice (Appendices 4–19 are available at www.radcliffe-oxford.com/financefordentists). The topics covered include the following.

➤ A brief overview of the current dental profession along with a look at the changes that may affect dentists and their patients in the next few years.

➤ The details of the income and expenditure that are included in the average dentist's set of accounts, with detailed key performance indices to enable dentists to benchmark their practice. This detail will also provide the information needed by dentists new to the profession to prepare budgets as part of an application for bank borrowing.

➤ An explanation of practice goodwill and other items included on the typical practice balance sheet. A detailed example is also included of the transactions which would usually make up the capital and current accounts of dentists in practice.

➤ Detail of the NHS contract in England and Wales and a brief comparison with the NHS contracts offered to dentists in Northern Ireland and Scotland.

➤ Details of the income earned by private practices and how they compare with NHS practices.

➤ An overview of the options available to dentists in respect of the provision and financing of their surgery premises.

➤ Details of the issues that need to be dealt with when buying or setting up a practice, including an explanation of the financing options available.

➤ Details of the differences between partnerships and expense-sharing arrangements, and the legal and accounting issues that need to be addressed when working with other dentists.

➤ Details of the staffing issues that affect dentists in practice and a look at the options available when 'employing' associates, technicians and hygienists.

➤ An explanation of the UK tax system and how it affects dentists, along with details of tax-saving measures, including the incorporation of the dental practice.

➤ Details of the superannuation scheme and how the pension is calculated, along with details of the differences in the two NHS superannuation schemes currently operating for dentists in practice.

The appendices include copies of the contracts and forms that the dentist will need to complete on a regular basis, along with detailed guidance on the completion of those documents (*see* www.radcliffe-oxford.com/financefordentists).

The examples of accounts, taxation workings and other items shown in the following chapters have been created purely for illustrative purposes, and do not refer to any particular practice. While every care has been taken to ensure that the detail is correct at the time of publication, legislation does change frequently and readers are advised to seek expert advice before following any of the recommendations included in this book.

There are a number of publications, journals and websites that are accessible and which provide further details of the topics covered in this book. A list of these can be found in Appendix 1.

WHO WILL BE INTERESTED IN THIS BOOK?

The dental profession consists of a number of separate disciplines, which are, as follows:

➤ hospital consultants
➤ general dental practitioners (GDPs) in NHS and private practice
➤ salaried hospital dentists
➤ other practitioners, such as orthodontists
➤ other dental professionals, such as hygienists.

Although this book will be of interest to dentists employed in hospitals and other organisations within the NHS, it has been written primarily for the benefit of dentists and orthodontists currently in or planning to set up in practice. Much of the content will relate to dentists in practice operating as:

➤ sole practitioners
➤ expense-sharing arrangements
➤ partnerships
➤ limited companies.

However, employed dentists may find the detail regarding the UK taxation system and the NHS Pension Scheme (NHSPS) of some relevance.

THE DENTAL PRACTICE TODAY

At the end of 2007 there were 35,419 dentists registered with the General Dental Council (GDC), of which 21,596 were male and 13,823 were female. Of that number 26,521 qualified in the UK, 5,053 within the European Economic Area and the balance of 3,845 qualified elsewhere overseas. Approximately 29,000 of that number are dentists in practice, with the balance working within hospitals and similar institutions within the NHS.

Also at that time there were 21,727 dental care professionals (DCPs) registered with the GDC, of which 20,219 were female and 1,508 were male. The different disciplines represented were as shown in Table 1.1.

TABLE 1.1 Dental care professionals registered with the GDC

Clinical/dental technicians	1 501
Hygienists	5 160
Nurses	14 757
Therapists	977
Total	22 395

The reason the total of the above breakdown of vocations is in excess of the number of DCPs registered is that a number have registered for more than one discipline. Since the end of 2007 there has been a significant increase in the number of registrations, as from July 2008 all dental professionals have been required to register with the GDC in order to continue to practise dentistry, and it is now an offence for a non-registered dental professional to practise in dentistry.

The two major changes that have impacted on the dental profession in practice over the last few years are the introduction of the new NHS contract (General Dental Services Contract) in England and Wales in April 2006, and the repeal of sections 40–4 of the Dentist Act 1984 in July 2006, allowing dentists to carry on their business as a corporate body. Both of these changes will be dealt with in detail later in this book, but are mentioned at this stage as they are responsible for bringing financial issues in dentistry to the fore. The introduction of the new NHS contract forced many practices to look at their finances and to expand upon their private dentistry to maintain levels of income, while the changes in the rules regarding incorporation allowed practices to make significant tax savings by reorganising the structure of their practice. In addition there have been recent changes to the NHSPS that have again prompted dentists to take a more active interest in their finances.

As a result of the above and earlier changes in dental finance, the dental professional has progressed from being, predominantly, a contractor within the NHS to being an independent business manager with a need for commercial and financial assistance. A number of organisations have evolved to provide that assistance.

SPECIALIST ADVISERS

Following the changes in dental finance over the years a small number of accountancy firms began to specialise in providing financial advice to the dental profession in the 1990s and built up a significant proportion of the profession as clients. In 1998 a number of these firms formed the National Association of Specialist Dental Accountants (NASDA) with the purpose of working together to improve the services they provided to the dental profession and to date they act for over 20% of dentists in practice. Their members need to display a high level of expertise to join the association and must contribute to forums and the provision of benchmarking information to maintain their membership (we shall look at some of their benchmarking information later in the book).

The Institute of Chartered Accountants in England and Wales (ICAEW) has created a Healthcare Group so that accountants in practice will be more able to assist the healthcare professional.

In addition, a number of successful entrepreneurs and dentists have created businesses to advise other dentists on practice management and marketing, to assist them run their practices. Two of the more successful are the Breathe Business Group and Chris Barrow. They have both been supplying training to the profession for over 15 years and have similar methods to help practices achieve their potential. They provide a very useful service to underperforming practices.

BENCHMARKING INFORMATION

The dental profession in the UK today is varied due to the wide variety of services that practices can provide, and with different contracts for the delivery of NHS services in England and Wales, Scotland and Northern Ireland it is difficult to benchmark a 'typical practice'. Examples of why there will be significant differences in practices are as follows.

➤ There are different payment procedures for provision of NHS services in different areas of the country.
➤ Practices may provide different mixes of private and NHS services; this will often be governed by the location of the practice and the income levels of patients.
➤ Practices may provide cosmetic dentistry and implant facilities, which are often expensive courses of treatment (CoTs). Again, the provision of these types of treatment will often be governed by the location of the practice.
➤ Practices may operate as partnerships, expense-sharing arrangements, limited companies, and sole practitioners or as expense-sharing arrangements of a number of different companies.
➤ Some practices may provide services which are subject to Value Added Tax (VAT), which will affect the way the practice is run, and their management and bookkeeping procedures.
➤ Practices may utilise the services of therapists and technicians to undertake the more basic work that the dentists provide.
➤ Practices may utilise the services of associates rather than have a larger number of principals.

As a consequence of the above the profits of practices can vary significantly and benchmarking can prove difficult. The NASDA benchmarking procedures go some way to try to overcome this difficulty by providing figures for NHS practices, mixed practices and private practices. Their method of distinguishing between the different types of practice will be used in this book to look at general practice in more detail. They define those practices that earn in excess of 80% of their income from NHS as NHS practices, and those practices that earn in excess of 80% of their income privately as private practices, with the balance being made up of mixed practices.

DENTAL PROFESSIONALS

Dental practitioners in practice can be divided into two groups, principals and associates. The principals are, in the main, the owners of the practice and associates supply their services to them on a self-employed basis. The associate is usually paid a proportion of the gross earnings that they bring to the practice, with deductions made for laboratory fees and other expenses. The associate will usually not have an interest in the capital assets of the practice. Further detail of the distinction between principals and associates will be dealt with in Chapter 9.

Along with the principal and associate dentist, the other dental professionals in practice would usually be dental therapists, dental technicians, hygienists and dental nurses, most of whom would be employed in the practice, although some can be contracted on a self-employed basis. Details of the distinction between employed and self-employed will also be dealt with in Chapter 9.

WHAT IS THE FUTURE FOR DENTISTRY?

Prior to the 'credit crunch' the demand for dental practices was high, with the banks willing to lend money to dentists at attractive rates of interest, and as a result the goodwill valuations of those practices were very high. Since then, the problem with the availability of finance has resulted in the interest rates charged to dentists increasing, and with the recession deepening the demand for expensive treatments appears to have tailed off. Early indications are, however, that there does not appear to have been a significant negative effect on the goodwill values of practices, and the demand for practices has remained high.

The corporates, such as Independent Dental Holdings, are still very active in the market, and other healthcare providers are looking at the merits of expansion into the provision of dental services. As with most other healthcare professions, it will not be long before a supermarket chain will experiment with in-store dental facilities. When this is coupled with the fact that there are still a significant number of independent dentists interested in buying practices, it is unlikely that there will be a significant drop in the values of practices being sold in the medium term.

The NHS contract in England and Wales appears to be continuing in its present format for the interim, and with generously funded services in Scotland and Northern Ireland the future provision of NHS services has been safeguarded. But with the current overall levels of funding, the provision of that service will not be able to meet the demand, with the result that demand for private treatments will be maintained.

Interestingly, recent proposals that new dentists should be forced to work for the NHS for a fixed period after qualifying, as an attempt to repay the NHS for their education, would have the effect of lowering the levels of profits that other NHS dentists could earn unless further funding was provided to pay for the additional dentists.

The demand for high-value treatments such as cosmetic work and implants appears to have fallen in the last year or so, and this has had an effect on the profitability of private practices. Whether this is seen as a short-term problem which will right itself when the economy improves will dictate what action those practices take. But there has been an increase in the number of practices offering finance packages to patients as a consequence of the recession.

Overall the future for dentistry in the medium term looks good, but there may be a move away from the current position where there are a large number of independent practices, to one where there will be an increase in the number of larger or corporate providers (probably undertaking larger scale NHS contracts). This move will be driven by a desire to reduce costs through economies of scale, and by the centralisation of healthcare facilities presently being introduced in the medical profession.

CHAPTER 2

Income and expenditure and where the money goes

As with any business a dentist in practice will have to submit an Income Tax Return to HM Revenue & Customs (HMRC) each year, and in order to do so the dentist will need to prepare accounts in order to identify the taxable profit of the practice. This will often be the prime reason for the preparation of the practice accounts, but there are a number of other reasons why this task is undertaken.

WHY DO I NEED TO PREPARE ACCOUNTS?

Apart from the need for dentists to prepare accounts for tax purposes, the other reasons for preparing accounts are as follows.

➤ The need to prepare a profit and loss account purely to identify whether a profit or loss is being made and to identify if the practice can afford to pay its overheads.
➤ The practice needs to identify the level of profit being made in order to ascertain an affordable amount of drawings for the principals, after taking into account the amount of taxation that will be due on the practice profits.
➤ The production of accounts will allow the principals to identify the efficiency of staff and contractors such as associate dentists and hygienists.
➤ Following the above the principal will be able to calculate the payments to contractors based on a percentage share of the income they produced (this will be discussed in further detail in Chapter 9).
➤ Without the production of accounts and the identification of expenses it is difficult to ascertain the amounts that will need to be charged to patients to ensure a profit will be made.

➤ The production of accounts will allow the principals to identify whether there are any excess profits that would allow a pay rise to be made to the staff or a profit share to be distributed to them.

➤ The production of accounts will enable the principals to identify the prior shares of income and expenditure that will be due to/from them as part of their partnership or expense-sharing contract.

➤ Often where a bank loan or overdraft is used to finance the practice, bank managers will require the practice to submit annual accounts to them in order that they can monitor the practice progress against forecasts.

➤ It would be difficult to sell a dental practice without some sort of profit and loss figures to show to prospective purchasers, and those with more detailed figures (in a profitable business) will be able to ask more for their business.

WHAT ACCOUNTING RECORDS DO I NEED TO KEEP?

While running a practice dentists will accumulate a lot of paperwork and documentation that they will need to keep in order that year-end accounts can be prepared for the practice. The more usual records are as follows.

➤ **Bank statements, cheque books and paying-in books**. As the analysis and balancing of the bank account are crucial to the preparation of practice accounts it is essential that these records are complete.

➤ **Petty cash records**. A lot of the day-to-day expenses in a dental practice are paid by way of cash and it is essential a record is kept of these expenses, whether funded from cash withdrawn from the bank or from cash receipts received from patients. It is preferable to bank the receipts from patients intact, as should HMRC decide to investigate the practice it will have a clear audit trail of the receipts from patients being banked. The downside to this approach is that it is quite expensive for a business to bank cash, so it is cheaper to use the cash received to fund cash expenses.

➤ **NHS schedules**. Practices that provide NHS services will receive a statement detailing the amount due to them in respect of those services each month. The statement/statements will split the contract value or the capitation payments between the performers/dentists and will also include details of the superannuation allocated to those dentists. The statements will also include details of other receipts and payments added onto or deducted from the monthly amount due to the practice. In order to prepare accounts, details of all the transactions on the statements are needed. In addition, the NHS amounts are usually paid one month in arrears; therefore, a copy of the NHS statements received after the year-end date will need to be included with the accounting records for that year.

➤ **Pay-as-you-earn (PAYE)/wages records**. The amounts paid to staff represent the net wages that they received after the deduction of PAYE and other amounts. In order to ensure the accounts are complete those net wages need to be grossed up from the PAYE records. Again, as the amount is usually paid one month in arrears the post-year-end details need to be included in the accounting records.

➤ **Purchase and expense invoices**. The invoices for all purchases need to be retained by the practice and submitted to the practice accountants with the accounting records. The reason is that there are different tax allowances available for different types of expenditure and the details of the type of expenditure are usually found on the invoice.

➤ **Details of income, laboratory bills and other expenses allocated to specific dentists**. In expense-sharing arrangements certain elements of income and expenditure are identified as belonging to individual dentists and shown as such within the accounts of the practice.

➤ **Details of payments to contractors such as associates and self-employed hygienists**. There are a number of different ways of structuring a payment system for contractors, some of which are based on the amount of units of dental activity (UDAs) that are completed, and others based on a percentage share of the gross income generated. It is important that the gross income and payment to the contractor are shown within the accounts, and not netted out.

➤ In order that the accounts can show different elements of income it is important to provide records of private fee per item income, monthly practice plan (e.g. Denplan) statements, and details of sales of toothbrushes and dental requisites.

➤ **Stock records**. In order to ensure that the practice has sufficient stock and can identify the unsold stock for the year-end accounts some type of stock record needs to be kept. For smaller practices the system can be quite basic, while larger practices would normally have computerised records to keep track of stock.

➤ **Expenses paid personally**. Often dentists, when away from the surgery, will buy items for use in the business, and will pay the amount due from their own resources. These items need recording or tax relief will not be given on the amounts.

➤ **Personal use of business expenses**. There are a number of areas of expenditure where there is an element of both business and personal use (e.g. motoring expenses), and it is important to identify the personal element that will be excluded from the accounts.

➤ **Statements from suppliers**. It is especially important to keep these at the year-end date in order that the creditors (the amounts that the practice owes) can be identified for the purposes of the accounts.

➤ **Details of income owed to the practice**. To ensure that patients pay for the treatment they receive it is important that the practice has some way of identifying the unpaid income of the practice at any given time. This is especially important at the year-end date as these amounts need to be included in the practice accounts. The details needed are as follows.

- Details of completed CoTs where the total fee remains unpaid.
- Details of incomplete CoTs, including an estimate of the amount of fees due in respect of the work to date.
- Details of laboratory fees, etc. yet to be charged to the patient.
- Details of any bad debts that the practice is likely to incur.

The list above represents the basic source documents from which an accountant will prepare the practice accounts. While there are a few practices that will deliver those records to their accountant and ask them to prepare their accounts from those source documents, most practices will have completed some bookkeeping procedures prior to submission in order to reduce the work the accountant needs to do. The main reason for this would be to reduce the accountancy costs which could be significant given that the accountant will charge an hourly rate for the work done.

The source documents need to be retained by the practice for a period of six years, and be available for inspection by HMRC at all times.

BOOKKEEPING AND MANAGEMENT ACCOUNTS
By completing some bookkeeping procedures the dentist will reduce the accountants' charges for the production of the year-end accounts; will also ensure that correct payments are made to staff, contractors and suppliers and will ensure all amounts due to the practice are received.

The minimum bookkeeping procedures to put in place, or to expect from an agency providing bookkeeping services, are:

➤ to balance the analysis of the bank transactions with the bank statements regularly, usually monthly
➤ to provide a list of suppliers that need paying at the end of the month, and write cheques out or prepare Bankers' Automated Cleaning Services (BACS) or similar banking instruction for automatic payment
➤ to provide a list of outstanding amounts due to the practice each month, in order that the practice staff can take action to collect those amounts.

The analysed and balanced bank account summary will be provided to the accountant at the end of the year for the purposes of preparing the accounts.

Some bookkeepers will also provide a PAYE service to assist practices with the paperwork necessary to process the payment of wages to staff. The rate of pay for a suitably qualified bookkeeper is in the region of £12 to £18 per hour.

Given the cost above, a number of practices will use a member of staff to complete the bookkeeping procedures, or in some cases the principal dentists will complete the procedures themselves. If a practice uses a member of staff to keep its books up to date it needs to bear in mind the following.

➤ Would the member of staff be more efficient at their original intended role, and would the cost of employing a bookkeeper be more or less than the cost of taking that member of staff away from their other duties?

➤ Has the member of staff got the ability to do the task at the same speed and as efficiently as a bookkeeper?

➤ Would the use of a member of staff give problems with confidentiality as to the dentists' level of earnings and drawings from the practice?

The bookkeeping can be undertaken manually in a cash book (increasingly rare), on Microsoft Excel spreadsheets or on a computerised accounting package, such as Sage or QuickBooks. There are also a number of suppliers of software to the dental profession who include accounting packages within their products. These packages are in their infancy and are yet to be adopted on a large scale, but they do offer, in some cases, access to benchmarking information and expert assistance with accounting records through an Internet link.

Some practices with more advanced accounting skills find it sufficient for them to e-mail a backup of their computerised accounts to their accountant to review and prepare the draft accounts. Following on from the preparation of those draft accounts a visit can be made to the practice to check invoices, etc. for tax purposes and to finalise the figures.

A number of practices which employ a bookkeeper or have more advanced accounting skills prepare management accounts regularly (either monthly or quarterly) by utilising one of the computer packages (above). Management accounts can show the practice its level of profitability and solvency through-out the year by effectively producing an income and expenditure account and balance sheet at given dates. While it is useful to know the financial position of the practice on a more regular basis it is costly for the practice to produce the management accounts, and would not be recommended unless:

➤ the level of bank funding is high and the bank requires regular management accounts as a covenant of the loan agreement

➤ the practice is new or has cash-flow issues which require it to keep a firm grip on practice finances

➤ the practice is large and/or has a profit/expense share calculation which is dependent upon regular updates of the level of income and expenditure.

One task that should be subcontracted to a bookkeeper or accountant is that of the completion of the PAYE records, as these are getting increasingly difficult to keep. The reason for this is the move to process the payment of benefits and collection of debts through the PAYE system. The weekly or monthly pay run can be complicated by the payments of working tax credits, maternity and paternity pay, and the deduction of student loans and other debts subject to deduction from the pay as a result of court orders and the like.

HOW DO I FIND A GOOD ACCOUNTANT?

Accountancy is one of the few professions where people can practise without having any type of qualification (although the government has indicated that it may bring this situation to an end soon, particularly in the realm of taxation advisers). In the meantime, however, anyone can open an office and tell the world that they are the best accountant in the world. So how do you ensure that the accountant you pick to deal with your personal and business affairs has sufficient knowledge of your profession and the tax legislation that is relevant to your income?

The following suggestions should help in the selection of an accountant who is knowledgeable in dental finances.

➤ Ask other dentists in practice who their accountants are and whether they would recommend them to you; although this will not always ensure that the accountant is knowledgeable, as that dentist may not be aware of the better services being offered by other accountants, it at least shows that the accountant has sufficient client skills to be recommended to you by his client.

➤ Look in the dental press at both the advertisements in the classified section and also in the body of the magazine for any finance or taxation articles written by accountants specifically for the dental profession.

➤ Look at the British Dental Association (BDA) list of recommended accountants. Although inclusion on this list is not a recommendation by the BDA, it shows that the dentists are sufficiently impressed by their accountant to include them on the list.

➤ Look on the websites of the ICAEW www.icaew.com or their corresponding site in Scotland and Northern Ireland, or the Association of Chartered Certified Accountants (ACCA) www.accaglobal.com for the members nearest to you. These associations have strict membership criteria and demand that members hold professional negligence insurance, which will ensure some type of recourse should the service be failing in any way.

➤ The ICAEW has a healthcare group which was set up to educate its members in finance issues relevant to the healthcare sector, so it would be prudent to ensure that the accountant to be appointed at least holds membership of that group.

➤ Find the local NASDA member nearest to you, as these accountants are experts in the field of dental finances. NASDA is an association of specialist dental accountants which was formed in 1998 by six accountants who were regularly sharing ideas and information. They decided that they wanted to form an organisation which would constantly work towards improving the standard of advice provided to dentists. There are now 37 members who between them have some 5,000 dentist clients, representing one-fifth of the dental profession. The combined knowledge and understanding of the finances of the UK's dentists in practice is unparalleled. The NASDA charter is an important aspect of the association and all members must adhere to it. NASDA members must also:

- be chartered or certified accountants
- have enough dentist clients to guarantee a specialist knowledge
- attend NASDA meetings
- share information among member colleagues.

➤ Every year all members pool information about their clients' accounts. This is done anonymously without names or any identifying factors, so that NASDA members can build an average profile. These figures also form benchmarking statistics to help NASDA members provide the best possible advice to their clients. Recently they have started gathering quarterly goodwill data for practices that have been sold or acquired by members' clients across the whole of the UK, again anonymously to maintain confidentiality. We shall be looking at some of the published statistics from NASDA later in this chapter.

➤ Given the expert knowledge that NASDA members have of the dental profession's finances, they are able to advise on the following.

- Benchmarking: with details from the annual NASDA survey they are able to advise on the level of practice profits, and where efficiencies and cost savings can be made.
- Goodwill: they produce a quarterly Goodwill database with details of practice sales. From this they can ascertain whether the value attributable to goodwill is reasonable.
- Incorporation: they can advise on the tax planning, structural planning and superannuation issues involved in the incorporation process and can highlight issues with income protection, associated companies and VAT.
- Practice sale or purchase: they can advise on the sale or purchase of a dental practice and can assist in the raising of finance and have a detailed knowledge of bank lending parameters.
- Primary care trust (PCT) attitudes: given their nationwide cover, NASDA members can advise on differing PCT attitudes to sales, purchases and incorporation of practices. They also have details of problems with PCTs regarding the sale of practices to large corporates and the effect on UDA rates.

- Private/NHS conversions: NASDA members have many clients that have converted from NHS to private and can advise on the process.
- VAT: there are issues in respect of VAT on cosmetic treatments, and on recharges between dental entities that are often missed by non-specialist accountants.
- Expense-sharing arrangements: NASDA members have extensive knowledge and regularly advise on these issues.
- Associates: again NASDA members have extensive knowledge of the arrangements with associates and can advise on the self-employed status and contract rates.
- Hygienists' status: there have been issues regarding the self-employed status of hygienists raised by HMRC, and NASDA members are best placed to advise on these.
- Practice profitability in relation to associates and vocational dental practitioners (VDPs): NASDA members can provide advice on the implementation of systems to monitor the efficiency or profitability of associates and VDPs.
- Large corporate dealings with smaller practices: many NASDA members' clients have been in negotiations with the corporates and they can advise on the procedures involved with a successful sale.
- Fee insurance: most NASDA members offer their client fee insurance in the event of a tax investigation.

➤ In addition to the above, most NASDA members provide advice on strategy, profit improvement and provide valuations for lending purposes.

WHAT DO I NEED TO ASK THE ACCOUNTANT?

Once an accountant or a number of different accountancy firms have been identified as possibly suitable for appointment the next step is to arrange a meeting. It is advisable to meet more than one accountant as it will be useful to compare the services being offered. Also, as the appointment of an accountant is of a long-term nature, it is important that you get on with the accountant on a personal basis, and the more that you meet the more likely you are to find one that you will get on with.

At the meeting you will need to cover the following areas:

➤ Explore their knowledge of dental finances by looking at the firm's literature, website and brochures, and enquire whether they regularly produce specialist newsletters.

➤ Find out whether they are proactive or reactive. You will want an adviser who provides proactive advice and not one that you have to chase all the time.

➤ Do they keep their clients up to date on financial and taxation issues?

Obtain references from the firm and ask their clients whether they consider that they are kept up to date.

➤ Will they make prudent choices on your behalf or will they explain the consequences of the options available to you and let you decide? Many dentists have not enjoyed the tax savings from incorporation as a result of their accountants considering that action as too aggressive from a tax-planning point of view (incidentally the Arctic Systems case decided in the House of Lords in June 2007 ruled that incorporating and obtaining the tax benefits as a result was perfectly legal, but there are still some accountants advising against it!).

➤ Discuss the level of fees as there will be a large variation in the fees that different firms charge. Usually, the larger international firms will charge higher fees and the smaller firms will charge lower fees. But you need to be aware that the old adage 'if you pay peanuts you get monkeys' applies to the accountancy profession, so be wary of low fee quotes, as they may reflect a low cost base (i.e. poorly paid non-specialist staff) or a loss leader, with additional fees being charged for extra services that may be included within other firms' fee quotes. The dental press often have details of average fees, and other dentists may give you an indication of what they pay. The fees will vary as the level of work varies and to give you an example of the levels charged in practice my firm currently quotes the following ranges:

● associates: £400 to £850 per year
● principals: £1,300 to £2,600 per year.

➤ The figures above are for dealing with the preparation of the annual accounts and tax returns and are pre-VAT. Any variation in the level of fee will be primarily due to the quality of the accounting records.

➤ Enquire as to whether the firm has had to deal with a number of tax investigations into its dental clients' accounts and if so the reasons for those enquiries. Also ask whether the accountant offers a fee insurance scheme, whereby their fees would be paid by an insurance policy in the event of a tax investigation.

➤ Enquire as to the number of other dental clients the accountant deals with personally, as often the larger national firms issue marketing material claiming that they act for a large number of dental clients but, given the number of offices they practise from, they often do not have individuals within the firm who deal with enough dentists to display an expertise.

➤ Does the accountant deal with all the dental clients personally or do they have the assistance of a team? Problems in respect of accessibility can occur when all the dental matters are dealt with by one member of the accountant's firm, and you should look for firms where there is a specialist team with a number of individuals available to deal with queries.

➤ Given that it is usual to meet with your accountant only once or twice a year, and with most issues being dealt with by phone, post or e-mail, it is not vital that the accountant is in your geographical area. Most specialists will travel to clients so look to those a bit further afield if there is not the expertise locally.

HOW DO I APPOINT AN ACCOUNTANT?

Once you have decided upon the accountant that you want to act for your practice all that you need to do is to advise them in writing. Should you be leaving an existing adviser at the same time, it would be courteous to write to them too. Clients regularly move between accountants so don't be too worried about upsetting the existing adviser.

Once those letters have been sent there is very little else you need to do, other than complete the paperwork necessary to inform HMRC of the change of adviser, and complete the forms necessary to comply with the money laundry regulations; this paperwork will be forwarded to you from your new adviser. At the same time you will often receive a direct debit form so that the agreed fee can be collected from your account.

The two accountants will deal with the transfer of information regarding the accounts and tax returns between themselves.

THE ANNUAL ACCOUNTS MEETING

Non-specialist accountants will often supply their dental clients with a standard set of accounts and a completed tax return, and provide very little else within their service. This is often as a result of a lack of knowledge of dental finance.

Dental practices should expect more than merely a set of accounts and a tax return from a specialist adviser, and should be provided with an interpretation of their results that will provide them with a high level of management information and advice. A specialist adviser should cover the following points at the client accounts meeting.

➤ Comment on the practice income and expenditure, and provide benchmarking information to compare the practice performance with industry averages and the practice's previous year data.
➤ Provide suggestions for increasing practice profitability.
➤ Highlight any weaknesses and opportunities that the practice should be aware of.
➤ Comment on internal accounting and management systems of the practice and provide advice as to how future accountancy fees can be reduced by the practice improving its records.

➤ Provide suggestions to equate current account balances (i.e. the money the principals have in the practice), and the draw-down options available.
➤ Provide advice on the levels of future drawings, with note to tax liabilities.
➤ Provide estimates of tax liabilities, and provide advice as to the reduction of future tax liabilities.
➤ Discuss current industry hot topics and the effect they may have on the practice.

Dentists should not accept a level of service that does not include the above.

WHAT DO THE ACCOUNTS LOOK LIKE?

There is a specimen set of dental practice accounts included in Appendix 2, but before looking at those in detail it would be advisable to examine the individual schedules that comprise a set of accounts. Usually, the first schedule in a set of accounts is a detailed summary of the income and expenditure which is often called a profit and loss account, as this schedule summarises the profit or loss made by the practice in the selected period.

Figure 2.1 shows a typical principal dentist profit and loss account. The figures included within the account are not intended to represent any industry averages, but provide ballpark figures within which the majority of dentists' results may fall. Averages for dentists in NHS, private and mixed practices are included later in this chapter.

Income

As you can see from the account, the income of the practice is usually shown at the top of the schedule, and will typically be made up of amounts received (and receivable) from the NHS, private fees and sundry other income from sales of dental requisites and reimbursements of expenses. As there are chapters devoted to all these sources of income later in the book it is not intended to provide any further detail of these amounts at this stage.

Expenses

There are many different types of expenditure that a dentist will incur in operating a dental surgery; the more usual ones are as follows.
➤ **Materials:** this category of expense usually relates to the materials and drugs used in the provision of dental treatments. In addition, this category includes all the consumables used in the provision of those treatments, such as disposable gloves, etc. This category of expense usually accounts for 5–7% of the total fee income of a practice.
➤ **Laboratory fees:** this category represents the costs of bridges, dentures, etc. produced at a dental laboratory for the use of patients as part of the dental

	£	£
Income		
NHS fees		220 000
Private fees		190 000
Other income		4 000
		414 000
Practice expenses		
Materials	21 000	
Laboratory fees	24 000	
Payments to associates	63 000	
Hygienists' costs	9 000	
Wages and salaries	64 000	
Recruitment costs	800	
Courses and staff training	500	
VDP salary	35 000	
Rates and water	3 000	
Light, heat and power	3 500	
Use of home as office	1 000	
Clinical waste	1 000	
Repairs and maintenance	7 000	
Telephone	3 000	
Printing, postage and stationery	5 000	
Subscriptions	10 000	
Equipment leasing	15 000	
Sundry expenses	5 000	
Insurance	3 500	
Motor expenses	500	
Advertising	6 000	
Accountancy	3 000	
Legal and professional fees	500	
Bank charges	500	
Credit card charges	2 500	
Depreciation charges	5 000	
Bank loan interest	14 000	
Hire purchase interest	3 000	
		309 300
Profit for the year		**104 700**

FIGURE 2.1 A typical principal dentist profit and loss account

treatment provided. This category of expense usually accounts for 6–7% of the total fee income of a practice; however, since the introduction of the new NHS contract in April 2006 the level of laboratory fees incurred by NHS practices has reduced to between 4–5% of fee income.

➤ **Payments to associates**: this expense represents the payments to associates which are usually calculated as a percentage of gross fees earned by those associates (or as an agreed amount per UDA), less any expenses allocated to those associates in respect of laboratory fees and hygienists' costs. Associates are self-employed contractors providing services to the practice and the payment to them will be subject to an agreement which often will provide the associate with approximately 50% of the gross fees earned. (Examples of the calculation of payments to associates can be found in Chapter 9.)

➤ **Hygienists' costs:** whether hygienists are employed by the practice as staff members or work as self-employed contractors it is important that their costs are separately classified for the purposes of benchmarking.

➤ **Wages and salaries:** this expense represents the gross salaries agreed payable plus employers' National Insurance Contributions (NICs), pensions and any other associated costs of employing staff. If the practice has incorporated (i.e. operates as a limited company) this expense will often also include the principals' salaries (and spouses if appropriate).The typical employees of a practice would include practice nurses, hygienists, therapists, and management, administration and reception staff.

➤ **Recruitment costs:** the costs of recruitment can be quite high, especially when advertising higher paid or clinical posts in the dental press. Even advertisements in the local press for vacancies for administration staff can prove costly. If these amounts are not distinguished from general advertising costs the benchmarking process can be adversely affected. Occasionally, the practice may use an agency to source staff members; the fee payable for this service would also be included within recruitment costs.

➤ **Courses and staff training:** with the requirement for dentists and their staff to undertake continuing professional development (CPD) the costs of training will increase over the next few years. The GDC requires all DCPs to complete 150 hours of CPD over a five-year period. All professionals on the DCP Register on 1 August 2008 start their cycle on that date. The cycle ends on 31 July 2013. Anyone who registers after 1 August 2008 will not start their cycle until August 2009.

➤ CPD can be verifiable or general. Examples of verifiable CPD are courses, lectures, online learning programmes and in-house training programmes. General CPD is any other learning activity which is beneficial but does not comply with these requirements. Examples of general CPD are the reading of books and journals, library or Internet research and informal meetings.

➤ The GDC asks all registrants for an annual declaration of CPD. At the end of the five-year cycle, the GDC will ask a percentage of all registrants to provide their records for inspection. If non-compliance is found, the professional's name can be taken off the register and will not be readmitted until the CPD requirement is fulfilled.

➤ Further details of the CDP requirements can be found in Appendix 4: CPD for DCPs (*see* www.radcliffe-oxford.com/financefordentists).

➤ Training costs will also be incurred in health and safety updates, national vocational qualifications (NVQs) and the introduction of new treatments such as cosmetic and implant surgery.

➤ **VDP salary:** the current salary paid to VDPs has been agreed at a gross amount of £2,486 a month. But National Insurance and other costs bring the total cost to the practice to approximately £35,000 a year. This amount is reimbursed to the practice and included in income (usually shown within NHS fees).

➤ **Rates and water:** a dental practice, like any other business, will be assessed for business rates, and that assessment will take into account location, property values and local economic conditions, among other factors dictated by government policy. The amount assessed will be payable to the local council. If the practice provides NHS services, a proportion of the business rates will be reimbursed to the practice.

➤ In addition the practice will also pay water rates to a utility company; this amount is not reimbursed as part of the NHS contract.

➤ **Light, heat and power:** this category of expense will include the costs of gas, oil and electricity; with the recent increases in the price of these utilities it has become a significant expense of a dental practice.

➤ **Use of home as office:** often the dentist in practice will do a significant amount of work from home, whether it is updating patient records or dealing with administration and financial matters. In addition, a number of dentists keep themselves updated by undertaking research on the Internet from their home computer. As a result of these activities they often incur additional expenses in their home, and it is these expenses that can be claimed as an expense against the practice income.

➤ **Clinical waste:** health and safety legislation dictates that clinical waste is disposed of by way of collection by authorised waste-disposal businesses, and the fees payable to those businesses are usually shown as a clinical waste cost within the accounts.

➤ **Repairs and maintenance:** there are many items within a dental practice that will need maintaining and often, in order to do this, service or maintenance agreements are taken out with manufacturers and suppliers of items such as dental chairs and computer equipment. The expense of these agreements plus the costs of general repairs within the practice are included in the category of repairs and maintenance expenses. However, any items of material value that are replaced would usually be shown within the equipment heading on the balance sheet (*see* Chapter 3 explaining the items included within the balance sheet).

➤ **Telephone:** this category of expense would usually include the costs of the practice landline and Internet costs, plus on occasions a proportion of the principals' home or mobile phone costs incurred on practice matters.

➤ **Printing, postage and stationery:** the advent of computerisation has increased this category of expense significantly with the cost of printing and toners accounting for the majority of the increase. This category also includes the costs of producing the practice headed paper and associated stationery, and the costs of postage of items to dental laboratories and correspondence to patients, etc.

➤ **Subscriptions:** in order to keep up to date with advances in dental matters the membership of the professional bodies and associations is essential, and it is the membership subscriptions of such bodies as the BDA and the GDC which make up this expense heading.

➤ **Equipment leasing:** prior to recent changes in taxation legislation it was financially advantageous to lease the practice equipment, such as computers and dental chairs, rather than buy them, and the lease payments, usually paid monthly, are allowed as an expense against practice income. Under a lease the ownership of the equipment remains with the leasing company, and the practice pays a rental while it effectively hires the assets.

➤ **Sundry expenses:** the expenses in this category are usually smaller amounts that do not fit within another category. Examples of usual expenses posted to sundries are refreshments, newspapers and magazines, window cleaning, staff parties and entertainment.

➤ **Insurance:** this expense heading will include the insurance costs for the following:
  • buildings
  • contents
  • public liability
  • professional indemnity
  • employers' liability
  • motor expenses (may alternatively be included in motor expenses).

➤ Often a dentist may take out insurances to protect income in the event of illness, or a life policy to repay loans, etc. upon death: these types of policies are not allowable as a deduction against income and are usually treated as the personal expense of the dentist in the accounts.

➤ **Motor expenses:** it is unusual for dentists to have significant motor expenses in their accounts as they will not use their cars to any great extent for business use. The home to work trip is not allowed as a business expense, so only the motoring costs for visiting dental exhibitions, conferences, attending courses, domiciliary visits, meeting with professional colleagues, looking for practices to work in or buy, going to the bank, visiting the accountant, etc. will be allowed as business expenses.

➤ **Advertising:** the more established practices and most NHS practices will not have to spend too much on advertising for new patients, as they will most often have waiting lists to replace any fall in patient numbers. However, newer practices, and sometimes those who have converted from NHS to private, will have to incur advertising costs to attract patients to their surgery.

➤ It is important for a practice to enquire from new patients how they found out about the services offered by the practice, as this information is crucial to assess the effectiveness of the practice's advertising policy. Many practices do not do this and waste large amounts of money on ineffective advertising. In the accountancy profession, for example, research has shown that in some cases fewer than 1% of new clients join a practice as a result of an advert in Yellow Pages, but many firms are unaware of this and spend thousands of pounds each year on expensive adverts in telephone directories.

➤ **Accountancy:** the cost of preparing the practice accounts and the partners' tax returns is often shown as an expense of the practice, but there are some practices that treat the partners' tax costs as their own and do not include them within the accounts. The accountancy costs will remain fairly static, except for when advice is needed on changes in the partnership, property issues and tax-planning arrangements.

➤ **Legal and professional fees:** from time to time the services of other professionals will be needed, whether it is a solicitor drafting a new partnership agreement or a surveyor providing a valuation of the practice premises. These expenses will often be shown in the profit and loss account, but sometimes they will not be allowed as a tax deductible expense given that they may relate to a capital project, such as the purchase of a property.

➤ **Bank charges:** most banks will provide free banking to new businesses for one year, but thereafter will calculate charges based on the number of items being paid in and out of the practice bank account. However, there are a number of building societies who offer professional practices free banking and this option ought to be considered by those who do not need to borrow any money.

➤ **Credit card charges:** given that most people would opt to pay for their treatment by way of credit card it is essential that the practice provides the facilities for this type of payment. There are only a small number of financial institutions who provide these services and the costs they charge are very similar. They charge a percentage of the gross fee being paid by the credit charge, with the percentage charge being based on the gross annual amount of fees. Basically, those with a higher amount of credit card sales will pay a smaller percentage fee.

➤ **Depreciation:** this is a non-cash expense often added to the accounts by the accountant while preparing the year-end accounts. The purpose of the provision is to show the decrease in value of the assets of the practice over time, and is usually charged as a fixed percentage of the cost of the asset each year. The rate of depreciation charged will depend upon what type of assets the practice owns. For example, computers are often charged with 33.3% depreciation in order to write them off over three years.

➤ **Bank loan interest:** the interest on any practice loans can be included in the profit and loss account as an expense; however, the capital element of the repayment cannot. Historically, dentists have been one of the professions that banks have been keen to lend to and they have been offered very competitive rates, but rates have increased as the credit crunch has reduced the available cash to lend, and the cost of borrowing has increased.

➤ **Hire purchase interest:** a hire purchase agreement is effectively a loan agreement, usually with a finance company allied to one of the main banks. Often the rates charged can be in excess of those offered by the banks, except when new equipment or vehicles are being bought where the manufacturer will often subsidise a low rate of interest.

The profit for the practice is calculated by deducting all the expenses incurred (as above) from the practice income from fees and reimbursements. The amount of profit can vary from 36–42% of the gross income depending upon the services the practice provides and how efficiently those services are delivered.

ASSOCIATE ACCOUNTS

The above profit and loss account includes a comprehensive list of income and expenses which can usually be found in a principal dentist's set of accounts. An associate's set of accounts in contrast are fairly simple, with usually only one source of income from the principal dentist, and very little expenditure, as there are no costs of employing staff or financing a property. Figure 2.2 shows a typical associate's profit and loss account.

As can be seen from Figure 2.2, the associate's expenses are fairly low, with the professional indemnity insurance being the main expense. Again, the figures included within the account are not intended to represent any industry averages, but provide ballpark figures within which the majority of associate dentists' results may fall.

	£	£
Income		
Gross NHS fees	42 000	
Gross private fees	39 000	
		81 000
Cost of Sales		
Laboratory fees	5 000	
		5 000
Direct Costs		
Payments to hygienists	2 000	
Other direct costs	100	
		2 100
Gross profit		73 900
Other income		1 100
Expenditure		
Payments to dental nurses	800	
Use of home as office	520	
Courses	450	
Motor expenses	300	
Accountancy	450	
Telephone	80	
Printing, stationery and postage	50	
Subscriptions	400	
Insurance	2 400	
		5 450
Profit for the year		**69 550**

FIGURE 2.2 A typical associate's profit and loss account

WHAT LEVEL OF PROFIT WILL I MAKE?

The level of profit dentists will make will depend upon whether they are a principal or an associate, and also whether they provide NHS services or private dentistry. Principals will earn more than associates as they will gain from the fees that their associates and hygienists can generate in excess of the amounts that they pay to them. The difference in the level of profits generated by practices providing different services can be seen in the NASDA profits analysis extract below. Each year NASDA publishes the average earnings of dentists in the UK, and split those averages into the following groups:

➤ NHS practices
➤ private practices
➤ mixed practices
➤ the typical practice
➤ associate.

The NASDA Profits Report published in April 2009 is reproduced below to give an indication of current levels of profit earned by dentists.

NASDA Profits Report 2009

Each year the National Association of Specialist Dental Accountants, which represents more than 20% of self-employed dentists in the UK, produces a profits report summarising the results of a sample of their dental clients. They look at both principals and associates and analyse income and expenditure. They provide the only comprehensive independent benchmarking figures against which clients can compare their performance.

This year's report includes the earnings of the second full year of the new National Health Service contract, showing the effect that the contract has had on dentists' net income. For those practices with year-ends set in 2008, the key results were as follows:

Principal practitioners

The average total fee income generated per principal practitioner in a typical dental practice increased in 2008 to £384,546. This was an increase of £17,232 (4.7%) on the figure achieved in 2007, when the average total gross income per principal was around £367,314. For the third year running private income has exceeded NHS income with the gap widening between the two, resulting in a ratio that is now 54% private to 46% NHS.

The shift towards more private work has again increased the gross profits in those practices, but an increase in turnover in NHS practices has not been enough to match an increase in material and laboratory fees, which has resulted in a decrease in gross profit in those practices. The gross profit is the total income minus the direct costs, for example dental materials, lab costs and payments to associates.

The average gross profit per principal practitioner in the typical dental practice rose by 2.9% from £249,904 in 2007 to £257,189 in 2008.

The net profit is the gross profit less all the practice overheads, including staff costs and premises costs. Increases in those costs and overheads have resulted in the average net profit per principal falling slightly in the year. The average net profit per principal practitioner in a typical dental practice in 2008 was £141,288 compared with £142,705 in 2007, a decrease of less than 1%.

The data shows that, in the typical practice, increases in both staff and administration costs have accounted for the fall in profits. The staff costs represent 18.0% (17.6% in 2007) of turnover and the administration costs represent 13.9% (13.1% in 2007).

The figures are based on a 'typical dental practice', which is calculated as an average of the results of NHS practices, private practices and mixed practices. The average net profits for these practices are shown below:

Type of practice	2008	2007
Typical practice	£141 288	£142 705
NHS practice	£148 020	£149 455
Private practice	£136 534	£130 942
Mixed practice	£140 661	£147 068

The decrease in NHS practices' net profits has been less than 1%, whereas private practices have shown a 4.3% rise. Mixed practices have seen their net profits fall by 4.3%.

The net profit percentage (the net profit as a percentage of the total income of the practice) has fallen in each type of practice as follows:

Type of practice	2008	2007
Typical practice	36.70%	38.90%
NHS practice	40.40%	42.60%
Private practice	34.60%	35.60%
Mixed practice	36.20%	39.10%

The net profit percentages have fallen as costs have risen faster than income in all types of practices. The private practices have been able to increase income to slightly offset the increase in costs whereas the NHS and mixed practices have been unable to do this.

The 'typical' practice average has been affected by the drop in the NHS and mixed practice profits. Whether the NHS practices will see a continued fall in their profits will depend on the number and value of the UDAs in their contracts, and whether they can achieve any cost savings. NASDA has seen UDA values as low as £16.20 and as high as £37.84 this year, with the average being £24.38.

Associate dental practitioners

Associate dental practitioners have seen an increase in their average gross earnings of 0.5% in 2008. The average gross earnings are £83,302 per associate after deducting the payment to principal; this figure was £82,864 per associate in 2007.

However, the average net profit per associate has decreased this year dropping from £70,396 in 2007 to £70,299 in 2008. This is the second year that their earnings have dropped. Although the drop in itself is relatively minor, when the cost of living is taken into account, they have suffered a significant drop in income over the past two years.

The above profits report was compiled from a survey of 500 practices and 500 associate dentists from across the UK and represents the only national survey of dentists' earnings.

Figures 2.3 and 2.4 have been extracted from the Doctors and Dentists Pay Review Body (DDRB) report for 2009.

The NHS Information Centre also provided a summary of NASDA statistics supplied to the DDRB for the years 2001/02 to 2006/07 which is reproduced as Figure 2.4. This shows that the level of NHS profits for that period increased by 72.8%, for mixed practices 84.3% and for private 38.8%.

NHS commitment	Population	Average gross earnings (£)	Expenses	Net profit	Net profit percentage
Over 75% private	1 160	£331 902	£214 296	£117 606	35.43%
Mixed	833	£357 080	£228 832	£128 249	35.92%
Over 75% NHS	2 614	£353 631	£207 033	£146 599	41.46%
All responders	4 607	£348 784	£212 806	£135 978	38.99%
No survey	3 373	£360 816	£227 561	£133 255	36.93%
All dentists	7 980	£353 869	£219,042	£134 827	38.10%

Information provided by NHS Information Centre for the DDRB 2009

FIGURE 2.3 Dentists' average earnings for 2006/07

	2001/02	2002/03	2003/04	2004/05	2005/06	2006/07
NASDA net profit per dentist	£	£	£	£	£	£
NHS	86 500	90 400	104 000	118 000	142 400	149 500
Mixed	79 800	87 200	98 800	100 400	129 600	147 100
Private	94 300	100 100	113 000	124 700	131 400	130 900

NHS practices are those where NHS earnings are 80% or more. Private practices are those where private earnings are 80%

FIGURE 2.4 Growth in dentists' earnings from 2001/02 to 2006/07

WHAT EXPENSES ARE NOT ALLOWABLE FOR TAX?

Most of the expenses listed above will be allowable as deductions from the gross income of the practice for tax purposes (*see* Chapter 10 for more details), but there are a few that are not and these are listed as follows.

➤ **Legal fees incurred in dealing with capital matters** such as the purchase or sale of a building. These fees will be allowed as an expense against the sales price of the building for capital gains tax (CGT) purposes only.

➤ **Course fees incurred in acquiring a new skill:** the cost of CPD is allowed as a tax deduction as this involves the updating of existing skills and learning, whereas the training involved in acquiring a new skill is not. A dentist attending a course on a new cosmetic non-dental procedure may find that the costs of that course will not be allowed as an expense against the dentistry income from the practice. There are a number of grey areas with respect to the training involved in implant surgery and some cosmetic dental procedures and advice from a tax expert should be sought before a claim is made.

➤ **Private element of motoring costs:** some dentists charge all their motoring costs to their practice, not in an attempt to claim the whole amount as a deduction, but merely to gain the cash-flow advantage of the practice paying the bills. In these instances it is important that an adjustment is made when transferring the detail to the tax return to ensure that the personal element is not claimed for. This applies to other expenses where there may be a personal element, such as telephone costs.

➤ **Some replacement costs of assets:** the tax rules regarding the expenses of maintaining properties are very complicated with some expenses being allowed in full against taxable income, some only being partially allowed each year against income, and others only allowed against the capital gain on an ultimate sale. For example, the replacement of a single-pane window with a similar one would be allowable against taxable income in full, whereas if it was replaced by a double-glazed window, there would be an element of improvement, and that expense would be added to the property cost to be ultimately relieved against a future property sale.

➤ Where a practice has taken a loan with a bank there is often a covenant that the principals take out **life cover** to the amount of the loan. Even though this insurance is very much a business expense it will not be allowed as a taxable expense. However, should a claim ever be made on these policies the proceeds are not taxable on the practice.

➤ **Permanent health insurance:** most dentists will pay premiums on insurance policies designed to provide for income during periods of sickness. These policies are invariably marketed as locum insurance, whether or not that is strictly speaking the case.

➤ A genuine locum policy is one where a direct refund is made, during or following a period of sickness, of costs directly incurred in payments to locum dentists, whereas a permanent health policy provides for a lump-sum payment which dentists can use at their discretion.

➤ There is often confusion regarding the tax treatment of locum insurance policies and permanent health insurance policies, and further confusion is often caused by the lack of paperwork for the policies, in most cases the policy document needs to be examined to determine what type of policy it is.

➤ A locum policy will attract tax relief on its premiums, but tax will become due on the receipt of a payout from the policy. As the expenses that the proceeds will pay for will mostly be tax allowable, there is a tax neutral situation with this policy. These policies are not very useful if it is difficult to find a locum dentist to undertake to cover for the dentist during a period of sickness. A permanent health policy, however, does not attract tax relief on its premiums, nor attract a tax charge upon the receipt of proceeds; it is also not dependent upon expenses actually being incurred. The expenses paid from the proceeds of these policies will still attract tax relief, if appropriate.

➤ **Accountancy costs for personal tax and financial matters:** only the cost of preparing the accounts and the compliance costs of the completion of the tax computations are allowable as a taxable expense in the accounts. The cost of completing the personal tax return of the dentist is not allowed; however, as most of the detail for the completion of the tax return is collated as part of the compliance work above, in most cases the cost of completion of the tax return is minimal.

➤ **Professional fees for the preparation of a partnership agreement** (although the cost of updating the agreement is allowable).

➤ **Bank interest on personal borrowings:** normally, the interest on a practice overdraft will be allowable as a taxable expense, but if the overdraft has been created by the principal drawing more from the practice than the profits have generated, that element of the excess will be deemed to be personal borrowings and the interest thereon will not be allowed. Given that depreciation is not a cash expense that amount should be added back in calculating the practice profit for this purpose.

➤ **Depreciation:** HMRC will not allow depreciation as a taxable expense, but instead allows a similar deduction called a capital allowance. The percentage rates of capital allowances vary and in some cases will be in excess of the depreciation charged in the accounts. Although some would argue it would make more sense to adopt the capital allowance rates within the accounts, International Accounting Standards dictate the types and levels of depreciation that may be used.

➤ **Entertainment costs:** other than costs that are allowable for staff functions the costs of entertaining patients and business colleagues are not allowable as taxable expenses.

HMRC ENQUIRIES

The above profit and loss information is useful for dentists to benchmark their performance against industry averages, and also provides the basis of the information that will be returned to HMRC on the dentist's Self Assessment Tax Return form. The tax return form includes a number of boxes within which expenses from the profit and loss account need to be entered, as can be seen in Appendix 5: Self-employed income tax return supplementary pages (*see* www. radcliffe-oxford.com/financefordentists). The description of expenses to be entered in each box does not often correspond to the headings in the accounts so some items will be combined upon completion of the return.

Once the return is completed it will be submitted to HMRC, increasingly by using the online filing facilities. Upon submission the return is not checked by an Inspector of Taxes, but may be selected by exception reporting if it appears items are omitted or figures do not conform to those expected from a dentist. If a tax return is selected at this stage it will usually be for confirmation of one item on the return. This type of enquiry is called an 'aspect enquiry' and will usually be closed if a satisfactory answer can be provided to the Inspector of Taxes regarding the item being queried. If a satisfactory answer cannot be provided it is likely that a full enquiry will be initiated into the tax return, which will involve HMRC requesting all the business accounting records for the period under review.

A full enquiry will usually commence with HMRC requesting the accounting records of the practice, which will be reviewed for completeness, with the Inspector of Taxes checking that all receipts are banked. It is usual for the practice diary to be inspected and random patient appointments selected. The accounting records are then checked to ensure the payment in respect of those appointments has been included within those records.

In addition the PAYE and petty cash records will be checked to ensure that all payments to employees have been treated correctly.

Finally, the dentists' claims for expenses will be examined to determine whether any personal items are being claimed for in error.

Following the inspection of the records, and usually after a number of letters to the accountants requesting details of items from the accounts, a meeting may be requested where the Inspector of Taxes will ask further questions as to how the practice is run and the accounting records completed. It is strongly recommended that a qualified adviser attends the meeting on the dentist's behalf, or at least accompanies the dentist to the meeting to advise on the correct etiquette at such meetings.

If the Inspector of Taxes does find personal items being claimed for in a cavalier fashion, or finds significant under-declarations of income, he or she has the right to open up the earlier five years' tax returns and raise an assessment for that whole period. Not only will the tax under-declared be assessed, but penalties will be issued and interest charged on the outstanding tax; the penalties can be as high as 100% of the tax due if the under-declaration is considered to be intentional.

If there are no errors in the year being examined, the Inspector will not open up the earlier years for investigation, unless intelligence is available which points to under-declarations in those earlier years.

Therefore, detailed enquiries can be initiated by the following.

➤ Unsatisfactory responses to an aspect enquiry.

➤ Random enquiry: each year HMRC selects a number of returns at random and undertakes full enquiries into those returns.

➤ Industry enquiry: often there may be a nationwide review of specific industries with local tax offices asked to enquire into a number of tax returns which have been submitted from those industries. For example, in the 1980s HMRC discovered an under-declaration of income from cremation fees in doctors' accounts and commenced a nationwide series of investigations specifically to look at that aspect of their accounts.

➤ Local intelligence: if the Inspector of Taxes comes across detail or is informed of taxpayers' under-declaring their income, he or she will inspect and may ultimately enquire into those taxpayers' affairs.

The average cost of professional fees incurred in dealing with an HMRC enquiry is £2,500 to £3,000, and it is strongly recommended that dentists take out insurance cover to provide for the fees in such an event.

MANAGEMENT ACCOUNTS, BUDGETING AND CASH FLOWS

As can be seen above, the practice accounts are predominately used to benchmark performance and provide the details for the completion of the principals' tax returns. There are, however, other uses for the information produced in a set of accounts.

Some practices use accounting software or Excel spreadsheets to produce accounts on a more frequent basis than the usual annual accounts produced by most practices. These management accounts will be quite detailed and will be prepared for a number of reasons, the most common being to compare the practice performance and cash flow with budgets.

Budgets are detailed financial projections prepared by the practice that will often allow it to borrow money for a specific project or to forecast a level of affordable drawings for the principals. A good example of a situation where budgets would be used is upon the setting up of a squat practice (a new practice), especially if bank borrowing is needed. Given it would be unusual for a squat practice to have a full complement of patients from day one, the practice will need to build a cash-flow model that will allow the payment of practice expenses and the drawings of the principal until such time that the income of the practice will match or exceed the expenses. The preparation of a budget will help identify the maximum level of borrowings that the practice will need and a bank could then be approached to lend that amount to the practice.

Often the bank will require the practice to provide management accounts throughout the year in order that it can monitor the risk on the facility it has provided to the practice. It would be usual to appoint a specialist dental accountant to assist in this process as they will have experience in the types of expenditure a squat practice will incur, and they will be able to assist in the production of the management accounts.

However, most dental practices will not need to produce management accounts and budgets as the practice cash flow will be fairly predictable, but there are some larger practices with quite sophisticated financial systems that monitor their finances for other purposes. These practices may have branch surgeries and will want to monitor their progress on an ongoing basis, and produce financial information that will allow those practices to do the following.

➤ Identify fees generated per dental chair, and monitor the efficiency of that surgery over time.

➤ Identify fees generated per fee earner and compare with their hours worked to produce efficiency comparisons. This is often done to compare the abilities of associates.

➤ Identify expenses to recharge to principals and associates in line with profit/expense-sharing arrangements.

➤ Identify the working capital of the practice to ensure that sufficient cash is retained within the accounts to pay the liabilities each month.

WHERE'S THE MONEY GONE?

One of the most common questions that dentists ask their accountants when they are presented with their year-end accounts is: where has all the profit gone? The typical dentist profit and loss account in Figure 2.1 above discloses a profit figure of £104,700; should that figure be available to draw from the practice? It would be very unusual if it was available, for a number of reasons.

➤ The finance for a practice comes from three main sources:
  - usually upon setting up a practice the initial source of funds would come from bank borrowing
  - other funds may be introduced by the principal from personal savings and the like
  - the main source of funds on an ongoing basis is from the profits generated from the practice each year.
➤ Therefore, if the practice buys, say, a dental chair during the year for £15,000 and doesn't increase its bank borrowings and the principal does not introduce any funds, the purchase of that chair must have come from the profits generated that year. Therefore, from the £104,700 the amount of £15,000 would need to be deducted, leaving only £89,700.
➤ The income of the practice shown in the profit and loss account will include amounts that have been earned by the practice but have not yet been received, whether it is from the provision of NHS services or amounts due from private patients. If these amounts totalled, say, £17,000 the amount of profits available to draw would be £72,700.
➤ The personal expenses of the principal are not allowable as an expense of the practice, but are charged to him or her via a 'capital' account, which basically summarises the profits allocated to that principal, less any amounts paid on his or her behalf and drawings taken by him or her. If in the example above the practice during the year had paid the principal's tax bill of, say, £23,700, there would only be £49,000 available to draw.

Therefore, in the above example, if the principal had paid himself or herself £3,000 a month during the year he or she would have only a balance of £13,000 to draw from the profits of £104,700. But even that amount may not be available if, since the year-end date, the practice had purchased even more stock or assets. The finances of a practice change from day to day and the profits are not ring-fenced but are utilised in the payment of daily expenses and asset purchases. However, cash will build up if on an ongoing basis the level of expenses and asset purchases are less than income.

An important note to make at this point is in respect of the calculation of the principal's taxable income. In the example above the principal has received only £36,000 throughout the year, with the possibility of another £13,000, a total of £49,000. However, the principal will be taxed on the profit of £104,700 (less some capital allowances on the chair, and corrections in respect of depreciation). So remember that self-employed dentists pay tax on the profits they *make* and not on the amount that they *draw* from their practices.

CHAPTER 3

The balance sheet and what I'm worth

In order to get a complete picture of your financial position you will need to have a balance sheet prepared. A balance sheet is made up of the following two parts.

1   A list of assets and liabilities that comprises the total business worth of the practice or the individual.
2   A capital account and/or a current account which equates to the list of assets and liabilities (hence the expression balance sheet).

Figure 3.1 shows what a typical balance sheet of a dental practice could look like, and the following notes provide explanations of the figures and descriptions more commonly used by accountants.

FIXED ASSETS

Fixed assets comprise assets such as goodwill, property, plant, fixtures and equipment. The term fixed assets is used in accountancy to describe assets and property which cannot easily be converted into cash. This can be compared with current assets such as stock, debtors, cash or bank accounts, which are described as liquid assets as they represent cash or items that can quickly be converted into cash.

The fixed assets usually found on a dental practice balance sheet would be goodwill, property, fixtures and equipment, and in some cases motor vehicles. Further details of these assets can be found below.

Fixed assets can be further divided into two subclasses, tangible and intangible assets. The tangible assets are those such as property and equipment, etc.

	2009		2008	
	£	£	£	£
Fixed assets				
Intangible assets		250 000		250 000
Tangible assets		450 000		450 000
		700 000		700 000
Current assets				
Stocks	3 500		3 200	
Debtors	17 500		18 300	
Cash at bank and in hand	34 500		43 500	
	55 500		65 000	
Current liabilities	22 500		46 500	
Net current assets		33 000		18 500
Long-term liabilities		235 000		250 000
Net assets		498 000		468 500
Financed by				
Capital accounts		465 000		450 000
Current accounts		33 000		18 500
		498 000		468 500

FIGURE 3.1 A typical dentist's balance sheet

and the intangible assets usually comprise goodwill and intellectual property. The intangible asset on the balance sheet in Figure 3.1 represents the goodwill of the practice.

Goodwill

It is usual upon a sale or transfer of a dental practice for the proceeds to exceed the value of the tangible assets of the practice. This excess payment or premium represents the 'goodwill' that will need to be paid to the dentist selling the practice in order to buy the rights to the future profits of the practice. Goodwill is calculated by reference to the continuing business that the practice is likely to retain after the sale or transfer. The level of goodwill is dependent upon the level of the practice profits, with the more profitable practices achieving higher levels of goodwill upon a sale or transfer. The goodwill value on the example balance sheet in Figure 3.1 is £250,000.

Goodwill valuations

The valuation of the goodwill of a practice will not only depend upon the level of profits, but also upon the following.

➤ **The level of fees:** usually those practices with a higher turnover will attract a higher price.

➤ **The mix of fees** between NHS/fee per item/Denplan or similar fees. As each different source of fees will have a different method of payment, and profit margin, there will be a difference in the goodwill valuation attached to each.

➤ **The number of associates working in the practice:** usually a practice with a large number of associates would attract a higher price, but the larger practices tend to require management skills that the average dentist often doesn't possess, leaving only the corporates interested in those practices. The corporates tend to negotiate hard on price.

➤ **The number of surgeries in operation:** if a practice has only one or two surgeries and no room for expansion, it will be very difficult to significantly increase the level of that practice's turnover and profit. As a consequence a multi-surgery practice would be of more interest to most prospective purchasers (because there will not be a limit on future earnings). Dentists should be advised not to purchase a one-surgery practice as this will not only reduce their earnings potential but also reduce the scope of services they could provide.

➤ **The level and type of staff employed:** the mix of staff in a practice can have a marked effect on that practice's level of profits, with the more experienced staff being able to produce a higher level of fees and remain efficient. A younger team will usually need more training, management and supervision.

➤ **The practice's use of hygienists and dental technicians:** to achieve an optimum level of profits the dentist should be available to perform the higher priced treatments. In order to do this the dentist needs to utilise the services of hygienists and associates to undertake the more routine procedures. Practices with an established number of hygienists and associates will be worth more than those without (subject to the management issue mentioned above).

➤ **The age and condition of the practice's fixtures and equipment:** a number of dentists when approaching retirement will refrain from updating their fixtures and equipment, with the result that following their retirement the new owner will need to incur the cost of a refit. Practices with old equipment will have their sales price discounted as a result of their underinvestment.

➤ **The type of property from which the practice operates:** the price of a practice may be affected by the property it operates from, whether it is modern or old, a converted house or a purpose-built surgery, or on the ground, first or second floor. Access for elderly patients and ability for them to travel to the practice and park their cars easily are increasingly important factors that can affect the value of a practice.

From the above factors a valuation can usually be made, but whether that amount is obtained upon a sale will depend upon the eagerness of the vendor to sell and the purchaser to buy. As always, a sale will be subject to market forces.

There are two or three specialist valuers of dental practices in the UK and most dentists will use these firms upon a sale or transfer of their practice. There are usually only five occasions where these valuers' services are needed.

➤ A sale of the practice to another local practice upon retirement. This would be an open-market sale to an expanding local practice or an independent dentist wishing to set up on his or her own.

➤ A sale of part of the practice to an associate who has worked within that practice for a period. This can be either as a result of the associate buying out one of the principals upon their retirement, or the practice increasing the number of principals. As part of this process the associate will buy a share of his or her own goodwill.

➤ A transfer of the practice into a limited company that has been formed and will be wholly owned by the existing principals. As HMRC can take an interest in the value of goodwill in this instance, from a tax point of view it is important that the practice accountant is involved in this process and advises on the level of goodwill.

➤ A sale of the practice to a corporate as part of their plans to expand the chain of dental practices they operate. Corporates are national chains of dental practices, such as Independent Dental Holdings (IDH) or James Hull & Associates; they have been very active over the last few years in increasing the number of practices that they own.

➤ A valuation as part of a legal dispute upon a dental practice breaking up. Often the fact that the practice is breaking up will have a depressing effect on the value of the goodwill.

Increasingly, specialist dental accountants are providing valuations, especially in the case of a sale to an associate or a transfer to a limited company.

Historically, the goodwill valuations of practices have averaged about 33% to 35% of the gross fees generated by those practices and have not varied very much from that range for a number of years. Obviously, practices did achieve much higher valuations if they demonstrated superior qualities as per the list above, and larger practices tended to achieve higher rates due to their attraction to the corporates. But, for the most part, practice sales and part sales to associates in the years up to 2005/06 fell into the 33–35% range.

Since that time, however, the valuations of goodwill have risen dramatically with some NHS practices in large towns and cities being sold at 100% of the recurring fees of those practices. The reasons for the increase in the levels of valuation of goodwill are as follows.

➤ As the European Community has expanded the UK has seen an increase in the number of dentists from the Community relocating here. As a consequence of this, and a general increase in numbers, there are more dentists wanting to buy into a practice. The result of this higher demand has been the increase in the prices that dentists have paid or are prepared to pay for a practice.

➤ The statistics produced by the specialist dental accountants show that the levels of dentists' profits from practice have increased consistently over the last few years (also *see* Figure 2.4 Growth in dentists' earnings from 2001/02 to 2006/07). They also show that dentists undertake more private dentistry, which as a proportion of the total dental services provided now exceeds NHS dentistry, as more dentists have reduced their commitment in that sector following the introduction of the new contract in England and Wales. As a result of this increase in income the level of goodwill, upon which it is ultimately based, has increased.

➤ The provision of funding to dentists is very popular with the financial institutions as there has been, historically, very little bad debt in this profession. As a consequence, the cost of borrowing was, until the credit crunch and subsequent recession, at an all-time low. The lack of funds caused by the resulting financial meltdown has forced the major lenders to the dental sector to increase their margins on their loans. Prior to the credit crunch the specialist bankers in this sector were lending up to £320,000 unsecured, at 1% (or slightly less!) over the Bank of England base rate, to dentists wishing to buy or expand their practices. These rates have risen by 0.5% to 0.75%, but the banks are still eager to lend to this sector, which will ultimately force the rates back down. Indications are that funding is becoming more available and, given this readily accessible finance, prospective purchasers can borrow more and afford to pay more for practices.

➤ The corporates are now being joined by multinational corporations that are looking for profit opportunities in healthcare. These organisations have deep pockets and are eager to build up portfolios of dental practices (predominately private) in a short period of time. As a result, the larger private practices are achieving high sales prices.

➤ More private practices have been set up, as there are an increasing number of practitioners who are eager to buy them to get out of the NHS sector for a less stressful working environment. This has resulted in an increase in the goodwill values in private practice. Private practices do not generate a higher level of profit than NHS practices as a whole, but the work rate tends to be less, and it is this factor that attracts dentists to private practice.

As can be seen above, there are a number of reasons for the current record levels of goodwill in dentistry. Indications are, however, that this situation will not continue into the future. The reason is that there is concern in England and Wales as to how NHS dentistry will be delivered as the existing contract evolves. Currently, there are a number of issues with the contract that need resolving.

➤ Most of the personal dental services (PDS) practices obtained higher levels of payments for their UDAs than the general dental services (GDS) practices, as the amount they received under the new contract was based on their levels of income prior to the introduction of that contract. Historically, PDS practices had higher levels of profits. But as the work that each type of practice currently performs is basically the same, there is an unfair situation which will most probably be corrected sometime in the future. It is more than likely to result in the reduction of the payments for UDAs for the PDS practices than an increase in the amounts paid to GDS practices.

➤ Upon the introduction of the new contract there were a large number of mixed practices that were given small contracts to continue dealing with the existing NHS patients registered at those practices. Most of those patients were exempt from NHS fees, being children, etc. Those practices were given UDA payments based upon the income that they received in respect of those patients under the old contract. As a consequence those practices have not increased the amount of work they have performed for the NHS.

➤ The health boards and primary care organisations (PCOs) have been under a lot of pressure to provide 'NHS Dentistry For All', and in some cases have not been renewing these exempt/small contracts when there has been a change of provider. They have, as an alternative, been concentrating their funding on larger NHS-only practices which will accept new patients or funding Access Centres where they can directly employ dentists to deal with patients who can drop in at any time.

➤ Many dentists underachieved their UDA targets in the first two years of the contract and are currently trying to make up part of the deficit in UDAs in their third year, but at the same time paying back a proportion of the shortfall. This has resulted in them working harder for less money! This will have an effect on a future sales price as the accounts will show falling profits.

➤ If, as the contract evolves, more practices start losing some or all of their NHS income, we may find that there will be more competition in the private sector in order to recoup some of that lost income. This could result in a reduction in prices and ultimately profits.

➤ Given the ease with which funding is currently available it is feasible that some NHS practices will be bought with a high percentage of borrowed monies. It is also feasible that those practices could lose some or possibly all of their income as the contract evolves. If this were to happen, there is a real possibility of some dentist practices going bankrupt. If this occurred, the banks could revise their lending criteria for dentists, thus making the raising of finance more difficult.

It is likely, therefore, that the NHS contract will have a depressing effect upon the level of profits and ultimately reduce goodwill values in England and Wales.

Before we leave the topic of goodwill there are a couple of issues to discuss which are peculiar to dentistry.

First, the goodwill valuations in dentistry are more often than not shown as a percentage of the level of fees that the practice generates, and in some cases it appears that the level of profitability has not been considered in full. This type of valuation is very different to the standard method of looking at historic profits and adjusting for material items. The reason for this method of valuation is that the number of patients (and ultimately the fees they generate) provide the ability to produce a profit and are considered key to the valuation of the practice. It is of interest that the two differing methods of valuation do not produce the same result in all cases!

Second, the issue of the purchase of goodwill by an associate can often produce tension, especially if the associate has been with the practice for many years. The reason is the associate has to effectively buy his or her own goodwill. This is because the valuation of the practice (or part thereof) will take into account the income and the net contribution that the associate makes to the practice. This is seldom popular to an associate who has built up a profitable patient list over a period of years.

One way to deal with this issue with associates is to price up the alternatives that they have, that is:

➤ to buy or rent a property
➤ to buy or lease fixtures and equipment and pay for the conversion of the building
➤ to survive for a period of six months to two years until a full list has been built up
➤ to deal with new patients and all the dental problems that they may bring.

Often when the above scenario is explained to them they willingly pay the price being asked.

There are a number of technical issues regarding goodwill and how it can be seen to have arisen as a result of different factors, such as location and personal service, that need to be explored, but it is outside the realm of this book to deal with such matters.

As mentioned above, goodwill is an area where HMRC take a keen interest, and it is paramount that specialist advice is sought regarding the valuation of goodwill.

Goodwill within the accounts

Goodwill that has been created by the proprietor within the existing business would usually not be included on the balance sheet of that business as it has not cost anything to buy (although it may have cost a lot of hours of hard work to generate). However, goodwill that has been purchased as part of the cost of buying a practice will be included within the accounts.

The accounting rules for un-incorporated practices (i.e. not limited companies) are fairly relaxed and the principals of those practices can decide how goodwill is disclosed in their accounts. In some cases a value will have been attributed to the goodwill that the principals have created, and the amount shown on the balance sheet, the reason for this will often be to give the principals a more complete picture of what their practice is worth on an ongoing basis.

Whether the goodwill on the balance sheet has been purchased or internally created it is seldom written off (amortised) in the accounts of un-incorporated practices. The reason often given is that, while the principals will recognise that value of the practice goodwill will fall as patients leave the practice, they also want to recognise the increase in value of the goodwill as new patients join, and as long as the net patient numbers remain the same there will not be a fall in the value of goodwill.

The rules regarding limited company accounts are, however, a lot stricter and the accounting rules dictate that goodwill will be subject to an annual amortisation charge (i.e. written off) based on the estimated useful life of the goodwill (to a maximum of 20 years), and/or subject to an annual impairment review.

But within a corporate arrangement there is a tax allowance available where the goodwill has been purchased or was created after April 2002. This tax allowance is not available to un-incorporated practices.

Future of goodwill values

It is probable as the recession starts to hit harder that goodwill values will fall, but by how much? There are many views as to the ability of the dental profession to weather the current financial crisis intact, and what the future holds for dentists, both private and NHS. The following points were made by Chris Barrow in his April 2009 e-zine:

Once again I risk being accused of influencing the market, but I can't help myself but to say that goodwill values in general practice seem to be on a steady decline – down from 100% of gross revenues last summer (2008) to maybe 75% or 60% of gross revenues this month.

I'm not sure that all of the valuation agents have caught up with the plot – but having supervised over 75 practice valuations in the six months I've enjoyed at IDH I can tell you that we have a very carefully developed valuation model which is constructed not only to calculate what we consider to be a 'fair price' in current market conditions but also a price that protects the future profitability of the business – for the sake of all of our employees, dentists and investors.

There will be exceptions to the numbers mentioned above – a golden opportunity based on location, professional specialisation, expansion plans, the desire of one dentist to live in a particular town. The accountants' valuation is sometimes superseded by the opportunity cost – but can we all please get used to the idea that the 'glory days' of high-profile dentists selling out for fortunes are over.

We have 46 practices in the Private and Specialist Division of IDH now – and we estimate our division to be the fourth largest business in UK dentistry in its own right – but I have to say that my acquisitions activity is slowing right down and we are taking a much closer look at any practice before we make an offer. I'm delighted to be representing a board who believe in growth where it's sensible and not just for the sake of it.

We are developing a talented team of business development managers, area managers and practice managers who are working 'hands on' to ensure that our practices move to the forefront of the private sector – some of our practices are already there, others will require monumental effort by the team.

Over the next three years we will be developing national brand standards to ensure that any of our division members will have access to centralised assistance and training on all aspects of 'perfect practice'.

My sentiment is that the 'conversation' about joining a private corporate has moved on from 'how big will my cheque be?' (the story of the last three years) to 'where best will I survive and prosper in the next 10 years?'

The opportunity to join a private corporate will be attractive to any principal who understands that there is strength in three commodities:
- more people with their minds and bodies at work on ideas to remain successful
- more money to invest in innovation
- more time to either do the dentistry or the business-building, depending on your passion.

I remain convinced that the dental market over the next 10 years will be populated by:

- NHS corporates
- private and specialist corporates
- retailers offering in-store services
- larger specialist dental poly-clinics
- four to six-surgery boutique independents that will offer NHS, mixed or private services – and sometimes working alongside two-surgery 'feeders' (see below).

But I am going to stick my neck on the block and suggest that the two-surgery loner is facing a serious challenge to their survival and will have to consider selling, joining or amalgamating into four to six-surgery mini-clinics.

The economies of scale, the need to constantly reinvest and the likely increase in compliance costs will, in my opinion, force the loners to either create the producer groups I have mentioned in recent years or create some other 'tribe' that will allow them to spread risk, cost, resources and people.

In that there is great opportunity for the business-minded. What we are doing at IDH is only one solution – and it will not suit everyone – but there are other solutions emerging in the marketplace.

I remain 100% confident that all principals have a bigger future, provided they can keep their minds open.

Just to prove my point – there is Willie and Xandra MacEachan at the brand new, two-surgery clinic they opened last week in Craiglockhart, Edinburgh.

Proof that I'm talking rubbish?

No – the two-surgery clinic is a satellite of their main clinic and will ultimately become a 'feeder' for the main clinic as well as a profitable mini-practice in its own right – and therein is a formula that requires much further discussion.

Whether Chris's predictions come true will depend, ultimately, on the patients and their expectations of a quality dental service provided for a reasonable price, but I do agree that a certain amount of amalgamation within the profession will raise quality, and also allow for economies of scale and a reduction in fees (especially NHS fees). As it is probable that there will be a change of government in the next few years, and this coupled with the austere spending cuts that the public sector needs to make will more than likely reduce the funding for NHS dentistry. I can see the larger NHS focused practices being given more work for agreed reductions in UDA values.

Property

The property that will usually be found on a dental practice's balance sheet will be the practice surgery premises, and will more often be shown at cost price, although some practices do increase the value of their premises to agree to the price paid by the most recent principal to join the practice. As property issues are looked at in greater detail in Chapter 6 there will be no further explanation of property related matters at this point.

Fixtures and equipment

The fixtures and equipment usually found in a dental practice can be broken down into the following categories:

➤ furniture such as desks, chairs, filing cabinets, bookcases, cupboards and some floor coverings

➤ dental equipment such as dental chairs, sterilising equipment, surgery units and hand pieces or tools

➤ office equipment such as computers, printers, telephones, faxes and cash registers and equipment to allow payment by credit card, etc.

➤ sundry other equipment such as vacuum cleaners, tea and coffee-making facilities, pictures and equipment for the provision of providing background music

➤ items of 'plant' that are integral to the building such as fitted cupboards and ambient lighting systems.

These items will be shown in the accounts at their purchase cost less a provision for depreciation to write off that cost over the estimated useful life of those assets.

When a practice is sold it is usual to have the fixtures and equipment valued by a dental equipment provider and that value used as the purchase price for the dentist buying the practice.

Tax allowances are available to reflect the loss in value of these assets over their estimated useful lives, with the allowance claimable being dependent upon the type of asset and the date it was purchased.

The different options as to the financing of these assets can be found further in this chapter.

Motor vehicles

In some un-incorporated accounts motor vehicles are included within the fixed assets on the balance sheet as a separate category, and these vehicles often represent the principal's own private car. As explained above, there is very little scope for dentists to claim a significant proportion of their motor expenses as business expenses. Therefore, the proportion of the loss in value of those vehicles that can be offset against taxable income is very low.

However, if the vehicles are not the principals' own cars but pool cars or commercial vehicles higher allowances can be claimed on them.

Given the very high taxes that will be payable by dentists as a result of being provided with a company car by their limited company, it is very rare to see motor vehicles on the balance sheet of a dental limited company.

The allowances that can be claimed against taxable income, on vehicles used by the practice, will be discussed in Chapter 10 on taxation.

CURRENT ASSETS

As mentioned above, current assets usually comprise of stock, debtors, cash and bank accounts, which can be described as liquid assets as they represent cash or items that can quickly be converted into cash.

Stock

A dental practice will usually hold the following items in stock:
➤ anaesthetics, sedatives, antibiotics and other medicines and pharmaceutical items
➤ consumables such as disposable instruments and rubber gloves
➤ stocks of over-the-counter dental products, such as toothbrushes, floss, interdental brushes, mouthwashes and toothpaste.

The amounts held can vary significantly depending upon the dentist's internal procedures and the ability of the wholesaler to supply the practice on a shorter time cycle, with the average stockholding in practice tending to be in the region of £1,000 to £2,000 per dentist.

There are two conflicting aims when it comes to buying stock for a dental practice. The first aim is to hold as little stock as possible, as that stock represents the principals' money which is tied up in the practice. The other aim is to buy the stock as cheaply as possible, but as that often results in having to buy in bulk, the level of stock rises! Most practitioners find a happy medium.

Where significant stocks are held, a proper stock-take should take place each year, valued with the addition of VAT, and that valuation should be included within the accounts. There will be stocks of drugs, amalgams, dental materials, rubber gloves, etc. which may prove to be of a material amount in a multi-surgery practice. With the recent changes to the rules regarding autoclaves and sterilising procedures there may also be holdings of disposable instruments.

A practice that does not perform a stock-take may include an estimate of the amounts held, on its balance sheet. If the estimate is for a round sum amount it could lead to an enquiry into the accounts from HMRC, who have stated that they expect more accurate records from businesses. They expect better records from larger practices.

Obviously, with smaller practices the level of stocks may be low and an estimate may be acceptable, but it should be noted that a significant misstatement would impact the profit and loss account.

No matter what size the practice is, a stock-take upon a partnership change-over should be mandatory. For the retiring principal it will provide comfort that they are receiving their share of the value, and for the continuing practice it is an opportunity to identify obsolete and outdated stock. A stock-take also provides the opportunity to test the accuracy of the stock estimate.

The smaller, less computer literate practices may have very basic stock-control procedures, while the more advanced practices may have online stock-ordering facilities. The former practice will find that they will have excess stock of some items and shortages of others and may suffer from obsolescence of items that may have been held for too long. In addition they will often estimate the amount of stock at the year end for accounts purposes, and as a consequence their margins may be inaccurate. By contrast, the latter practice will hold the minimum amounts of stock to reduce working capital, and be able to provide accurate stock figures for accounts purposes. In addition their systems will highlight any stocks likely to become obsolete.

Most practices will hold stocks of dental items for sale to their patients, but very few make a significant amount of profit from it, usually for the following reasons.

➤ The principals don't view these sales as an important part of the practice, and view it as an incidental operation which is superfluous to the main business.

➤ The principals don't feel comfortable in asking their patients to spend more with them.

➤ The principals don't know how to sell and don't highlight the benefits of the items on sale to their patients.

➤ Staff are often not trained or motivated to sell the items to patients.

As there can be significant profit margins on some of the items, dentists should put more effort into increasing these sales. They can sell the items to patients by explaining to them that they are complementary to or necessary for their treatment, and inform the reception staff to have the items ready and priced in with the treatment costs when the patient is ready to pay upon leaving the practice.

If the dentist is not interested in selling dental care products one option is to let the practice staff operate that part of the business with, possibly, a profit-share arrangement with them, linked to the sales income, as part of the agreement. This arrangement has proved successful in increasing sales levels in a number of practices.

Debtors

Dental accounts need to be drafted on an earnings basis, and not to merely show receipts and payments during the accounting year. Therefore, at the year end, account needs to be taken of all outstanding items that remain unpaid at the year end.

The debtors of a practice represent the amounts that are owed *to* that practice at the year-end date and would usually comprise of the following.

➤ **Amounts due to the practice from the NHS:** in England and Wales this amount would represent the arrears of the monthly on-account payment for UDAs, whereas in Scotland and Northern Ireland the amount would be in respect of outstanding fees and allowances. As most practices demand the payment of patient charges and private fees as the patients leave the practice following their treatment, the major debtor will be the amount owed to the practice for its NHS services.

➤ As a result, most accounts will include a debtor for the payment due under the NHS contract, payable one month in arrears. Given the number of NHS practices and the number of transactions that are processed, the NHS formulated a system where schedules were processed at different dates during the month, in order to avoid all the work being concentrated at the month end. They managed this by allocating dental practices to specific groups, with each group being processed at a different time in the month (Appendix 6: Dentist NHS payment schedule 2009, *see* www.radcliffe-oxford.com/financefordentists. This shows 20 such groups and details the dates up to which their schedules are processed. From this schedule it is possible to identify the period for which NHS monies will be outstanding to a practice at their year-end date.)

➤ **Practice plan payments:** where the practice has a payment plan in place, such as British Union Provident Association (BUPA) or Denplan, there may be outstanding subscriptions due to the practice at the year-end date, but most of these plans tend to forward the payment to the practice in the month in which they are received.

➤ **Outstanding fees:** where the practice charges fees per item there may be amounts due to the practice for treatments that have been completed and invoiced. There also may be on-account payments outstanding in respect of longer courses of continuing treatment.

➤ **Work in progress:** at the year-end date there may be time spent and costs incurred on treatments that have not yet been completed where no invoice or payment request has been raised. Accounting rules and tax legislation require that the sale price of that work be included in the accounts as owing to the practice at that date.

➤ **Prepayments:** at the year-end date there may have been payments made for items in advance, for example a year's insurance paid upfront.

The advance payment is calculated and shown in the accounts as a prepayment, with the amount being carried forward.

Most dental practices will manage their fees, both private and the collection of patient charges, very well and will incur very little expense in the way of bad debts, but inevitably there will be a number of patients that it will be very difficult to extract money from. In order to manage the process to ensure that bad debts are kept to a minimum, successful practices adopt the following procedures.

➤ The dentist gives something (a file or similar) for the patient to return to the reception staff upon leaving.
➤ The dentist asks the patient to arrange another appointment with the receptionist on their way out.
➤ The dentist notifies the receptionist of the charge to make to the patient by way of internal computer link.
➤ The practice provides facilities for patients to pay by credit and debit cards.

The above procedures minimise the chance of patients leaving without paying their fees. In addition, those practices will not carry out further treatment where there are outstanding fees due for earlier work.

The level of unpaid fees should be relatively low if the above procedures are adopted, with the amount of debt relating mainly to the last course of treatment undertaken. If the amounts are less than, say, £150 there is very little action that could be taken that would be worthwhile, other than writing a few strongly worded letters from the practice and visiting the patient personally to ask for the payment.

Although most solicitors provide an excellent service when it comes to chasing customers for the non-payment of debt, the amounts are often too small to warrant their fees, if the debt remains unpaid, and most claims are just not economical to be dealt with in this way.

This leaves a dentist with a problem when there are fees in excess of £150 outstanding and all efforts from the practice have not produced a result.

This is where Money Claim Online can be a benefit to a business. Money Claim provides an online process, from Her Majesty's Courts Service, that allows County Court proceedings to be initiated for a fee as low as £30. This site allows for a claim to be made online in England and Wales for up to £99,999.99. (Unfortunately, there is no equivalent in Scotland at present.)

The site provides a tutorial to guide you through the process, and is very easy to use.

The costs increase in line with the amount of the claim, but debts up to £3,000 can be dealt with for as little as £30 to £85 per claim.

This site provides a cost-effective option for proceedings involving smaller debts, and can avoid the situation where escalating costs can negate the debt recovery action. Further details can be found on www.moneyclaim.gov.uk.

Cash at bank and in hand

The figures included on a practice balance sheet for cash at bank and in hand represent the reconciled balances at the year-end date. The reconciled bank balance rarely matches the amounts on the bank statement as it represents the balance in the bank account at the year-end date, less the cheques written out and not presented at that date, plus the receipts banked but not yet cleared in the bank account.

There will usually be a small amount of cash included on the balance sheet; this amount will represent the petty cash held at the year-end date. The petty cash is either obtained by utilising some of the cash received from patients as they pay their fees or by withdrawing cash from the practice bank account. Petty cash will normally be used to pay trivial bills such as coffee, tea, newspapers, window cleaning, etc.

Historically, dentist practices have been fairly lucrative and often built up amounts of surplus cash in deposit accounts, and these deposit accounts may be shown on their balance sheets. For those practices which have incorporated, surplus fees may have built up within the company as a result of tax-planning initiatives, and may be similarly held in deposit accounts.

In some cases these deposits may be shown on the balance sheet of a company but the amounts may actually be held in accounts in the dentist's own name. These funds will remain the company's but will be held 'on trust' by the dentist for the following reasons.

➤ Limited companies are not offered high investment rates on their surplus funds, and the amounts that can be earned are often derisory compared with the amounts an individual can earn on a personal account. For that reason some dentists have been withdrawing money from their companies to invest in their own name to obtain a higher level of interest. They have done this by way of a trust and have completed paperwork to the effect that the funds and the interest earned remain with the company. HMRC have accepted these arrangements in the past as long as there is a valid trust deed signed by the relevant parties.

➤ The recent banking crisis resulted in an increase in this type of arrangement, the main reason being the transfer to the personal accounts of the directors to obtain the deposit guarantee of £50,000 that was not available to corporate structures. Without these transfers the companies' funds were at risk of a bank collapse.

CURRENT LIABILITIES

The liabilities of a practice represent the amounts that the practice owes *to* others, and they are usually split in the accounts (especially limited company accounts, where it is a legal requirement) between current and long-term liabilities. Current liabilities are those which are due for repayment within 12 months of the balance sheet date, and long-term liabilities represent those amounts that are due thereafter.

The current liabilities of a dental practice would usually be made up of the following.

➤ **UDA overpayments:** where NHS practices have failed to achieve their contract level of UDAs, for which they have been paid, a provision is made in the accounts for the amount that may need to be repaid, or for the additional work that may be necessary to make up the shortfall in the following year. Most PCOs have accepted a combination of repayments and UDA catch up in the following year to deal with this problem. Usually, PCOs would require the repayment of an underachievement of more than 10% of the target, and would allow an underachievement of less than 10% to be carried forward to be completed in the next year.

➤ **Amounts due to suppliers:** most suppliers of dental equipment and materials, and providers of expense items, will give dentists 30 to 60 days to pay for their orders, so it is usual to have outstanding bills at the year end in dental accounts.

➤ **Dental laboratory fees:** similarly, at the year-end date there would usually be dental laboratory bills outstanding. Some Denplan practices will wait to obtain payments from their patients, for their laboratory fees, before paying the amount to the laboratory.

➤ **Associates' fees:** it is usual for associates to be paid in arrears, usually towards the end of the month or earlier the following month, for the work they have undertaken. The main reason for the delay is to await details of the income they have earned (from NHS and private treatments), and the expenses that they have incurred, in order to calculate the amount due to them per their agreements.

➤ **Hygienists' fees:** some hygienists will be employed by practices and receive payment for their work through the amounts paid through payroll. Other hygienists will work on a self-employed basis and will usually invoice practices at the end of a month for the work that they have done. It would be usual for hygienists on the payroll to be paid by the end of the month, but those who raise invoices will usually find that their fees are outstanding at the month end.

➤ **Accruals:** there may be expenses that have been incurred by the practice by the year-end date but for which an invoice has not been raised; for example, the cost of producing the year-end accounts would normally be included as an expense in those accounts, but the invoice for those services will often not be raised until the accounts are completed after the year end. These types of expenses are 'accrued' in the accounts (other similar items are phone costs or utility costs where invoices have not been received by the year-end date).

➤ **Bank overdraft:** as most bank overdrafts are repayable upon demand they will be shown as a current liability in the accounts.

➤ **PAYE and corporation tax:** if the practice is incorporated, making profits and providing employment, it will create liabilities for both PAYE and corporation tax. These should be provided in the accounts as liabilities at the year-end date.

➤ **Balances due within one year on loans and hire purchase arrangements:** the balances due after 12 months will be shown within long-term liabilities (see next section).

➤ **Director's loan account:** where practices are incorporated the transactions between the dentist and his or her company would usually be recorded in a director's loan account. Examples of such transactions are:

  • capital introduced from own resources or financed by personal borrowings
  • amounts drawn from the practice, usually in lieu of dividends declared
  • company expenses funded personally by the dentist
  • personal expenses of the dentist funded by the company.

➤ It would be usual to find the director's loan account in creditors, reflecting the fact that the company owed the director for excess funds introduced to the company. If it is found as a debtor it means that the director has taken excess funds from the company and will be subject to a tax charge on the amount, plus interest.

LONG-TERM LIABILITIES

Usually the long-term liabilities of a dental practice consist wholly of balances due on loans and hire purchase arrangements.

Given the cost of funding the stock of drugs, appliances and consumables until payment is received from the NHS, payment plan provider or the patient, a practice requires a level of money to operate; this is known as working capital. In addition, funds may have been required to purchase the practice and to renovate the property to a reasonable standard. This funding is often provided by way of bank borrowing, either an overdraft or a loan. A loan will be disclosed on the balance sheet, and the element within long-term liabilities will represent that part of the loan which will be due for repayment after one year.

The purchase of dental equipment is often funded by hire purchase agreements which can be taken out over a period of years, usually three to five.

From the repayment schedule it is possible to identify the amount that will be due within, and after, one year, and disclose those amounts in the accounts as appropriate.

It would be normal, if the amount of borrowing was significant, for the lender to ask the borrower for some form of security or guarantee, and often principals or directors sign personal guarantees to secure their company borrowings. These guarantees will give the banks access to the dentist's personal assets should the loan not be repaid within the agreed timetable. In addition, there are government-funded guarantee schemes where the banks are guaranteed a percentage of the loan should the dentists default on the loan. The premiums on these schemes are quite expensive, and are usually paid for by the borrower. Up until 2008, the specialist lenders did not often ask for guarantees, but since the credit crunch it has become more the norm to do so.

PURCHASE OF ASSETS AND EQUIPMENT: CASH, HP OR LEASE?

Accountants are often asked: what is the best way to finance the purchase of new assets? In most cases if cash is available it is preferable to use that to buy the asset outright, because the cost of the interest on a loan will often be more than the return the cash was achieving on deposit. But often dentists, especially those setting up a practice for the first time, have limited cash flow and it is often preferable to spread the payments over a period of time, but is it better to buy an asset on hire purchase, with a loan, or to lease it?

The following paragraphs summarise the differences in the way assets are treated when they are financed by different methods.

➤ **Purchase with own cash:** if dentists use their own funds to buy the asset, they will own that asset from the outset and be able to get 100% tax relief on the cost in the year of purchase, up to the annual investment allowance of £50,000.

➤ **Purchase with an unsecured loan:** again, the dentists will own that asset from the outset and be able to get 100% tax relief on the cost in the year of purchase, up to the annual investment allowance of £50,000. (An unsecured loan is one given by the lender free of any security. A secured loan would give the lender a security over the asset being purchased, or other assets of the borrower. Given the lender is in a safer position with a secured loan, the rates charged on those loans are usually less than those charged on unsecured loans.)

➤ **Purchase under a hire purchase agreement:** under a hire purchase agreement, the dentists are treated as owning the asset from the outset, but legal ownership only passes to them on the payment of final 'option to purchase' fee. Again, the full cost gets 100% tax relief in year of purchase, up to the annual investment allowance of £50,000. Usually, a hire purchase loan is secured on the asset to which it relates.

➤ **Purchase by way of a lease:** under this arrangement the leasing company owns the asset for the period of the lease and the monthly leasing payments get tax relief, as they are paid, through the profit and loss account. Often at the end of the initial lease period (usually three to five years), a secondary lease period will commence with the asset being leased to the dentists at a peppercorn rent in perpetuity, effectively giving the dentists ownership of the asset.

So when an asset is bought, 100% tax relief can be obtained in the year of purchase (this does not include cars). If the asset is leased, tax relief can be obtained only over the period of the lease, so there are significant cash flow benefits to choosing purchase over leasing, as shown in the above examples.

Under current tax legislation it is generally better to buy rather than lease assets, but if you are considering purchasing assets in the future check with your accountant as to the current rules.

NET ASSETS

This figure should represent the net worth of the practice at the year-end date. In the example balance sheet above the net asset value is £498,000, and this is the amount, in theory, that would be generated by a sale of the business items on that day. So if the goodwill and fixed assets were sold for £700,000, the stock sold, the debtors monies collected, and the funds utilised in paying of the debts, including loans, the amount left in the bank would be £498,000. This is a theoretical exercise, as the amount collected would depend on whether the values on the balance sheet were up to date, and actually achieved upon a sale. However, the balance sheet is a useful indicator of the value of a practice, and can be brought up to date quite easily by obtaining current valuations, in the event of a sale of whole or part of the practice.

The net asset position of the practice in the example above was £498,000 on 31 March 2009 and £468,500 on 31 March 2008; the increase in value of £29,500 in that year could only have occurred as a result of one or all of the following.

➤ **Excess profits being retained:** this is the most common reason for an increase in the value of a balance sheet, and occurs when principals take less from the practice by way of drawings than they have earned in profits. As they have under-drawn those profits, they have been retained within the practice and increased its value. It is very rare, however, for those under-drawn profits to be represented by extra cash in the bank account because they may have been used for the following:

- purchase of additional fixtures and equipment
- an increase in the level of stocks held
- some of the profits may be represented by fees that have yet to be received for treatments undertaken prior to the year-end date
- the profits may have been used in reducing the bank overdraft, paying off creditors or reducing the balance on the practice loan.

➤ **The input of funds by the principal:** in some cases when there is a need to upgrade the practice facilities the principals can input from their own resources some, or all, of the funding that will be necessary to pay for the upgrade. Dentists may also introduce funds to repay excess drawings in earlier periods.

➤ **Revaluation of assets:** often the property shown on a practice balance sheet will be shown at its purchase price, and will only be revalued upon a sale of all, or part, of the practice. In addition, the value of the practice's equipment may be understated by a high level of depreciation being charged on it; these may also be revalued upon a sale and the increase (or decrease!) be reflected on the balance sheet.

In the example balance sheet in Figure 3.1 the increase in the value has occurred as a result of excess profits being retained, and Figure 3.2 shows how the excess profits have been utilised. In the year to 2009 the stock has increased by £300, current liabilities have been reduced by £24,000 and the loans have been reduced by £15,000. This total increase in value is £39,300, and has been financed by the retained excess profits of £29,500, monies from debtors of £800 and monies from the bank account of £9,000.

Next we will look at how the net asset position is reflected in the principals' capital and current accounts balances, and provide an explanation as to the distinction between these accounts.

	2009	2008	Increase/ Decrease
	£	£	£
Stocks	3 500	3 200	300
Debtors	17 500	18 300	−800
Cash at bank and in hand	34 500	43 500	−9 000
Current liabilities	22 500	46 500	24 000
Loans	235 000	250 000	15 000
Net increase in value			29 500

FIGURE 3.2 Example balance sheet – increase in value

FUNDING OF DENTAL ACCOUNTS

One aspect of dental accounts that is often queried by dentists is that of capital. How does this capital accumulate, how it is distributed between the principals and why it cannot be drawn out. These are the more usual questions asked on this topic, along with the matter of the introduction of the capital into the dental practice, how it is described in the accounts and by what means it should be contributed to by an incoming principal. If the capital in a practice is managed correctly, it can assist the principals in future planning and in some cases present significant tax advantages.

The capital in the majority of dental practices can be fairly easily allocated under three headings, as follows.

➤ **Property capital:** this usually represents the principals' interest in the equity in the surgery building, and in some cases the fixed assets of the practice. This is often separately identified in the accounts as the 'capital accounts' of those principals with an interest in those assets. As this capital is represented by physical assets it cannot easily be withdrawn from the practice.

➤ **Other (or fixed asset) capital:** this represents the principals' interest in the non-building fixed assets of the practice, i.e. the fixtures and fittings, dental equipment, computers, etc. These are the assets from which the principals earn their general practice income and would normally be held in the same proportions as those in which the principals share the practice costs. However, a number of practices operate a system whereby each principal funds their own surgery equipment personally; in these cases the costs need to be attributed to the partners and shown as separate 'capital' accordingly.

➤ **Working capital:** this represents the funds needed to finance the day-to-day operation of the practice, and is often called the 'current account'. This amount is usually made up by the net investment in the practice assets as follows:

  • stocks of drugs and consumables
  • amounts owed to the practice
  • work in progress or un-invoiced work
  • cash and bank balances
  • amounts owed by the practice.

Although the capital has been broken down into three headings above, it is more usual to see it broken down into two headings in dental accounts; these are more usually known as the 'capital' and the 'current' account.

Capital accounts

Although there are no set rules as to which assets are financed by a principal's capital and current accounts, it is usual to see the net equity of the property reflected by the capital accounts with the balance of the practice finance (i.e. the 'other capital' and the 'working capital') being funded by the current accounts. The capital and current accounts are often held in equal shares by the principals, or in line with the percentage of practice costs they each fund. This is especially so where the practice agreement provides for a fully equipped surgery for each principal.

However, there are a number of expense-sharing dental practices where the capital of the practice is not funded equally. In these practices the principals are responsible for equipping their own surgeries as well as contributing an agreed amount to the shared equipment. In these cases their capital accounts will not only reflect their share of the property equity, but also their share of the other (or fixed asset) capital of the practice. This arrangement is popular with a number of practices as it gives the individual dentist the freedom to carry out improvements to the surgery irrespective of his or her colleagues' intentions. It is particularly of use where there is a range in the ages of the principals, as the younger dentists can carry out improvements to their own facilities without forcing their older colleagues, who are nearer to retirement, to do likewise.

In the example in Figure 3.1 the capital accounts of the dentists represent the costs of the property and all of the other fixed assets less the balance on the property loans as at the year-end date, as follows:

Fixed assets	£700 000
Loans	£235 000
Capital account	£465 000

However, for the rest of this section we will assume that the capital account reflects only the net equity of the practice premises (i.e. the value of the property less the outstanding balance on the loan).

Capital accounts are often based on the cost of the property on the balance sheet, and this cost is often an accumulation of the expense on the property over a number of years. It is important to regularly review the cost of the property against an estimation of its actual market value, for the following reasons.

➤ If the market value is less than the accumulated cost in the accounts, there is a negative equity situation and the principals would need to reflect this loss in value with a deduction from their capital accounts. This often happens when an extension is built onto an existing surgery, where the building costs are in excess of the added value of the extended surgery. It is important that the practice agreement includes a section to deal with this so that the principals are aware of the cash-flow implications of a change in partners. This is especially important for smaller practices where there is the possibility of one principal being left with the property and mortgage for more than the market value of that property.

➤ If the market value is in excess of the cost per the accounts, the equity position needs to be discussed with the practice so that they are aware of the cash they would need to raise to buy a principal out. By amending the accounts to show the market value the accounts show a more complete picture of the true value of the practice.

➤ By taking note of the market value of the building, the practice can identify the investment (or not) that each partner has in the practice, and plan for the funding needed should there be a change in the partnership in the future.

➤ It is often useful to provide the practice bankers with accounts with the property shown at current market value, so that they can assess the loan-to-value ratio on any funding secured on the property. The practice could renegotiate the terms of its loan if the value of the net equity in the property has increased significantly.

Often the purchase of the practice premises has been funded by a loan, which is being paid off out of the practice profits each year. As the practice profits are posted to the principals' current accounts it is important, therefore, to make an annual adjustment to reflect the amount of profits that have been used in repaying the loan capital, by way of a transfer from the current to the capital accounts. The adjustment will reflect the fact that the principals will have an increased level of funds in the premises' equity, and a reduced amount of profits from which to draw against.

In the example balance sheets in Figures 3.1 and 3.2 (above) the loans have been repaid by £15,000 in the year to 2009 and the capital account has been increased to reflect this additional equity.

Current accounts

Current accounts usually reflect the amounts that the principals initially introduced to the practice when they joined as well as their accumulated undrawn profits of the practice to date, and provide the funding for the working capital of the practice.

Each year the individual principal's profit share will be posted to his or her current account, plus any monies he or she has introduced to the practice (or amounts that have been received by the practice on his or her behalf). Amounts in respect of his or her drawings and liabilities paid on his or her behalf (e.g. income tax) are then deducted from the current account. If at the end of the year the current account balance has risen, the principal will have under-drawn his or her profits, likewise a reduction in the balance will represent an overdrawing of the profits in the year.

It is important that the principals understand how their current accounts work and that items, other than the cash they take from the practice, can reduce the balance on those accounts. Taxation and superannuation paid on the principals' behalf by the practice and personal expenses can be charged to the principals' current accounts to reduce the amounts available to draw.

As explained above, the current account balance provides the monies for the practice assets and the working capital of the practice.

To encourage good working capital management, practices should work to an agreed overall level of current account. This level should be sufficient to provide for the cash that the practice needs to operate, plus to provide for any future planned increases in fixed assets. It is important for the practice to set this figure as it represents a target for them to aim for, and to ensure that excesses do not build up within the practice that could otherwise be drawn by the principals.

Based on this agreed level, an annual equalisation can be calculated following the drafting of the accounts. This equalisation will allow those principals who have accumulated excesses to draw down, while those who have overdrawn will need to either reduce their drawings or input further funds to the practice. It is important for an equalisation to take place annually for the following reasons.

➤ It ensures that no principal's current account is too far out of line with those of his or her colleagues that it could cause a problem should that principal decide to retire. Problems can arise if a principal is allowed to accumulate a large current account, as the practice could be forced to obtain funding from its bankers to affect a payout on that principal's retirement. Likewise, if a principal is allowed to operate a negative current account, he or she will need to find monies to pay into the practice upon leaving.

➤ It ensures that the working capital of the practice is contributed to in line with the profit/expense-sharing ratios of the principals.

➤ It ensures that the overall level of the working capital is not allowed to build up or fall below the agreed level.

The agreed level of current account may need to be increased on an annual basis to match inflation and any increases in activity in the practice.

DRAWINGS AND THE PAYMENT OF TAX
The calculation of the principals' drawings in a dental practice is a relatively simple operation and the usual way of allocating the distributable income at the end of each month would be as follows.

➤ The gross income received by the practice in respect of each principal would be noted and allocated to the relevant principal.

➤ The general income received by the practice would be noted and a share allocated to each principal.
➤ The laboratory bills and other individual costs are then allocated to specific principals.
➤ The outstanding bills for the practice in total and wages costs for that month are collated and a share of the amount would be allocated to each principal.

The net of the amounts above is paid to each principal, and a schedule provided detailing the calculation. This method produces a fairly accurate way of keeping the current accounts in balance, although there may be one or two adjustments to be made at the year end that may affect the equalisation, such as superannuation and depreciation on separately owned assets. This method allows the principals to draw their gross income and is reliant upon them paying their own tax bills.

Where the practice has agreed to pay the principals' tax, the calculation of the drawings is more complicated and the tax liability needs to be taken into account. It would be very unusual for each principal to have the same tax bill given that they earn different amounts of profits, and especially in the case of a new principal, who may be paying tax on a different basis. Therefore, the calculation would need to deduct from the workings, above, an amount each month equal to a twelfth of the individual's tax liability. On the face of it, this appears reasonably straightforward, but in practice the individual principal's tax liabilities are not all notified to the practice at the same time, and refunds and reductions in the tax on-account payments can confuse matters.

INCOME TAX RESERVES

The calculations above provide for the principal's personal tax liabilities in respect of earlier years' profits to be deducted from the principal's current account as they fall due for payment. The calculations do not take into account the tax due on the profits in the current year, which will have not yet been calculated and will not be payable until the following year.

Historically, the tax liabilities of partners in a partnership were deemed to be a joint liability, in that the HMRC could claim from the partnership the unpaid tax of an errant partner. As a result of this many practices which operated as partnerships accrued for all the partners' future tax liabilities within the accounts to ensure that the funds were there in the event of a partner facing financial difficulty.

Given that, under self-assessment, the partners' tax liabilities are no longer a partnership liability, very few practices retain a reserve for future tax bills any longer. In fact most practices operate a gross drawings calculation, as above, which allows the partners to save up personally for their tax and, where appropriate, to use their tax monies in an offset mortgage account, to reduce their interest costs.

TREATMENT OF SUPERANNUATION CONTRIBUTIONS

Superannuation contributions deducted from the practice income on behalf of the principals are not an expense of running the practice, but rather a payment of a pension on behalf of those partners. As such, those contributions should not be shown as an expense in the annual accounts, but charged to the individual partners through their respective current accounts.

However, there is some debate as to how those deductions from income should be shown in the accounts of an incorporated practice. The treatment of the deductions will depend upon the nature of the NHS contract and the remuneration package agreed with the dentist, and is still an area of confusion with accountants when accounts are prepared.

DETAILS OF TRANSACTIONS IN CURRENT ACCOUNTS

There can often be disagreements between the principals in a practice and their accountant regarding differences in the balances on their current account. It is often a case of shooting the messenger when principals are informed that they have overdrawn their profits in the year and need to input funds to the practice.

It is important, therefore, for the current accounts to show sufficient detail, and for the accountant to provide explanations for variances in the partners' current accounts. It is essential that the principals understand what they have been allocated with and charged for in the accounts. Bookkeeping errors can result in income and expenses being allocated to the wrong principals, and only a detailed analysis will allow the principals to double check that their current accounts are correct.

CHAPTER 4

NHS dentistry

Before we look at the detail of how dentists are paid under their NHS contracts it would be useful to look at how the NHS is organised to deliver dental services.

The NHS was formed in 1948 and since then there have been numerous changes in the delivery of its services as each new government applies new policies to achieve their goals. The latest change involving dentistry was the introduction on 1 April 2006 of the New NHS General Dental Services Contract, which was introduced in England and Wales.

The NHS in England is controlled by the UK government through the Department of Health (DoH), which takes political responsibility for the service. The DoH controls the strategic health authorities (SHAs), which oversee all NHS operations, particularly the PCOs, in their area. The 10 SHAs in England are coterminous with the nine Government Office Regions, but with the South East region split into South East Coast and South Central SHAs. The SHAs are responsible for the NHS trusts in their area, and there are several different types of NHS trust as follows.

➤ PCOs, which administer primary care and public health. On 1 October 2006 the number of PCOs was reduced from 303 to 152 in an attempt to bring services closer together and cut costs. These oversee around 21,000 NHS dentists. In addition, they commission acute services from other NHS trusts and the private sector, provide primary care in their locations, and oversee such matters as primary and secondary prevention, vaccination administration and control of epidemics. PCOs control 80% of the total NHS budget.

➤ NHS hospital trusts. Approximately 290 organisations administer hospitals, treatment centres and specialist care centres in about 1,600 NHS hospitals (many trusts maintain between two and eight different hospital sites).

➤ NHS ambulance service trusts.
➤ NHS care trusts.
➤ NHS mental health services trusts.

Dentists providing NHS services in practice deliver their services under a contract with a PCO. In England the authority is a PCT. In Wales the equivalent authority is termed the local health board (LHB), in Scotland the local healthcare cooperative (LHCC) and in Northern Ireland the health and social service board (HSSB).

The dentists' contract to deliver services can either be between the practice and the contractual authority (PCO) or, in England and Wales, directly between the individual dentists (or performers) and the contractual authority.

INDEPENDENT CONTRACTOR STATUS

In conjunction with doctors, dentists contracting with the NHS have an independent contractor status, which is a halfway house between a genuine self-employed businessperson and a salaried employee of the state. On the one hand, the dentist pays tax and National Insurance under the self-employed Schedule D taxation system, he or she is responsible for his or her own business, has to finance the practice and take responsibility for staff, etc. On the other hand, he or she is not entirely independent as to how his or her income is calculated. As we shall see, this is based upon a formula which utilises UDAs in England and Wales (separate formulas are used in Scotland and Northern Ireland), the price of which the dentist has little input in. Those dentists who concentrate on NHS work find that their ability to increase their income is reliant upon the PCO increasing their NHS contract, and this level of control limits their independence which would not be appropriate to other self-employed individuals.

In the provision for retirement the NHS dentist appears to obtain the best of both worlds, as he or she is simultaneously self-employed and a member of a very good occupational pension scheme. The superannuation scheme as it affects dentists will be covered at length in Chapter 11.

As independent contractors, NHS dentists are responsible not only for dental care that they provide to patients but also for the organisation and financing of their practices. So, although their gross income is limited by their contract with the PCT, their ability to increase their profits relies upon their management skills.

In some practices, however, due to lack of training or focus on finance the level of profit can fall far beneath that of the average practice, even though the practice runs as a model of efficiency in respect of its dental care. It is these practices that can gain most from a specialist dental financial adviser.

There is a popular misconception that NHS dentists, like most workers within the NHS, are paid on a salaried basis. Historical earnings figures are issued by the DoH from time to time which seem to suggest a level of earnings, but these just reflect an average of the sample of accounts that they have selected at that time. The level of profits of NHS dentists can vary depending upon their ability to deliver services within a low-cost framework. The Standard General Services Contract (The New Contract – The National Health Service (General Dental Services Contracts) Regulations 2005) has produced a system where the level of income a dentist receives can differ from other dentists providing exactly the same level of service, so it is not possible to provide an accurate snapshot of the amount the average dentist should earn by providing NHS services.

THE GENERAL DENTAL SERVICES CONTRACT

On 1 April 2006 the New NHS General Dental Services Contract (*see* Appendix 7: General Dental Services Statement of Financial Entitlements at www.radcliffe-oxford.com/financefordentists) was introduced in England and Wales, and instituted a new way of paying dentists for supplying dental services under the NHS contract. The Personal Dental Services Statement of Financial Entitlements came into force on the same date. Prior to that date, dentists had been paid by a combination of capitation fees and item of service fees, as they currently are in Scotland and Northern Ireland.

The rest of this chapter will concentrate on payments to dentists providing NHS services within England and Wales, and further brief details of the NHS payments to dentists in Scotland and Northern Ireland can be found in:
➤ Appendix 8: Scottish Dental Allowances Guide
➤ Appendix 9: Scottish Dental Information Guide
➤ Appendix 10: Summary contents of Northern Ireland Statement of Dental Remuneration.
(*See* www.radcliffe-oxford.com/financefordentists.)

Further details can be obtained:
➤ for dentists practicing in Scotland, from: www.psd.scot.nhs.uk/dentists/index.html
➤ for dentists practicing in Northern Ireland, from: www.centralservicesagency.com.

It is interesting to note the emergence of different approaches to NHS dentistry in England, Wales, Northern Ireland and Scotland. Future studies should be able to determine which country has the better system for protecting the nation's teeth!

PAYMENT FOR NHS SERVICES IN ENGLAND AND WALES

From 1 April 2006 GDS and PDS dentists have had local contracts with PCOs, which hold budgets to provide dental services for their areas. The PCOs have agreed contract values with either providers (practices or companies) or performers (individual dentists) for a particular level of service.

This level of service has been specified in terms of an annual level of UDAs that have to be achieved by the dentist. The level of service takes into account CoTs, which are converted into UDAs based on the most complex component of the CoT.

The initial contract service level, from which the target number of UDAs to be achieved was calculated, was based on the level of dental activity performed by the dentist during the reference period October 2004 to September 2005.

This figure was then reduced by 5% in England and 10% in Wales to establish the contract level of activity. In 2009 most practices still have the same target level of UDAs that they were allocated in 2006. The payment of the contract values is made on a monthly basis.

The contract value is paid to dentists monthly in arrears, after deduction of 'patient charges'; these are payments which dentists receive directly from their non-exempt patients, a further explanation of these amounts can be found in Table 4.3.

The CoT payments work on a three-band system where each band comprises a range of treatments. The higher the band, the higher the charge, but within any one band the charge is uniform, although the cost and complexity of the treatment may vary.

The contract is constructed around the contractor (either a practice or an individual dentist) undertaking a course of treatment, with that treatment being given a value or banding and a UDA applied to that banding, as shown in Tables 4.1 and 4.2.

TABLE 4.1 UDAs provided under the contract in respect of banded courses of treatment

Type of course of treatment	UDAs provided
Band 1 course of treatment (excluding urgent treatment)	1.0
Band 1 course of treatment (urgent treatment only)	1.2
Band 2 course of treatment	3.0
Band 3 course of treatment	12.0

➤ **Band 1** CoTs cover check-ups and simple treatments such as examination, diagnosis (e.g. X-rays), advice on preventative measures, and a scale and polish.

➤ **Band 2** CoTs cover mid-range treatments such as fillings, extractions and root canal work.
➤ **Band 3** CoTs cover complex treatments such as crowns, dentures and bridges.

TABLE 4.2 UDAs provided under the contract in respect of charge exempt courses of treatment

Type of charge exempt course	UDAs of treatment
Issue a prescription	0.75
Repair of a dental appliance (denture)	1.00
Repair of a dental appliance (bridge)	1.20
Removal of sutures	1.00
Arrest of bleeding	1.20

Practices which opted to provide services under the contract were given a target level of UDAs to achieve in their first year. A value was applied to each UDA, and that value was calculated to give the practice an income in line with the level of income it had previously earned from supplying NHS services under the old contract (less the deduction of either 5% or 10%, as mentioned above).

The practice annual contract income, as calculated above, is paid over in 12 equal monthly payments, in arrears. However, the monthly payment is reduced by the amount of 'patient charges' that the practice should have received in respect of the work undertaken. Patient charges are the amounts that the non-exempt patients (i.e. those patients not eligible for a reduction in their dental costs) pay as a contribution to their dental work. These charges used to be set as a percentage of the cost of the treatment but have now been simplified to agree to the banding system and from 1 April 2009 have been as shown in Table 4.3.

TABLE 4.3 Patient charges

	England	Wales
Band 1	£16.20	£12.00
Band 2	£44.60	£39.00
Band 3	£198.00	£177.00

This figure increases each year in line with agreed NHS increases. Further details regarding patient charges can be found in Appendix 11: NHS dental charges: what you should pay, and Appendix 12: Patient charges explained (*see* www. radcliffe-oxford.com/financefordentists).

A dental practice will have its monthly NHS income reduced by the amount that it should have collected from its patients under the scheme, and not by the actual amount of patient charges that the practice receives. The difference between what the practice should have received and the actual amount collected can be due to a number of factors, such as the inability of the practice to obtain the money from patients as they leave the practice or errors in form filling by the dentist.

In order for the PCO to obtain details of the number and type of UDAs that a practice has performed, and how much the practice should have collected from patients, a form is completed after each task performed by the dentist. This form is called FP17 (*see* Appendix 13: Form FP17 and completion of form guidance, at www.radcliffe-oxford.com/financefordentists) and it has to include the following:

➤ details of the patient (name, address, etc.)
➤ details of the dentist performing the work
➤ details of what charge band the treatment falls into and any other services provided
➤ whether the patient is exempt from paying the patient charges
➤ signed by both the patient and the dentist.

Upon the receipt of the FP17 form the PCO is able to monitor the progress that the practice is making in achieving its UDA target and also calculate the amount to deduct from the practice payment for the patient charges. The PCO then sends a schedule to the practice detailing the following:

➤ annual contract value for the practice
➤ contract value for the month analysed into performers' shares
➤ the amount of patient charges deducted from each performer's share
➤ the amount of seniority receivable (if applicable)
➤ the deduction for the superannuation contributions for each of the performers
➤ notification of how much the PCT has contributed to the performers' superannuation
➤ details of the total annual activity (UDAs) for the contract
➤ details of UDAs achieved per performer
➤ details of how many CoTs have been processed in the period
➤ details of VDP salary reimbursement and National Insurance costs, if appropriate
➤ total local dental committee (LDC) levy (statutory or voluntary) collected against the contract. (The levy is an amount collected from dentists to fund the LDC.)

More detail regarding this schedule can be found in Appendix 14: Guidance to pay schedule, part 1, and Appendix 15: Guidance to new-look schedule, and

Appendix 16: Guidance to pay schedule, part 2 (*see* www.radcliffe-oxford.com/financefordentists).

As mentioned above, in order to ease workload, the processing of the monthly FP17 forms has been staggered so that some practices receive their pay based on a date early in the month, while others' monthly cut-off dates may be towards the end of the month. In order to facilitate this process practices are given group and schedule numbers that correspond to certain dates within the month. Details of the group numbers and payment dates can be found in Appendix 6: Dentist NHS payment schedule 2009 (*see* www.radcliffe-oxford.com/financefordentists).

The values of the UDAs are uplifted by the DDRB each year.

NASDA has recently revealed that the average UDA value under the new contract in 2008 was £24.38, with the highest rate being £37.84 and the lowest being £16.20.

Superannuation is deducted from the payments received by contractors and allocated to performers' pension records. Further details of the superannuation scheme can be found in Chapter 11.

SUPPLY OF NHS SERVICES

The General Dental Services Contract states that the contractor must provide to its patients, during the period of normal surgery hours, all proper and necessary dental care and treatment which includes:
➤ the care which a dental practitioner usually undertakes for a patient and which the patient is willing to undergo
➤ treatment, including urgent treatment
➤ where appropriate, the referral of the patient for advanced mandatory services, domiciliary services, sedation services or other relevant services.

The contractor must provide urgent treatment and:
➤ examination
➤ diagnosis
➤ advice and planning of treatment
➤ preventative care and treatment
➤ periodontal treatment
➤ conservative treatment
➤ surgical treatment
➤ supply and repair of dental appliances
➤ the taking of radiographs
➤ the supply of listed drugs and listed appliances
➤ the issue of prescriptions.

It was hoped that the new contract would have improved NHS services in England and Wales and make those services available to more patients; it is questionable whether or not that this has happened. But the following extract from the NHS Dental Statistics for England report issued on 26 February 2009 suggests that the availability of NHS treatments may be improving.

The proportion of people seeing an NHS dentist in England has risen very slightly for the first time in nearly two years, figures from the NHS Information Centre show today.

NHS dentists saw 52.9% (27.0 million) of the population in the 24-month period ending 30 September 2008. This compares to 52.7% (26.9 million) seen in the previous 24-month period ending 30 June 2008.

However, the number of patients seen is still 3.9% (1.1 million) less than the number seen in the 24-month period ending 31 March 2006, immediately before the new dental contractual arrangements began.

Findings from the report NHS Dental Statistics for England, Quarter 2: 30 September 2008, also show a higher proportion of the population was seen in the north of England compared to the south in the 24-month period ending 30 September 2008. This ranged from 60.6% in North East Strategic Health Authority (SHA) to 44.5% in South Central SHA.

However, the number of patients seen during the same period, compared to the previous 24-month period ending 30 June 2008, increased across all SHAs. This ranged from a 0.7% increase in South West SHA to a marginal increase below 0.05% in North East SHA.

Other key findings for the 24-month period ending 30 September 2008 are:

- 7.6 million children (69.1% of the child population) were seen by an NHS dentist. This is 7,000 more than in the previous 24-month period ending 30 June 2008, but 0.2 million less than the 24-month period ending 31 March 2006.
- 19.4 million adults (48.5% of the 18-and-over adult population) were seen by an NHS dentist. This is 0.1 million more than in the previous 24-month period ending 30 June 2008, but 0.9 million less than the 24-month period ending 31 March 2006.

In the quarter ending 30 September 2008, provisional figures suggest dentists carried out 9.1 million Courses of Treatment (CoTs) – 0.2 million (2.4%) more than the final figure for the same period in the previous year, and 19.4 million units of dental activity (UDAs) – 0.6 million (3.3%) more than the final figure for the same period in the previous year.

Provisional figures also suggest dentists carried out more complex CoTs. In the first two quarters of 2008/09, the proportion of CoTs that were Band 1 decreased by 0.6 percentage points compared to the first two quarters of 2007/08. During the same period, the proportion of Band 2, Band 3 and Urgent CoTs each increased by 0.2 percentage points.

NHS Information Centre chief executive Tim Straughan said: 'Our figures suggest the decline in the number of patients seen by NHS dentists may have halted. However, it is worth noting that the figure is still more than a million down on the number seen in the 24-month period ending 31 March 2006.'

One of the reasons for the reduction in the number of patients seeing an NHS dentist is that a lot of practices took the opportunity to go private upon the introduction of the new contract as many objected to the reduction of 5–10% of their income and their perceptions of the conditions being imposed on them. This had the effect of reducing the number of dentists providing that service.

This can be seen by the detail in Table 4.4.

TABLE 4.4 Movement in numbers of dentists offering NHS treatments

Dentists on PCT lists and their assistants	2003/4	19 026
	2004/5	19 797
	2005/6	21 111
Dentists doing NHS work in the year	2006/7	20 160
	2007/8	20 815

However, the increase in the number of dentists offering NHS services in 2007/08 appears to confirm the findings of the NHS Information Centre (above).

Among those dentists that took up the new contract there are many who were less than happy with the results.

For example, a BDA sample survey in 2007 of LDCs and PCTs suggested that around a third of all dentists were being penalised for either overshooting or undershooting their target. In addition, the BDA passed on evidence to the DDRB from the NHS obtained through a Freedom of Information request showing that, from information on 8,507 contracts, 47% had not achieved the minimum target of 96% of contracted UDAs. The BDA evidence this year included the results of a survey of 194 dentists (representing 650 providers). This revealed that 49.5% of those surveyed were angry, and a further 37.6% disappointed, with the present NHS GDS terms and conditions. This same survey also showed that 61.8% described their practice UDA target as difficult or impossible.

As a result of the above, the BDA is calling for the scrapping of the UDA system of payment, and proposes:

➤ that the whole of a PCO's dental commissioning budget should be paid directly to the PCO. (The BDA states that currently around 25% of a PCT's budget has to be collected through the patient charge revenue, but lack of predictability over receipts understandably leads them to be nervous about fully commissioning all the services that their budgets could potentially support.)

➤ that the restoration of the link between the NHS patient charge revenue and the overall spend on dentistry be re-established in order to maintain a safeguard on the total expenditure available to commission NHS dentistry.

The BDA suggest that the UDA system be replaced by a range of qualitative and quantitative performance indicators which will allow dental practitioners to provide a more satisfactory service.

In March 2008 Susie Sanderson, Chair of the Executive Board of the BDA, issued a statement to mark the second anniversary of the new NHS dental contract, introduced in England and Wales on 1 April 2006.

She stated:

This is a bleak second birthday for the new dental contract with criticism from the profession and patients continuing to gain momentum. The level of concern is starkly revealed in the evidence given to the Health Select Committee, currently investigating the impact of the government's troubled and controversial reforms of NHS dentistry.

In the course of this second year, we have seen:

- statistics released that revealed 47% of dentists failed to meet their first-year UDA targets
- figures that show access to NHS dentistry has still not been improved by the reforms
- a Patients Association survey of MPs that found dentistry was the health issue that caused most concern to their constituents
- the decision by the House of Commons' Health Select Committee to undertake an enquiry into the dental reforms.

The BDA will continue to call for action to tackle the flaws in this target-driven system and is also working proactively at a local level to encourage the commissioning of dentistry which genuinely meets local people's needs.

However, the latest information from the DDRB appears to suggest that there are less disputes with dentists and the delivery of NHS dental services is improving. The following extract is taken from the *Doctors and Dentists Pay Review Body Report 2009*.

CHAPTER 7: DENTISTS

Introduction:

The new arrangements for commissioning primary dental services in the NHS have now been in place for two and a half years. The transition to a system of locally commissioned services has been completed. We are now focusing on ensuring that the NHS is using the opportunities of local commissioning to their full advantage to meet local needs and to reflect the wider objectives for primary and community care identified as part of the NHS Next Stage Review. This includes ensuring that services are not just easily accessible but are much more responsive to individual patient needs; putting a stronger emphasis on promoting health at a practice-based level, for instance by ensuring the use of the evidence-based guidance contained in *Delivering Better Oral Health* – the preventive toolkit; and promoting continuous improvements in quality working with the profession, patient groups and clinical advisors.

This approach needs to be underpinned by more effective PCT commissioning and clinical engagement, areas where there is room for improvement. We need to ensure that the NHS is using the opportunities of local commissioning to their full advantage to meet local needs. Nonetheless, we have already seen:

- new dental services commissioned with a local focus on the needs of patients
- better working arrangements for dentists
- the NHS beginning to build on the secure funding now in place to improve patient access, and undertaking procurement exercises across the country to further expand dental provision
- excellent examples of PCTs using the new commissioning arrangements to improve patient access through local dental help lines and improved access to out-of-hours and emergency services.

It is notable that, in 2007/08:

- units of dental activity (UDA) increased by 4.5% to a level higher than was delivered in the last year of the old system. Courses of treatment increased by 2.7%. However, these increases are not yet reflected in the dental access indicator recording patients seen in the preceding 24 months, which has fallen by 1.1 million since March 2006. This statistic still reflects the temporary loss of some services in the immediate wake of the April 2006 changeover.
- PCTs continue to commission new services to improve patient access with no significant reported shortage of dentists offering to expand their services or establish new practices in tendering exercises for new services

- the number of dentists providing NHS services increased by 655 or 3.2%
- the government's investment in expansion of undergraduate dental education will help to sustain this healthier workforce position
- there were more Vocational Trainee (VT) places for dentists wishing to enter general practice and an increase in dentists wishing to participate in the scheme as trainers.

We believe that the award for dentists in 2009/10 should reflect the notable increase in net earnings for all groups of dentists – at least 10% for those holding contracts. It is possible to make the case from these earnings data that there should be no increase in gross contract values this year. However, we recognise the need to consider implications for motivation and morale, and we therefore recommend that there should instead be **a simple increase in gross contract values for 2009/10 of 1.0%**. This would start to take account of the effects of the large reduction in expenses caused by the move towards more preventative and simpler courses of treatment with a lower expenses element.

An award of around this level would also allow a greater proportion of growth funding to be used to improve access for patients. The large national increase in the dental budget was designed to provide additional access for patients and to improve services, not simply to increase the net incomes of dental providers. The new funding presents significant opportunities for contractors to bid for new work and increase their income through providing additional services.

Many PCTs are making good progress through strong commissioning plans, improved partnership with local dentists, good use of data, competitive procurements and a new focus on patient needs. Some recent examples can be found at **Annex F**, varying from major procurement exercises to expanding existing practices. Our challenge is to spread this good commissioning practice but this depends on having the resources to spend on new services, which has been reduced by high automatic increases in contract values through the pay awards. We should now be working to increase incentives for dental providers to work with PCTs to increase patient access, not reducing flexibility through high 'automatic' awards.

Significant Issues

There are two main issues for this year's Review:

- the current balance between net income and expenses, the effect on dentists' net remuneration and the implications for the Review Body's dental formula – which in our view needs to take specific account of the evidence on movements in dental expenses

- the trade-off between increasing dentists' income and improving access for patients.

The evidence submitted by the NHS Information Centre (IC) (as agreed by both the Department of Health and the BDA) shows that net dental income continues to rise at a rate well above the recommendations of the Review Body. Although this year's data is clouded by the effects of changes in the contractual system and the population of dentists surveyed, it still gives a clear picture of increased net earnings and reduced expenses. We calculate that total income for all dentists has increased from about £80,000 in 2004/05 to around £96,000 in 2006/07. Figures for all NHS dentists derived from the IC figures are shown in the table below.

Population	Average gross income	Expenses		Net profit	Expenses ratio
2004/05 GDS only	13 309	£193 215	£113 187	£80 032	58.6
2005/06	18 796	£205 368	£89 919	£89 919	56.2
2006/07	19 547	£206 255	£96 135	£96 135	53.4

The main reasons for the changes appear to be an overestimation of the increase in practice expenses in the past (fuelled by the use of RPI as an indicator rather than GDP as is used, for example, in the pharmacists' expense formula), the lack of an efficiency requirement in the uplift, and the recent reduction in expenses resulting from changes in treatment patterns (as demonstrated in this year's NHS IC evidence on treatment complexity and, we understand, information from the Dental Laboratories Association).

This has a direct effect on PCTs' ability to improve patient access to NHS dentistry: each 1% increase in gross contract values represents about £27.5 million of resources that could otherwise commission services for an additional 400,000 NHS patients.

Overall context: progress through reform
The Department launched reforms to NHS dental services in April 2006 against a background of widespread discontent with the previous arrangements. There had previously been no fundamental change to the system originally set up in 1948 and no significant change to the contractual arrangements established in 1990. Dentistry had fallen significantly out of step with the mainstream NHS. The key problems included:

- *access to services:* the location and volume of services were previously decided by dentists, not by the NHS. When some dentists began to drift away from the NHS in the 1990s, significant access problems emerged in some areas
- *remuneration system:* dentists were paid on a fee-per-item system which created incentives for more invasive and complex treatment and increased costs – this was not consistent with reducing disease incidence, or with a population with an increasing number of citizens with good oral health
- *patient charges:* there were over 400 patient charges for different treatments, which caused confusion for patients and made it hard to distinguish between NHS and private treatment.

The new system was designed to:
- support access improvements by putting the local NHS in charge of commissioning local services and deciding where to locate new services
- provide dentists with the stability of an agreed annual income in return for an agreed level of patient care, measured through overall courses of treatment (rather than individual items)
- simplify the charging system by introducing just three charges, linked to overall courses of treatment (rather than individual items).

Old national contract	New local contracts
Separate fees for each individual item of treatment (fee-per-item) created a 'treadmill' effect.	Provide security and predictability of agreed annual NHS income, in return for carrying out an agreed number of courses of treatment each year (with a simple weighting to reflect relative complexity).
Dentists wishing to provide simpler courses of treatment, e.g. with greater emphasis on prevention, were financially penalised.	Dentists can carry out less complex and invasive courses of treatment without financial penalty. This allows dentists to spend more time on prevention and is likely to reduce average workload and expenses.

Despite the predictions of the British Dental Association (BDA) of a mass exodus of dentists, the vast majority of practices signed up to the new system and PCTs have commissioned new services to replace those lost, though some did so more quickly than others. The time-lags involved in commissioning new services and having these services build up to full capacity is reflected in comparative activity figures for the first two years of the new arrangements. Overall activity reduced by about 4% in 2006/07 but was reversed in 2007/08 by a rise of 4.5% and further increases are expected this year.

There were also initial concerns, repeatedly emphasised by the BDA, that a high proportion of those contracts which were initially signed 'in dispute' between the dental provider and the PCT would result in further dentists leaving the NHS. In fact, in over 99% of cases, the disputes process has ended with dentists deciding to stay with the NHS. By the end of 2007/08, in only 14 cases had dentists given up their NHS contracts after these disputes.

Following this transitional period, the Department is now supporting PCTs to focus on using commissioning to drive up access, support and improve quality, and enhance oral health. Overall, two and a half years into the new system, we now have a secure basis for developing dental services over the coming years. The local NHS now has a statutory duty to provide dental services and the flexibilities needed to develop services to reflect local needs. In many areas, patients are already experiencing the positive results of this in terms of new or developed services, as illustrated by the examples at **Annex F**.

This is supported by the inclusion of NHS dentistry in the NHS Operating Framework which requires PCTs to develop commissioning plans that will deliver year-on-year increases in dental access.

Factors in the Review Body's remit

The remit for the Review Body has remained constant for a number of years, and our comments on specific aspects of this are set out below. It may also, however, be timely to consider if there are aspects of the new contractual arrangements that require recommendations outside the traditional remit. In particular, the uplift recommended by the DDRB now only directly affects the income of those dentists who hold provider contracts, and increasingly limited companies rather than individual dentists hold these contracts: the pay and conditions of individual dentist performers are now entirely set by the local dental market. There is considerable anecdotal evidence, backed by PCT intelligence, that many practice owners did not pass on last year's 3.4% award to their performers, increasing their own profit margins instead. NASDA, the association of dentists' accountants, reports that gross payments to performers fell from £84,308 in 2005/06 to £82,864 in 2006/07 and although their costs fell, their average net profit reduced from £70,695 to £70,306.

Recruitment and retention

The most important aspect of the pay review system is to ensure that there is a sufficient incentive for dentists to provide NHS services for a reasonable, but not excessive, reward. The numbers of dentists providing NHS services continues to increase.

The best indicator of dentists' willingness to provide NHS services under the new contracts is the continued success of the tendering exercises undertaken by PCTs. PCTs who have put services out to tender have reported no shortage of potential applicants. The commissioning requests from PCTs have brought a response from a variety of providers including corporate bodies, partnerships and existing practices seeking to expand. For example, Devon PCT recently received 28 expressions of interest in response to an invitation to establish a large general dental practice, and the PCT was able to select a contractor after interviewing a final shortlist of six tenderers. This suggests that NHS dentistry is now seen as a valuable commodity and, to dentists, is no longer seen as poorly remunerated when compared with private work. The NHS IC statistics for dentists who hold contracts and also perform NHS dentistry shows that highly committed NHS dentists had the highest net profit in 2006/07 – an average of £146,600 compared to an average of £122,000 for dentists with NHS commitment below 75%. Some of the difference is due to additional payments in 2006/07 from the ending of the old arrangements.

Practice profits for practices with high NHS commitment have been rising strongly and now exceed the profits in mainly private practices; the IC statistics show NHS practices 20% higher with some temporary effect from the ending of the old pay arrangements, whilst NASDA report NHS practices 14% higher.

The willingness of dentists to bid for and undertake NHS contracts, including in areas where dentists had previously chosen not to set up or provide NHS services, clearly demonstrates that recruitment and retention issues are not acting as a bar to improving access. The rate-limiting factor in the first two years of the new contract was the strategic capacity and capability of PCTs to commission services at a rate to reflect levels of local need, not the availability of dentists to provide services. That is why we have used the Operating Framework to ensure that PCTs rapidly enhance their commissioning capacity and why we have increased dental budgets to support increased levels of commissioning.

The detail from the DDRB in the extract above is included as part of their report into the level of earnings of NHS dentists, and their recommendations on the increase to be applied to those earnings. Further detail of this process can be found below.

DENTISTS' PAY AND THE REVIEW BODY

We have seen how NHS dentists, while not a salaried service, are nevertheless not entirely in control of their own income levels. Their income, in an almost unique situation, is determined by the DDRB, which normally reports in January or February each year, making recommendations as to the level of dentists' pay increases for the ensuing year.

Usually, the Review Body pay awards are granted in line with the fiscal policy of the government of the day.

The Review Body was formed in 1960 following the recommendations of a Royal Commission, charged with making recommendations as regards to the level of remuneration for doctors and dentists working within the NHS. Their work extends not only to general dental and medical practitioners but also to doctors and dentists who are employed in the Health Service. The Royal Commission recommended the establishment of an independent Review Body and laid down rules by which it should operate. The Review Body receives evidence from all interested parties, but in practice concentrates upon that received from a number of established sources, as can be seen in the next section.

Principal sources of evidence to the Review Body

Principal sources of evidence to the Review Body include the following:
➤ written evidence from the profession, prepared by a committee of the BDA
➤ written evidence from Health Departments
➤ joint written evidence between the profession and the Health Departments, usually dealing with matters which have been agreed in negotiations
➤ jointly agreed statistical information, for example evidence of dentists' earnings and expenses
➤ independent evidence prepared by the Review Body's Secretariat.

When its enquiries are complete, the Review Body reports to the Prime Minister, after which the report is published and a decision is announced.

It is fair to say that the degree of independence of the Review Body is not as absolute as might at first appear, as there have been several occasions when their recommendations have been moderated so as to accord with the policies of the government of the day.

The Review Body Report for 2009 was published on 15 October 2008 and recommended that the contract value for providers of NHS dental services in England and Wales should be increased by 1% from 1 April 2009. An uplift of 1% also applies to gross fees from 1 April 2009 in Scotland and Northern Ireland.

The contracts above were in fact only uplifted by 0.21%.

OTHER PAYMENTS UNDER THE STATEMENT OF FINANCIAL ENTITLEMENTS

Detailed below are a number of other payments which dentists can claim under the Statement of Financial Entitlements.

Commitment payments

Dentists in Scotland and Northern Ireland receive commitment payments, as a reward for their commitment to providing NHS services. Dentists in England and Wales no longer receive these payments as they are deemed to be included in the UDA calculations.

Commitment payments are an allowance paid to a dentist based on the number of years served in GDS, subject to certain criteria. More details of these payments can be found on the following websites:

➤ www.psd.scot.nhs.uk
➤ www.centralservicesagency.com.

Seniority payments

Seniority payments are additional monies that are paid to NHS dentists who have reached the age of 55. They are designed primarily to reward practitioners for staying within the NHS and to compensate them for the perceived reduction in their ability to perform their role in the NHS at the same pace as younger colleagues. The seniority payments scheme is self-funded by the profession in that all fees and allowances have been reduced by a very small percentage to pay for the scheme.

Seniority payments cannot be backdated, so if a dentist forgets to claim until they are 56 or older they will lose payments for those earlier years. They are no longer eligible to claim seniority payments once they start receiving superannuation benefits – their NHS pension.

The system of payment used is rather complex and is based on the accumulated earnings at the end of each quarter. The amount to which the contractor is entitled to is 21.72% of the Dentist Performer's net monthly Pensionable Earnings under the contractor's GDS contract in the month to which the payment relates, but the maximum amount payable in respect of each Dentist Performer in any month is £662.

It was planned for seniority to be phased out in England and Wales in 2008, but the allowance has now been retained until 31 March 2011.

Continuing professional development allowances

The payment of travel and subsistence for dentists undertaking verifiable CPD is delegated to PCTs along with the delegation of the commissioning of primary care dental services. Funds from the DoH are allocated for the postgraduate training of dentists under Section 63 of the Public Health Act 1968, and these are delegated to PCTs to make the payments.

Dentists need to send a form to their PCTs, if they are claiming travel and subsistence expenditure and it is important for them to keep a copy of the form for their records, as it acts as a certificate of attendance which may be required as evidence of their completion of their compulsory CPD requirement.

The form required is FP84-0306(1) (Appendix 17, *see* www.radcliffe-oxford. com/financefordentists) and it shows the rates at which expenses are reimbursed. Dentists are permitted to claim their expenses as there is a general understanding that as much as possible of the Section 63 funding should be used to support the delivery of training without burdening dentists, who work long distances from dental education centres, with unreasonable travel costs.

The current rates are as follows.

➤ **Mileage:** using their own vehicle taking the shortest practical route between either practice or home and place to be visited 23p per mile; dentists carrying one or more named eligible dentists to the same course can claim an extra 2p per mile.

➤ **Overnight stays:** actual receipted cost of bed and breakfast up to a maximum of £55 per night; non-commercial accommodation (i.e. friends or relatives) £25 per night.

➤ **Meals:** lunch (applicable when more than five hours away from the practice) £5; evening meal (applicable when away from the practice for more than 10 hours) £15, to a maximum of £20 in any 24-hour period.

Reimbursement of non-domestic rates

A dentist undertaking a NHS contract who pays business rates is entitled to claim reimbursement of the rates payable in any financial year for any building where GDS are provided. However, the amount payable may be 'abated' according to the proportion of private work carried out as a proportion of the total gross income of the practice.

The dentists making the claim must be on the dental list of the PCT as a principal.

The reimbursement will not be received if the gross NHS earnings of all the dentists practising in the premises for the financial year before application for reimbursement are below a minimum threshold of £25,000.

The PCO has the discretionary power to waive this criterion when it considers it reasonable to do so, for example for a new practice.

The amount reimbursed is the whole of the rates bill if the practice's total income is 90% derived from the NHS.

Otherwise, the amount is abated according to the level of NHS income as a proportion of total income, until, if the NHS proportion is less than 10% then the reimbursement is abated by 90%. This can be seen in the table below:

TABLE 4.5 Reimbursement rates

Proportion which the GDS contract income bears to the gross income of the hereditament	Proportion of non-domestic rates to be abated
90% or more	No abatement
80% or more but less than 80%	10%
70% or more but less than 80%	20%
60% or more but less than 80%	30%
50% or more but less than 80%	40%
40% or more but less than 80%	50%
30% or more but less than 80%	60%
20% or more but less than 80%	70%
10% or more but less than 80%	80%
Less than 10%	90%

The amount payable will be paid on the principal's normal schedule(s) by the Dental Practice Board (DPB). As this is a reimbursement of expenses the rates reimbursement is not pensionable and is not counted towards gross income for the purposes of the other allowances such as seniority and commitment payments.

The backdating of payments by PCOs is not permitted after six months, with this rule being absolute and PCOs unlikely to waive it.

Vocational training allowances

Historically, dentists upon finishing Dental College went straight into self-employment as associates in practice. Many found the transition between study and self-employment difficult.

As a result the VDP system was introduced whereby the trainee takes up employment at a registered practice for a period of 12 months. In return the practice receives reimbursement of the trainee's salary plus a training grant.

For the practice to receive the reimbursement the following qualifying criteria must be present.

➤ The trainer's name must be included in the dental list of his or her PCT.
➤ The dentist has been approved to act as a trainer in a vocational training scheme for general dental practice by the local postgraduate dental dean or director, acting on the advice of a trainer selection committee established by the Local Postgraduate Dental Education Committee.
➤ The trainer has entered into a contract of employment with the VDP as an assistant for a period of one year's full-time employment (or the part-time equivalent).
➤ The trainee has a basic dental qualification that may be registered by the GDC and is a UK or EEA national.

The allowances are payable by the DPB each month on the trainer's schedule, during the existence of the employment contract to the trainer.

The training grant to a trainer for a full-time trainee as at 1 April 2009 is currently being paid at a rate of £746 a month (£8,952 annually).

The salary reimbursement for a full-time trainee as at 1 April 2009 is currently being paid at a rate of £2,486 a month (£29,832 annually).

The trainer can claim 100% of the NICs for the VDP.

VDPs also attract an additional contract value of UDAs for the practice, in order to ensure there is sufficient NHS work within the practice for the VDP to do. The contract value varies in different PCT areas, as funding may permit, but would usually be in the region of £60,000 to £70,000 a year.

Long-term sickness absence payments

If an employee, a partner in a partnership or a contractor is a Dentist Performer, the contractor that employs or engages that Dentist Performer will be entitled to payments from the PCO in respect of a period of long-term sickness absence taken by that Dentist Performer, provided the eligibility criteria are satisfied and the relevant payment conditions are not breached.

A contractor is entitled to receive sickness leave payments in respect of a Dentist Performer that it employs or engages if, in respect of a complete week of sickness absence:

1 the Dentist Performer's name has been included in a Dental List for a period of at least two years, which need not be a continuous period and part or all of that period need not immediately precede the period of sickness, but during those two years (or that aggregate of two years) he must have been performing dental services as part of the NHS

2 the Dentist Performer has been unable to provide dental services under the contractor's GDS contract because of sickness, but sickness leave payments are not payable in respect of the first four weeks of absence

3 the Dentist Performer has been in receipt of payments under this Section for less than the maximum of 22 weeks during a period of sickness.

Sickness leave payments are only payable in respect of a maximum of 22 weeks in any period of 52 weeks. So, for example, once sickness leave payments have been made in respect of a Dentist Performer for a continuous period of 22 weeks, it will be a further 30 weeks before the PCT could again be obliged to make sickness leave payments in respect of that Dentist Performer. However, the PCT may waive the eligibility criterion set out in this paragraph in any case where it considers it is reasonable in all the circumstances to do so. The computation of periods of sickness leave is to take into account periods of sickness leave before this SFE comes into force.

The amount to which the contractor is entitled in respect of sickness leave payments is a weekly amount, calculated on the basis of the Dentist Performer's estimated monthly Pensionable Earnings (which should usually be the amount that features in respect of that Dentist Performer on the contractor's Monthly Payment Schedule, plus his or her estimated monthly Pensionable Earnings in respect of any Monthly Seniority Payment to which the Dentist Performer is entitled immediately before the sickness leave is taken).

This amount is to be multiplied by 12 and then divided by 52 to produce the weekly amount of the sickness leave payments.

The weekly amount determined in accordance is the amount to which the contractor is entitled in respect of each complete week during which the Dentist Performer is absent and continues to satisfy the eligibility criteria.

Payments, or any part of such payments, are only payable if the following conditions are satisfied:

1 the contractor must, if the PCT so requests, provide the PCT with medical certificates or other statements to the effect that the Dentist Performer is incapable of work by reason of sickness, completed by a registered medical practitioner, covering any period of absence in respect of which a sickness leave payment is being claimed
2 the Dentist Performer must not perform any dental services under a GDS contract or PDS agreement during any period of absence in respect of which a sickness leave payment is claimed, except with the written approval of the PCT
3 unless he or she dies, the Dentist Performer in respect of whom the payments are made continues to be a Dentist Performer and continues to be employed or engaged by the contractor
4 the contractor must continue to pay the Dentist Performer at least the Dentist Performer's estimated net Pensionable Earnings during the Dentist Performer's absence (or pay this to the Dentist Performer's estate if the Dentist Performer dies).

Maternity, paternity and adoption leave payments

These are allowances paid to principal and associate dentists when they or, in the case of paternity leave, their partner either gives birth to a child or adopts a child.

The dentist must have been included in a dental list for two years. However, they should have been on a dental list continuously for the six months immediately preceding 15 weeks before the expected date of birth of the baby – it is vital that a break is not taken during this period.

The amount to which the contractor is entitled in respect of parental leave payments is a weekly amount, calculated on the basis of the Dentist Performer's estimated monthly Pensionable Earnings (which should usually be the amount that features in respect of that Dentist Performer on the contractor's Monthly Payment Schedule, plus the Dentist Performer's estimated monthly Pensionable

Earnings in respect of any Monthly Seniority Payment to which the Dentist Performer is entitled immediately before the parental leave is taken).

This monthly amount is to be multiplied by 12 and then divided by 52 to produce the weekly amount of the parental leave payments.

That weekly amount is the amount to which the contractor is entitled in respect of each complete week of the Dentist Performer's Parental Leave Pay Period.

They will be paid their net earnings for up to 26 weeks, subject to a maximum payment.

If the dentist does not return to work within a year of the birth they may be asked to repay their payments.

There is a form entitled 'Application for personal payment under Statement of Financial Entitlements' (*see* Appendix 3 at www.radcliffe-oxford.com/financefordentists) which needs to be submitted to make any of the claims above.

CHAPTER 5

Private practice

Private practices have been defined by the NHS Information Centre and the DDRB as those practices whose private income exceeds 75% of their total fees; whereas NASDA defines private practices as those whose private income exceeds 80% of their total fees. Suffice to say that private practices predominately provide private treatments.

The relatively small amount of NHS work that they provide is usually as a result of their retaining their NHS-exempt patients upon the introduction of the new contract in 2006, and at that time being given a UDA target based on those patients.

The exempt patients in these cases usually comprised children, and private practices will often continue to provide NHS services for children while supplying private dentistry to their parents.

Private dentistry can either be delivered by way of 'fee per item', where the patient is charged a specific fee for each course of treatment, or by way of a 'payment plan' where the patient pays a monthly premium, which will cover various CoTs, either to the practice or a third-party provider such as Denplan or Simplyhealth.

FEE PER ITEM

The fee per item that dentists charge can vary from practice to practice, with the treatment charges being calculated in numerous different ways. The level of fees charged should be at least sufficient to cover the practice overheads and the drawings of the principals, and the practice accounts should detail these amounts, to ensure that the practice can check and pitch its fees at the correct level. However, many practices do not calculate the level of fees that they charge with reference to their accounts. Instead, they often adopt the level of fees that their predecessors charged, often inflating the amount by a small margin to take into account inflation. Others set their levels of fees to be in line with other dental practices in their area.

To calculate a sustainable level of fees a practice should undertake the following exercise.

➤ Ascertain the level of practice fixed costs, i.e. non-clinical staff costs and the practice running expenses.

➤ Ascertain the level of variable costs that are incurred by clinical staff and principals while providing treatments.

➤ Decide on an affordable level of profit for the principal, which will provide for sufficient monies to pay a reasonable level of drawings, pay the tax bill and provide for pension payments, if appropriate. The level of drawings should be set to afford the dentist the lifestyle he or she wants.

➤ Calculate the number of chargeable hours available in the year from all clinical staff fee earners (principals, associates, technicians, therapists and hygienists). Note that not all working hours will be chargeable as there may be administrative and management issues that will need dealing with.

➤ Allocate an hourly rate to all fee earners which will produce an annual turnover that will cover the practice overheads, the variable costs and produce the desired level of profit. Note that the BDA publishes average hourly rates of pay for DCPs.

➤ Monitor the levels of chargeable hours achieved against a budget on a regular basis to ensure the targeted level of turnover is being achieved.

Most dentists do not maximise the profits that they could make from their practice as they charge their patients too little. They are not aware of the price insensitivity of their patients, and do not realise that the majority of their patients would not consider leaving the practice if the level of their fees were to increase significantly. Obviously, this is not the case when a new dentist takes over a practice, but is certainly the case when there has been a long-term relationship between the dentist and his patient.

Most patients are not aware of the current level of fees that their dentists charge and accept those fees as a necessary cost. Given the infrequency of their visits I would doubt that any patient would notice if their dentist increased their fees marginally, say by 3% every six months, and if that amount was applied to the practice's turnover, the increase in profit could be quite significant.

There are very few individuals who would shop around by asking a number of different dental practices for quotes, although this may become more popular with the increase in the number of new treatments and products that may not be provided by their own dentist.

Although there has been an increase in the number of practices that have adopted a practice payment plan there are still a significant number of practices that provide a fee per item service, and the reasons for that are as follows.

➤ The main reason that payment plans with third parties are not adopted by practices is the cost of running the plan. The provider deducts an administration fee from the premium paid by the patient, and only the net amount is received by the practice. Some practices consider the administration fee too excessive and prefer to retain their fee per item system.

➤ Some dentists consider the monthly amounts payable under a payment plan to be excessive for some patients, especially those with good oral hygiene, and do not encourage those patients to adopt the scheme.

➤ There are a number of practices that have been running fee per item methods of payment for a number of years very successfully, and cannot see the financial benefit to them of switching to a payment plan.

As the price dentists charge for their services should be dependent upon the costs of running the practice, and the cost of materials and laboratory fees, their fees will vary in line with changes in those costs.

Although patients may not actively look for another dentist if they feel that the charges are too high, they may, especially in times of recession, delay routine treatments or opt for a cheaper extraction than a more expensive restorative treatment. Therefore, the level of fees may need to be reviewed if the practice appointment diaries are not fully booked up.

Table 5.1 gives examples of prices that dentists have charged for various CoTs. The information can be found on the website 'Whatprice' (www.whatprice.co.uk), and has been produced from a survey of the prices that dental patients say they have paid for specific CoTs.

TABLE 5.1 Examples of private dental charges (2009)

Dental work required	Private prices (£)
Apiectomy	388
Braces – ceramic	2586
Braces – Invisalign	3500
Braces – lingual	2167
Braces – metal	1064
Bridge	574
Cancellation fee	37
Dental crown – composite	379
Dental crown – gold	403
Dental crown – porcelain	375
Dental examination	43

(continued)

Dentures – full	560
First consultation	53
Hygiene clean	66
Implants	1 116
Large tooth filling – non-white	100
Large tooth filling – white	106
Root canal	356
Sedated tooth removal	140
Small tooth filling – non-white	81
Small tooth filling – white	77
Tooth extraction	87
Tooth scale and polish	46
Veneer	342
Whitening	306
Wisdom tooth extraction	179
X-ray	28

Table 5.1 gives an example of the prices that dentists currently charge for treatment in the UK. But dental treatment charges will vary significantly depending upon the geographical area, local competition, deprivation, etc.

If dentists do encounter problems in setting the level of fees there are a number of 'business coaches' within the dental profession who assist practices with their pricing structures, should their accountants or financial advisers not be providing that assistance.

The following is an extract of a recent article by Chris Barrow, which provides a useful insight in practice profitability:

What would you think if I suggested that the financial performance of your business could be predicted, up to three years in advance – and to an accuracy of +/– 10%?

Wouldn't that make supporting your practice, your family, your lifestyle and the tax man more tolerable?

Here's the formula:

Number of dentists (D) × Average Daily Productivity (ADP) × Number of clinical days (CD) = Gross Revenues (GR).

and . . .

Gross Revenues (GR) – Fixed Costs (FC) – Variable Expenses (VE) = Net Profit before Tax (NPBT).

So, to summarise:

$$D \times ADP \times CD = GR \qquad GR - FC - VE = NPBT$$

With me so far?

OK, now what I want to do is take a look at each of these input figures again, and make an assessment as to how predictable they are – let's say on a scale of 1–10, with 10 being 100% predictable.

number of dentists = 9/10

You can determine how many dentists will work in the building and, happily, they are quite secure in their environment if two conditions have been fulfilled – either

1 they have been there a long time (and tend to stay)

2 they have been recruited properly (forget about courses and qualification and determine their previous ADP – see below).

average daily productivity = 9/10

I've been measuring the ADP of principals and associates (even specialists) for some years now – and report that it's an amazingly consistent number. Elsewhere I have written that ADPs tend to cluster – around £800 per day, £1,000 a day, and £1,250 a day depending on the associate, and around £1,500 per day, £1,750 a day and £2,000 a day for the GDP principal.

It's another conversation to point out that the £800 a day associate on a 50% contract (or the £1,500 a day principal) is probably losing the business money.

number of clinical days = 9/10

One of my clients, principal of a 10-dentist, 6-hygienist practice, sits down with ALL the clinical team once a year and determines how many days in the year they will be showing up. If he can do it, so can you – and then it's just weddings, funerals and illness that screw up the figures. Of course, the beauty of a multi-surgery practice is that one clinician's absence can be replaced by another's extra attendance – especially when they have similar ADPs.

Fixed costs – are what they say they are = 9/10

So provided you don't go mad at a dental exhibition and buy another toy off another salesperson who tells you 'it will pay for itself', then your fixed costs will only move in line with interest rates.

Variable expenses – surely not predictable? Of course they are – 9/10.

If you measure your KPIs (key performance indicators) and measure variable costs as a percentage of sales for a given period you will find the following:
- lab costs (GDP) 10%
- lab costs (cosmetic and implants) up to 14%
- material costs 7%
- staff costs (excluding hygiene) 17.5%.

And your net profit before tax should be:
- up to £500k sales = 35%
- £500k – £1.2m = 30%
- £1.2m – £2.5m = 25%
- over £2.5m = 20%.

So there you have it – a 90% predictable business.

You may have noticed the absence of a couple of apparently important factors.
- What about prices?
- What about membership schemes or UDAs?

The fact is they make no difference at all. Why? Because dentists are 100% disciplined to their existing ADP. It just doesn't change:
- no matter how many plan patients or UDAs you give them
- no matter how big any financial carrot or employment stick.

They just find their ADP level – and stay there. I challenge you to start measuring and prove me wrong. So, the most experienced clients I work with do sit down at the start of their trading year, they interview the existing clinical team to assess CD's – and they predict their business performance.

There's only one factor that can destroy the predictability. If you stop putting fuel in the engine, the most efficient machine in the world grinds to a halt. And the fuel? Patients.
- Existing patients.

- Reactivated patients.
- New patients.

And the systems with which these numbers are maintained are critical – especially now – hence all the marketing seminars you are seeing. Take control of the numbers and they will look after you. I love mathematics in business. Numbers are like the machines in the *Terminator* movies.
They don't throw 'sickies'.
They don't have moods.
They don't bitch, moan and whine.
Numbers are just numbers. But unlike the robots – you can control them. And just like the robots, if you take your eye off them, they will destroy you. If you are more than 10% down in each of the categories we described above, the cumulative effect will bring you down.

Food for thought?

When the prices of treatments which are provided by private practices are compared with the NHS patient charges that patients will pay for similar work performed on the NHS, the cost is much higher, as can be seen in Table 5.2. This is partly because there are only three fixed bandings of NHS patient charges, £198.00, £44.60 and £16.20.

However, there may not be a lot of NHS practices offering the more complex treatments listed in Table 5.2, mainly due to the low income levels that they will generate.

TABLE 5.2 Comparison of charges of NHS and private practices

Dental work required	Private prices (£)	NHS prices (£)*
Apiectomy	388.00	198.00
Braces – metal	1 064.00	198.00
Bridge	574.00	n/a
Cancellation fee	37.00	n/a
Dental crown – gold	403.00	198.00
Dental examination	43.00	16.20
Dentures – full	560.00	198.00
First consultation	53.00	16.20
Hygiene clean	66.00	n/a
Implants	1 116.00	n/a
Large tooth filling – non-white	100.00	44.60
Root canal	356.00	198.00

(continued)

Sedated tooth removal	140.00	44.60
Small tooth filling – non-white	81.00	44.60
Tooth extraction	87.00	n/a
Tooth scale and polish	46.00	16.20
Veneer	342.00	n/a
Whitening	306.00	n/a
Wisdom tooth extraction	179.00	n/a
X-ray	28.00	16.20

* NHS prices in 2009/10

Historically, one of the disadvantages of a fee per item scheme when it was compared to a payment plan was in relation to insurance, as most payment plans will provide cover for emergency dental work on a worldwide basis. However, it is now possible for dentists to source an independent insurance policy for their patients, should this be an additional service they wish to provide for them.

PAYMENT PLANS

There are a large number of private providers of payment plans for dental services. Some offer pure emergency medical and dental insurance cover while others include cover for certain courses of dental treatment. There is a large range of policies that allow the patient to select the treatment that they wish to pay for, and the costs and treatments available can also vary significantly.

Practices who have adopted a payment plan from a third party are often given assistance from the plan provider in setting a level of fees suitable for their practice.

Purely as an example of the cover provided by some of these policies I have included details below of the 'Denplan Care' plan:

Denplan Care is a care contract that allows the treating dentist to provide an ongoing preventive dental care treatment programme. It also includes Supplementary Insurance and Denplan's Insurance Services.

Denplan Care is a comprehensive package and offers:
- examinations
- X-rays
- necessary fillings
- hygiene treatment (including scale and polishes)
- preventive dental advice and therapy
- any necessary extractions
- periodontal (gum) treatment

- crowns, bridges, dentures, inlays (excluding laboratory fees)
- root fillings.

It does not provide funding for the following, however:
- laboratory fees/prescriptions
- any treatment specified as excluded by the dentist in your contract
- referral to a specialist and specialist treatment
- treatment carried out anywhere other than at your registered dentist except when covered under your Supplementary Insurance
- orthodontics, implants, cosmetic treatment
- sedation fees.

A payment plan has the following benefits for a practice.
➤ Ensuring predictable practice income and better cash flow, as the patients' premiums (less an administration fee) are received by the practice monthly, irrespective of whether any treatment has been carried out.
➤ The level of the payment plan premiums is flexible and the practice can set the level of monthly premiums to suit its profit forecasts.
➤ The patients often pay their premiums early in the month, and the practice receives that income towards the end of the same month, so there is no need to finance the payment of fees for up to a month, as can be the case when providing NHS dentistry or fee per item.
➤ Payment plans allow patients to budget for their dental costs, and they will be less likely to complain or refuse to pay their liabilities. This can save a lot of management time.

The main provider of payment plans is Denplan with around 6,000 UK dentists being Denplan members. They deal with approximately 1.3 million patients under Denplan schemes. Denplan provides:
➤ a range of plans to suit all patients
➤ a conversion programme providing full support and advice for practices moving from NHS to private dentistry
➤ support and experience for practice development, business planning, marketing and team development programmes
➤ Professional Development Team and network of specialist consultants across the UK
➤ a range of products and services.

There has been a marked increase in the number of practices providing payment plans in the last few years and, in particular, the number of practices signing up for Denplan schemes.

The reason for the increase has been the number of practices converting from NHS dentistry to providing private dentistry services, and the assistance those practices can obtain in the process of the conversion from Denplan. As a lot of the correspondence regarding the conversion is dealt with direct between Denplan and the patients, the dentist does not experience a lot of the resistance that this process can sometimes attract.

However, there may be a number of practices which have signed up with Denplan, upon their conversion from providing NHS services, to obtain the above assistance, but with the intention that within a few years they would set up their own in-practice payment plans. The benefit being that their patients by that time will have accepted the method of monthly payment to pay for their dental care, but that the practice could operate an in-practice scheme cheaper by saving the administration fee that they would otherwise have to pay to the payment plan provider.

There are a number of independent providers that can assist practices set up their own payment plan and provide insurance cover if it is required.

Below is an extract from the literature of an actual independent practice plan:

PRACTICE DENTAL CARE PLAN

(1) We are delighted to offer our Dental Care Plan – our own membership scheme, which enables us to provide you with the treatment and support necessary to control dental disease and restore your mouth to full fitness.

(2) As individuals we have to make more and more provision for our own health needs. We at Practice Dental Care believe that the best way of making treatment affordable, without compromising our high quality of care, is to offer you membership of our own Dental Care Plan which provides the following benefits.

- A convenient payment scheme for routine treatment.
- Greater choice of treatment and materials.
- More time to help prevent decay and gum disease.
- An extended payment facility to spread additional costs.
- A fair and equitable system where everybody pays the same.
- Substantial discount on additional treatment and sundries.
- Worldwide Trauma and Emergency Callout Insurance.
- Redundancy Protection.

(3) Children are born free of dental disease, yet by adulthood 95% of the population has active gum disease and most people have experienced some tooth decay and even tooth loss. It is our belief that disease can be prevented. Our aim is to provide your child with the best Dental Care available to secure their dental health. We ask parents to register their children from birth so that we can see them twice a year on the NHS to help them grow up free from dental disease. However, if they do need treatment, we can offer them

alternatives not generally available on the NHS. To the children of members of our Dental Care Plans, we can offer these alternatives on the same terms as their parents.

CHOICE OF MEMBERSHIP PLANS

Option 1 – Gold Plan £8.95 per month
- Regular and detailed examinations, including checking for signs of possible oral cancer.
- Regular scale and polish visits with the dentist to maintain the highest standard of oral health.
- Continual advice, coaching and discussion about alternative treatments to suit your individual needs.
- 20% discounts on treatments.
- 10% discounts on oral hygiene items sold in the practice.
- A convenient monthly payment by Direct Debit.
- Worldwide Trauma and Emergency Callout Insurance.
- Extended Payment Scheme for large-cost treatments.
- Redundancy Protection.

Option 1 – Platinum Plan £11.95 per month
As for the Gold Plan, but with one additional hygienist appointment per year.

Option 1 – Periodontal plan £15.25 per month
As for the Gold Plan but with two additional hygienist appointments.

Option 1 – Denture Plan £3.55
Members who have full dentures are entitled to an annual examination to check the soft tissue. Members will receive a discount on denture repairs and new dentures, as well as receiving the same insurance benefit as patients on the Gold Plan.

Option 2 – Registration and Insurance
Some of our patients will prefer to pay in full for clinical examinations and treatments as and when they are needed. For those people, we can offer a second alternative, to register with the practice and pay an annual registration fee of £30.00, which gives our registered patients the same level of insurance as our Plan patients. We have listed the details of this option below.
- Worldwide Trauma and Emergency Callout Insurance.
- Patients pay for each examination and treatment as it is provided, at the standard price.
- There is no discount on treatments or items for sale in the practice.
- There is no Extended Payment Scheme.
- Registered patients must attend an examination at least once per year.
- No Redundancy Protection.

In order to maintain high standards of oral and dental health, we would recommend regular visits to the practice so that we can spot problems early and monitor the effectiveness of treatments. We hope that you will see, therefore, that we have designed a scheme that enables us to provide you with the highest standards of service and enables you to budget monthly for quality preventive dentistry.

The above example shows that the practice has packaged the services it provides and produced a number of options for its patients. In doing so it will gain all the cash-flow benefits of a scheme with a third-party payment plan provider, but without the costs associated with those plans.

It also provides an insurance policy, which not only provides a benefit for the patients but also will generate a receipt of commission from the insurance provider.

It is possible for a well-run practice operating a fee per item payment scheme to generate a decent level of profit, and with good working capital management to maintain good cash flow, but it is far easier if the practice is operating a payment plan. For this reason you will find that most of the higher earning practices will be those with payment plans.

COMMISSIONS ON INSURANCE AND FINANCE PACKAGES

With an increasing number of practices providing more complex dental treatments, such as implants and braces, and some practices expanding into cosmetic treatments, the costs of treatment to the patient have been rising, in some cases quite significantly.

While there has been an increase in disposable income, and an increase in demand for these additional expensive services from patients with sufficient funds to pay for them, there has also been a market for these services from a proportion of the population without the ready cash available to pay for them.

As a result of this there has been an increase in the number of finance packages being made available for patients to effectively borrow the money to pay for expensive dental and cosmetic treatments.

There are currently two types of loans being made available to patients, as follows.

➤ **Interest-free loans**, usually offered for a period of 12 months. These loans are financed by the dentist, and are effectively paid by the profit made on the dental procedure provided. Often these loans are offered to increase the amount of the complex work that the dentist can provide within the practice.

➤ These loans often work as follows.

- The cost of initial treatment is divided over the agreed term, to give the amount of the monthly repayments.
- The first instalment will usually be due a month after the treatment starts; the practice will send the patient a welcome letter advising them of their credit limit, should they ever need to use the account again in the future.
- They can spend up to their credit limit, so once they have started to reduce their account, their credit limit is available to be reused, on a revolving basis.
- So if they need further treatment, this will simply be added to the outstanding balance on their account, and the repayments will be recalculated on the new, total value. The revised repayments will continue, until the balance reaches zero, or they have further treatment.
- The minimum payment each month will be set and no interest will be charged, so long as they continue to make their payments on time.
- They will receive a monthly statement, keeping them up to date on their treatment bills and payments made.
➤ The cost to the dentist of providing the interest-free credit varies according to the length of the term. For example, six months interest-free credit could cost the dentist 6.5% while 12 months could cost 7.5% and 24 months 11.5% (at current rates for £5,000 to £25,000).
➤ **Loans which attract an interest charge**, which is paid by the patient. These loans are often for a period in excess of 12 months. The terms and structure of these loans are very similar to bank loans.

Both types of loans can be sourced from third parties, with finance facilities being offered to provide interest-free and interest-bearing credit for treatments usually up to £5,000.

Experience has shown that practices who offer credit are able to provide more advanced and interesting treatments, increasing both job satisfaction and practice success. The benefits to the practice are as follows.
➤ The opportunity to practice more advanced and enjoyable dentistry through the increased take-up of advanced treatments.
➤ Cash flow will improve as the payment for each full course of treatment is sent to the practice bank account at the beginning of the course of treatment.
➤ Fewer bad debts, as the credit company takes the risk of non-payment.
➤ Greater patient satisfaction.

Some practices provide a hybrid loan where the patient and the practice share the interest cost; these loans are called co-payment loans.

When dentists provide their patients with insurance cover for dental emergencies, these policies will usually cover the following.

➤ Dental accident cover (up to a predetermined amount per incident).
➤ Temporary emergency dental treatment in the UK (up to a predetermined amount per incident, with a total limit payable per calendar year).
➤ Temporary emergency dental treatment when overseas (up to a predetermined amount per incident, with a total limit payable per calendar year).
➤ An amount for every night spent in hospital under the care of a dental or oral/maxillofacial surgeon for treatment to head and neck.
➤ An amount for mouth cancer treatment costs for up to 18 months following a positive diagnosis.

Given the high costs of dental treatment patients are very interested in these policies, especially if not covered under a payment plan scheme.

Dentists receive commissions from insurance companies on the sale of these policies, and receive further commissions from finance providers for the interest-bearing loans they initiate. The level of the commissions will be dependent upon the agreed level of premium to charge the patients for the insurance policies and the level of interest to be charged on the loans. These commissions are becoming more significant as the demand for more complex treatments increases.

Practices that are offering credit products will need to apply for a consumer credit licence.

COSMETIC PROCEDURES

Dentistry is no longer just a case of maintaining, filling and extracting teeth, as it was for many years. Nowadays, many people turn to cosmetic dentistry, as a way of improving their appearance, much as they would use cosmetic surgery or even a new hairstyle. The treatments can be used to straighten, lighten, reshape and repair teeth. Cosmetic treatments include the following.

➤ **Veneers:** these are thin slices of porcelain. These are precisely made to fit over the visible surface of front teeth.
➤ **White fillings:** are now becoming a popular alternative to amalgam fillings. The new dental materials mean it is much easier to find a perfect match for the shade of a particular tooth. In most cases, it is quite impossible to see that the tooth even has a filling. Sometimes white filling material can be used to cover unsightly marks on the teeth, in a similar way to veneers.
➤ **Crowns:** when a tooth is badly broken or heavily filled, the dentist may need to crown or 'cap' it to restore its appearance and strength.
➤ **Dentures:** if a tooth is missing, or needs extracting, there are several ways

to fill the gap that is left. In some cases it is important to try to replace any missing teeth in order to balance the jaw. A partial denture is the simplest way of replacing missing teeth. However, some people find dentures uncomfortable and eventually decide to look at alternatives.

➤ **Bridges:** are ideal for people who don't like dentures or only have one or two teeth missing. Conventional bridges are made by crowning the teeth on either side of the gap and attaching a false tooth in the middle. They are fixed in the same way as crowns. These bridges are usually made of precious metal bonded to porcelain. Sometimes other non-precious metals are used in the base for strength.

➤ **Implants**: are an alternative to dentures or bridgework, but they are more expensive. Implants are titanium rods, which are surgically placed into the jawbone and act as anchors for fastening dentures or crowns onto.

➤ **Tooth whitening**: can be a highly effective way of lightening the natural colour of your teeth without removing any of the tooth surfaces. It cannot make a complete colour change, but it will lighten the existing shade.

➤ **Teeth straightening:** with orthodontics (braces). This is usually done during the teenage years, when the teeth are going through a period of growth. However, many adults also have treatment to straighten their crooked teeth or to improve their appearance. The procedure can take much longer in adults and is therefore more expensive. For cosmetic reasons, clear or plastic braces can be used, which are hardly noticeable.

➤ **Tooth jewellery:** involves sticking small accessories onto the teeth.

These cosmetic treatments are highly profitable and are providing lucrative alternatives to dentists that have opted not to continue as NHS dentists.

MIXED PRACTICE

By the NASDA definition, mixed practices are those that do not provide either 80% NHS services or 80% private dentistry, but on the whole are carrying out the same CoTs as those listed above.

With practices opting to take on more cosmetic procedures and others converting their patients to private patient plans, the number of practices within the 'mixed practice' definition is reducing each year and looks likely to continue to do so given that there currently appears to be a polarisation of NHS services.

Many PCOs are under a lot of pressure to deliver 'NHS dentistry for all' from the limited budgets they have been provided with, and often try to obtain economies of scale by reassessing contracts to ensure more funding goes to the NHS practices to expand their services, or to PCO access centres, often at the expense of the practices with small exempt contracts.

CHAPTER 6

Property matters

The purchase of a practice will most often include the purchase or the assignment of a property, which will usually account for a large part of the agreed price. In order that the more common property pitfalls are avoided it is essential to obtain specialist legal and taxation advice prior to the purchase.

A specialist adviser will have experience of all the things that can go wrong with property ownership and can advise accordingly, whether it is to reduce the tax on the eventual sale of the property or to preserve the rights of the continuing principals upon a dispute.

Accountants will, at times, find themselves drawn into advising their surgery-owning clients on the financial aspects of surgery ownership, including the potential taxation advantages. It is necessary, therefore, that they have a sound working knowledge of this topic. Similarly, a solicitor with an understanding of dental practice can assist in preventing any property-related problems in the future.

This chapter will attempt to highlight the more common problems related to property ownership and will offer advice on how to deal with them.

WHAT TYPE OF PROPERTY IS BEST FOR A PRACTICE?
The type and standard of accommodation provided by practices for use as surgery premises can come in many forms, the more usual are:
➤ converted residential or commercial property
➤ first-floor premises over high street shopping areas
➤ purpose-built premises.

The more common premises tend to be converted houses or shop units, which have often been operating as dental surgeries for a number of years, and their present condition will be as a result of a number of extensions and conversions over the years as the need for accommodation has increased.

Whether viewing a practice to purchase or another property to move into the following issues need to taken into account.

➤ The area in which the property stands can affect the type of work that a practice can charge for, with more deprived areas offering fewer opportunities for private, more profitable treatments. More deprived areas tend to bring with them a higher cost in securing a property such as a dental practice, with bars to windows and heavy-duty locks being needed to protect the property from break-ins.

➤ The number of rooms that the property has can affect the practice's ability to generate a decent level of profit. The least profitable practice that I have encountered was a one-surgery NHS practice in a deprived area. A one-surgery practice will result in the principal undertaking less profitable procedures which an associate or hygienist could do.

➤ A restriction on the number of rooms or available space can limit the practice's ability to expand and increase its income.

➤ Recent legislative changes have required practices to construct a sterilisation room; this has resulted in some practices losing a surgery!

➤ Older properties and listed buildings can be a headache when new surgeries are planned and the installation of chairs and drainage systems can need planning permission and cause problems that will increase the cost of such works.

➤ If the plan is to convert from NHS to private or to provide more private procedures the standard of the décor, etc. needs to be of a high quality. The cost of providing a higher standard of accommodation needs to be factored into the purchase price.

➤ Purpose-built properties tend to provide the best facilities, but beware those properties built more than 20 years ago as they may not meet current standards and further expense may be needed to bring them up to date.

➤ Some properties are easy to sell; others seem to stay on the market for ever. When buying it is advisable to think ahead and try to identify if there are any negative aspects to the property that may affect its eventual sale (consider neighbouring properties and the area the property is situated in).

➤ Private practices normally provide a higher level of facilities for patients, whether it is a bigger waiting room with tea and coffee facilities, or privacy areas for dealing with sensitive issues with the practice support staff. If you are considering providing private treatments ensure the premises are suitable.

➤ Likewise, ensure that there will be sufficient room to display dental products for retail sales.

➤ Legislation in respect of disabled access needs to be considered before

purchasing a property. There is nothing worse than patients negotiating a Stannah stairlift on the way to the surgery.
➤ With parking restrictions generally increasing a surgery with a free car park would be popular with patients.

In summary, the ideal property will be of a high quality, roomy, on the ground floor, with parking, in a good area, near to other facilities and offer room for expansion if needed. Do such properties exist? Yes they do . . . dentists need to look no further than 'out of town' developments of shops and offices where all the requirements on the list above can be satisfied, with the added attraction of possible new patients from neighbouring businesses.

The above advice is aimed at the dentist starting up or expanding a practice. For those nearing retirement there is another option which is increasingly being offered to NHS dentists by PCOs, that is the 'Darzi' type health centre, where the PCO relocate a number of medical practices within one building and offer other healthcare services by similarly relocating a local NHS dental practice and pharmacist to the centre. There are often incentives to join these initiatives, with assistance in the sale of the existing premises being offered. This type of arrangement can ease the process of retirement.

FREEHOLD OR LEASEHOLD: SHOULD I BUY OR RENT?

The distinction between freehold and leasehold property can be explained by the following definitions.
➤ **Freehold:** any interest in real property which is of uncertain or undetermined duration (having no stated end), as distinguished from a leasehold which may have declining value towards the end of a long-term lease (such as the 99-year variety).
➤ **Leasehold:** an estate, or interest, in real property held under a rental agreement by which the owner gives another the right to occupy or use land for a period of time.

Leasehold property can be further defined as:
➤ **short leasehold:** where the portion of the term remaining unexpired under the rental agreement is less than 5–10 years
➤ **long leasehold:** where the portion of the term remaining unexpired under the rental agreement is more than 10 years.

The above distinction between short and long leasehold is not cast in stone, as different industries have their own classifications; for example, residential lets over 12 months can sometimes be classed as long term!

It would be usual to pay a premium to buy a long leasehold as it effectively gives you a right to occupy a property for a substantial period; for example, there are long leasehold properties with leases of 999 years (effectively a freehold). Long leaseholds of such length are generally treated in the same way as freehold properties.

It would be unusual to pay a premium for a short leasehold as it does not provide safety of tenure past the date of the termination of the short-term rental agreement.

There are a lot of legal issues that need to be taken account of in relation to leases which dentists must discuss with their solicitors prior to signing any agreements. Failure to do so can result in the dentist paying rent for periods in excess of their tenure.

The following issues need to be taken into account in deciding whether to buy a freehold property or rent a leasehold property.

➤ **Risk:** there is a school of thought that it is riskier to sign a mortgage deed and purchase a freehold (as the liability on the mortgage could be 'a millstone around your neck'), than it is to sign a leasehold agreement. My personal view is that it is a lot riskier to sign a long leasehold, say for 25 years, as the landlord can claim the rent from you for the whole of the period of the lease, even if you have retired before that period and assigned the lease to your successors! At least if you have purchased the property you will have the option to sell it to pay off the mortgage.

➤ Some landlords will let you sign the lease through a limited liability company, which effectively means that you are protected personally in the event of a dispute with the landlord. Given that this option gives you protection there are a lot of landlords who will not accept this arrangement.

➤ **Freehold property ownership problems:** when more than one person owns a freehold property the owners will hold it as either:
  • **tenants in common:** each of the property owners owns an agreed share of the property. That share can be bequeathed to dependants in a will.
  • **joint tenants:** the property owners own all of the property together. If one of the owners passes away the surviving owners automatically own all of it, no matter what it says in the deceased's will.

➤ It is important that a commercial property such as a dental surgery is held by the principals as tenants in common.

➤ **Advantages:** taking on a lease, rather than buying a freehold property, can be of benefit in the following circumstances:
  • where there are no suitable properties in the chosen area
  • where there are no funds to pay a deposit on the purchase of a property; however, the specialist lenders are willing to lend more than 100% to dentists buying practices, subject to a higher rate of interest being charged on the loan

- where there are no long-term plans to stay in that location
- where the practice has been resited as part of a PCO-led surgery development
- where the retiring dentist is not willing to sell the freehold to the purchasing dentist.

➤ **Disadvantages:** leaseholders, however, suffer the following disadvantages.

- The payment of rent, although allowable as a taxable expense, is effectively dead money.
- The repayments on a loan to purchase a property will often be of a similar amount as the rental that property would attract. It is therefore often better to purchase a property with a loan, as the repayments will help buy an investment that should increase in value over time.
- The leaseholder will ultimately not benefit from the increase in value from any improvements that he or she makes to the property. This is often a reason why leaseholders do not make significant improvements to rented property.
- The leaseholder may be prohibited from extending or developing the property which may impact upon the growth of the practice.
- There may be aspects of the expenditure that the leaseholder incurs on the property that may not be allowed as a taxable expense, whereas if the property was owned these expenses would be allowed against any future capital gain made on the sale of the property.
- A leaseholder will ultimately have to move out of the property at the end of the lease period, although there are a number of regulations that may allow the tenant to unilaterally extend the period of the lease if the landlord cannot prove that he needs the property for his or her own business.
- Improvements to leasehold premises may present problems in the accounts of the individuals that lease those premises. When improvements are made to the property there is no real value added from the tenants' perspective, in that if they were to vacate the premises the next day they would receive no payment for the work done. However, those improvements will provide benefits to them over the remaining period of the lease. So how should that expense be treated in the accounts?
  - (a) Written off in the year it was incurred, recognising there is no real value added?
  - (b) Written off over the remaining period of the lease, recognising the benefits that the work will provide for many years to come?

There is no right answer to this question, as it is up to the individuals involved to decide, and it will be dependent upon their circumstances at that time. But it is important to note that the decision will affect the value in the accounts and ultimately the amount the principals will receive when they retire from the practice.

SALE AND LEASEBACK OF THE SURGERY

Although much more popular in the medical world, there are organisations that specialise in the purchase of dental surgeries in order to lease them back to their former owners. The types of property that are more suited to this type of sale are the purpose-built dental surgeries rather than the converted residential property.

The advantage to the dentists from this type of arrangement is that the capital investment in the property is released and paid back to them to be available for other business or non-business use. The advantage to the property investor is a long-term investment in property with the receipt of a rent in the interim.

The disadvantage to the dentists is that they have lost any share in the growth in value of the property. Also the dentists will lose out on any increase in value that could arise from any improvements that they make to the property. This can act as a disincentive to do any major improvements, with the result that the standard of the practice falls.

WHO SHOULD OWN THE SURGERY?

Dental surgeries are usually owned by the principals who are in practice together, often on an equal basis. However, there are practices where the surgery is owned by a limited company that is controlled by the principals, and a number of practices that have transferred their surgeries to self-invested personal pensions (SIPPs) to obtain the significant tax advantages that are available in doing so.

Although there are significant tax advantages to be gained by transferring the practice property to a SIPP, it is mostly those dentists with a significant amount of income taxed at higher rates that will benefit. Given the increased use of incorporation to reduce the tax paid by dentists in practice there has been a slowing down in the number of dental surgeries being transferred to SIPPs.

As mentioned above there are a few practices that hold the practice property within a limited company, usually the decision to do this was made many years ago, and as this arrangement can bring with it a lot of negative tax issues it is not to be recommended. Briefly, the tax disadvantages arise in the following situations.

➤ If the property ever needs to be extracted from the company, both the company *and* the shareholders may pay tax on the increase in the value of the property while it has been held within the company.

➤ In addition companies do not benefit from the allowances that individuals can offset against their capital gains.

➤ Another problem of holding the property within a company is that if a rent is charged to the principals (and directors) at less than market rate, there is the possibility of a taxable benefit-in-kind being assessed on the directors.
➤ There are also potential problems in obtaining tax relief on loans that may be necessary to allow new partners to buy in to the shares of the company.

Where the premises are held by the principals it is usual that they are owned by the principals currently in practice, but there are a number of practices where the premises are still partly owned by retired principals. In these cases, and in others where the ownership of the property is not on an equal basis, it is common to see a rent charged in the accounts. This can present problems with CGT upon retirement, and dentists should ask their accountants to look at other ways of recompensing themselves for property ownership.

If the property is not owned by the principals in equal shares, conflicts can arise as to which expenses should be charged to the practice and which are the responsibility of the property owners. The more stable practices are those where each principal is given the opportunity to take a full share of the assets of that practice, and I would advise that this approach is taken to the ownership of the premises.

Those practices that operate as limited companies will not include the property that they own, and operate from, on the balance sheet. The principal reason for this is taxation, with more allowances, etc. being available to an individual than to a corporate body, upon the eventual disposal of that property. Therefore, it would be unusual to see a freehold property on the balance sheet of a dental company.

TRANSFER OF THE SURGERY TO A SELF-INVESTED PERSONAL PENSION

The benefits of the transfer of the practice property into a SIPP were mentioned briefly above. In the following paragraphs we will look at the benefits in a little more detail. The transfer of the practice property into a SIPP brings with it significant tax advantages.
➤ Tax relief on the value of the property being transferred to the SIPP.
➤ Any growth in the value of the property within the SIPP is tax free.
➤ The practice will get tax relief on the rental paid to the SIPP, but the SIPP receives the rent tax free.

The disadvantages of a transfer are as follows.
➤ CGT will be payable on the value of the property being transferred to the SIPP.

➤ The value of the asset is locked away in the pension fund until the dentist attains the age of at least 55.

A simplified example showing the benefits is as follows:

A dentist with earnings of £100,000 a year after superannuation, which will all be subject to higher rates of tax, owns a surgery valued at £100,000 which cost him £70,000 five years ago. By allowing the SIPP to take the surgery over he will gain £40,000 in tax relief but incur a CGT bill of £3,582 (a net gain of £36,418).

The mechanics of the transfer would be as follows.

1 The dentist takes a loan from his bankers for £80,000.
2 He pays £80,000 to his SIPP as a pension contribution.
3 As the amount paid or transferred into a SIPP is treated as a net of tax contribution the SIPP can reclaim 20% tax back from HMRC (i.e. £20,000).
4 The SIPP buys the surgery from the dentist for £100,000.
5 The dentist repays his loan from the proceeds.
6 The dentist claims back 20% tax relief on the pension contribution from HMRC (i.e. £20,000).
7 The dentist pays CGT of £3,582.

The reason for the rather convoluted way in which the surgery is transferred to the SIPP is to ensure that the dentist retains all of the tax relief personally. If he were to transfer the property direct to the SIPP, the value of the contribution (i.e. £100,000) would be treated as a net of tax amount and the SIPP would be able to reclaim £25,000 in tax relief. Although the tax relief would be higher the dentist could not withdraw that amount from the SIPP.

Obviously, not all dentists will be in the position in the example above, as the situation can be complicated by partnership shares and borrowings secured on the property. But there are specialist SIPP providers and financiers who can assist in the more complicated cases.

Although the tax advantages are significant, the transfer to the SIPP will inherently be an investment decision and as such should only be made following the advice of an independent financial adviser (IFA).

This course of action is not to be recommended to younger dentists who may consider a change of life or country at some stage, as the result of transferring the property to a SIPP will prevent the use of any capital relating to the property being made available until the age of 55.

This course of action is also not to be recommended to those who may be subject to higher rate tax liability in retirement, as, although the tax relief now is quite attractive, higher rate tax will be payable on any income received post retirement from that investment. Depending upon the age the dentist lives to he or she may pay more higher rate tax post retirement than he or she has claimed back on the transfer of the property to the SIPP.

DO WE NEED A PROPERTY OWNERSHIP AGREEMENT?

A substantial amount of fees are paid to professionals, such as lawyers and accountants, as a result of 'partnership' disputes, and although most dentist practices are not partnerships *per se* the way in which the property is held can result in problems similar to those found in partnerships. Examples of the common problem areas include the following.

➤ Disputes in respect of the valuation of the property upon changes in principals.
➤ Disputes with new principals not wanting to take on shares in high fixed-rate loans and early-redemption penalty clauses.
➤ Disputes regarding refurbishment expenditure near to a principal retiring.
➤ Disputes regarding negative equity as a consequence of excessive development costs.
➤ Disputes regarding the payment of a property share to a former partner.

In order to avoid the above problem areas dentists are strongly advised to have a property deed drafted to cover all matters that relate to the property. The property deed should cover the following points.

➤ Clearly define the property and the principals' individual interests in the property. This would normally be facilitated by the inclusion of a schedule listing the percentage share of the building owned by each principal.
➤ Describe what the property can be used for. In order to prevent problems with principals using the building, or part of it, for activities that may not have the agreement of all the owners, a restriction on allowable activities should be included within the agreement. This restriction may also have an effect on the market value of the property (see below).
➤ Set out the procedures regarding the transfer of the property following a partner's death, retirement, or expulsion from the partnership, etc. This section should list the provisions for the sale of the property share upon retirement and time frame within which any payment should be made to the former partner or their estate (and/or the payment of any rent or interest on the capital amounts involved).
➤ List partners' options to buy upon a partner leaving. This section should deal with the options the continuing partners have for buying the former partners' share of the property. It could also provide a time limit within which former partners could continue to retain ownership of a share of the property, and could include restrictions upon non-principals owning a share of the building.

➤ Set out the responsibilities for costs in connection with the occupation, maintenance and insurance of the property, especially if there are principals within the practice who do not own a share of the premises. In those instances it would be usual for there to be a tenancy agreement between the property-owning partners and the practice.

➤ Provide for the method of valuation upon partnership changes. The agreement should provide for a valuation to be undertaken when there are partnership changes and it should also dictate the basis of the valuation (i.e. open market value or a value as a dental surgery). The Royal Institute of Chartered Surveyors (RICS) has specific instructions on how to value surgeries. Most good partnership agreements include an arbitration clause, so that in the event of a dispute the valuation can be decided upon by the local chairperson of RICS.

➤ In some cases the market value of a surgery will be less than the cost of the building and development costs and negative equity arises. Some larger practices in this situation fund their practices based on the cost of investment and require all partners to have a capital balance in excess of the market value of the premises. This capital requirement (unless drawn previously) is fully repayable upon leaving the practice and is not treated as 'buying in' but more as providing a share of capital. At some stage in the future the market value should equate or exceed the capital requirement. This approach will not work in small practices where there is a real possibility that one partner could end up owning the surgery in his or her own name with responsibility for borrowings in excess of the market value of the premises.

➤ This section should also cover the way that refurbishment expenditure should be treated in the accounts in order that there are no disputes regarding this expenditure upon the retirement of a partner. This eventuality can be dealt with by the inclusion of clauses to provide for the following.
  • An early sale to the continuing partners at the current market value.
  • The sale price fixed at the current market value if the actual market value in two years' time is less.

➤ As the refurbishment will benefit the continuing partners in the long run they should agree to this approach. A problem could arise, however, if a new partner joining in, say, two years' time refused to pay in excess of the equivalent current market value for his or her share!

Ultimately, if the property owners do not draft an agreement, any unresolved dispute could result in a court applying to dissolve the partnership and force the sale of the surgery on the open market.

An agreement is pretty standard and most firms of solicitors should be able to draft one to cover a dental practice for a modest fee. Without it a practice could find itself in a dispute with a partner, which may only be resolved by resorting to legal action.

HOW DO I FINANCE OR REFINANCE THE PROPERTY?

There are a number of occasions when dentists will need to raise finance in respect of a property transaction. They can either provide the finance from their own resources, or, as is more usual, approach a bank to ask them to provide the finance. The usual situations where finance is required are:

➤ upon the purchase or construction of a new surgery for the practice
➤ upon the retirement or appointment of partners, where partners' shares in the premises are transferred
➤ upon the refinancing of the surgery premises to allow a draw-down of the partners' capital accounts
➤ upon the refinancing of the surgery premises to allow funding for further development to those premises
➤ upon the transfer of the practice borrowings to another lender to achieve savings from lower interest and bank charges.

Historically, the dental profession has been a sector that the banks have been very keen to lend to, and the banks were offering dentists very good rates on surgery borrowings for any purpose up until spring 2008. However, as the result of the financial meltdown in 2008/09 they have tightened up their lending criteria significantly. Banks will look at all propositions now on an individual basis and are under a lot of pressure to increase margins in their lending. While it was possible up until 2008 to obtain a business loan to purchase a practice at a rate of 1% above the Bank of England base rate, at the current time (summer 2009) the minimum rates being offered are in the region of 2–2.5% above Bank of England base rate.

When dentists approach a bank they may be asked whether they would like a fixed- or a variable-rate loan. A fixed-rate loan is one where the interest rate charged for the entire period of the loan is fixed at the start, whereas a variable-rate loan is one where the rate of interest changes when the Bank of England alters the base rate. Although a fixed-rate deal will give the practice financial stability, in that the repayments on the loan will remain fixed (even though interest rates may rise), the practice could lose out should the rate of interest drop. The rates offered under fixed-rate deals tend to be a lot higher than the current variable rates, so are only to be considered if it is forecast that interest rates will rise. There are capped rate offers where the practice will benefit from a reduction in the level of interest rates, and still be protected from interest rate rises, but the premiums charged on these arrangements are high and reduce the benefits that the practice could make. With hindsight it is easy to advise on fixed- versus variable-rate offers, but the instability of the financial markets means it is always going to be a gamble.

Those that opt for fixed-rate borrowings gain financial stability, but do they do it at a cost or a benefit? In truth there is no correct answer to this query without resorting to a crystal ball.

Interest charged on a loan taken out by a practice, or individual dentist, to purchase a property from which to practise will attract tax relief. In order to maximise this tax relief some practices opt for an interest-only loan with the intention that they will pay off all personal, non-tax efficient borrowings prior to the repayment of the capital on the practice loan. As well as maximising the tax relief, this arrangement ensures that there is more cash available to draw, and as long as the additional drawings are used in paying down personal borrowings or building up investments, this arrangement will benefit all the principals.

But there may be partners in a practice that do not have any personal non-tax efficient borrowings and they may object to a high level of practice borrowings. They can usually be persuaded to agree to this type of arrangement as follows.
1 Interest rates are currently at 0.5% and monies are currently being made available to practices at 2.5% over base rate.
2 Therefore, the gross cost of borrowing will be 3%.
3 The net rate after tax relief at 40% will be 1.8%.
4 There are a number of relatively safe or deposit-based investments that will secure an after-tax rate of return in excess of 1.8%.
5 Therefore, the partners would be better off maximising their borrowings and investing the funds that they have available to repay the loan.

A number of banks are restricting the number of years that they will allow capital-repayment holidays or interest-only loans, so practices are often advised to take on a repayment loan. In this situation the practice should look at the benefits of re-banking the loan to the original level of borrowing, say, every five years or so.

Normally, over time the property loan will be paid down and the value of the property will increase with the result that the net equity in the premises will increase, but this may not always be in the best interest of the practice. If the net equity is allowed to build up over the years it may become a problem upon the retirement of a partner, as this may present a hurdle to a new partner considering buying into the practice. Often a new partner will quite happily sign up to a share of a large partnership loan, as opposed to approaching the bank on an individual basis to arrange a separate large loan for his or her share of the property.

To summarise at this point, the practice would be better off borrowing the maximum amount it can for tax purposes, and borrowing the amount as a practice rather than by way of individual loans. Other benefits from this approach to practice financing are as follows.

➤ It is less likely that the bank would require any form of life assurance if the loan is in the partnership's name.

➤ Given there would not be a refinancing every time a partner joins or leaves, there would be savings in bank charges.

➤ Equality in the equity shares in the property of the partners could be maintained at all times at a level to be agreed.

The legislation that grants tax relief on interest on partnership loans is complicated and care needs to be taken in the order in which loan finance and draw-downs are taken to ensure that tax relief is allowable on the borrowing.

Tax relief will not be available on interest on that part of a loan that has been taken out in excess of the cost of the property, as it will result in the partners' capital accounts going overdrawn upon its withdrawal by the partners from the practice.

Below is an example of the tax savings that can be obtained through refinancing of capital accounts.

The Churchill practice is a three-dentist practice based in a city in the North of England.

The three principals are as follows.

• Mr A lives with his wife and two children in a £300,000 house and his only borrowing is the mortgage on the house of £180,000. His mortgage is a repayment mortgage at a rate of 5.95%.

• Mr B lives with his wife and new baby in a £250,000 house upon which he has an interest-only mortgage of £100,000 at 5.39%. His pride and joy is his Audi TT upon which he has a £10,000 bank loan at a rate of 7.2%. He uses this car 20% of the time for the practice.

• Mr C is the senior partner and lives with his wife in a £450,000 house. He has no borrowings. His daughter is due to marry soon and he plans to help her buy her first house. He is nearing retirement and is interested in improving his pension position.

The practice premises are based in the city centre and cost £700,000; the outstanding loan on the property is £370,000.

The practice approaches the bank and arranges to borrow a further £330,000 on the practice premises and each partner will draw £110,000.

Mr A will use the money to pay £110,000 off his mortgage and his annual savings will be £4,565.

Mr B will use his money to pay off his car loan and the balance of his mortgage. His annual savings will be £4,022.

Mr C will give his daughter a gift of £25,000 and will use the balance for investments and pensions. His annual excess will be £3,375 (plus £34,000 tax relief on the contribution to his pension).

The total annual gain to the partnership is £10,882.

The above savings were achieved by maximising the partners' tax reliefs, and they have not caused the partners as a whole to go deeper into debt than they already were.

NEGATIVE EQUITY AND VALUATIONS

Given the vagaries of the property market, and the high levels of borrowings taken on by dentists, the possibility of a negative equity situation arising is very real. The banks have been known to lend up to 120% upon the set-up of a squat practice (a new practice set-up), so in the early years of ownership of those practices there is a negative equity situation. This can also be the case upon the construction of a purpose-built dental surgery, where the building value after completion can be worth less than the cost of construction.

A lot of practices have been established in converted residential properties, and are valued on the basis of the market value of that property as a residence (less any costs of conversion to make it so). When there is a fall in the value of residential property, there will be a corresponding drop in the value of the surgery, which if below the amount paid for it will result in negative equity.

In most cases, however, practices, particularly those with a relatively high level of income and comprised of principals not nearing retirement, will be able to weather this problem without too much difficulty. Provided that there are no retirements pending and they can afford to repay the loan from their income, they could wait for a few years with the reasonable expectation that property prices will increase over the medium term so that the negative equity will be extinguished.

Often practices in this situation protect themselves by inserting a clause in their agreement to the effect that a principal retiring or leaving the practice within a specified period would be protected, in that his or her share of the property would never be sold at less than cost. But this type of arrangement is not suited to smaller practices, where there is the possibility of one principal being left with a property worth less than the loans secured upon it!

Basis of valuation

For many years the accepted basis for valuation of dental practice surgeries was to be based upon the continuing use of the building as a dental surgery. This is especially so where the property is purpose built or subject to planning restrictions. However, there are instances, especially with surgeries in residential areas, where the property will be worth more as a residence than a surgery. How does a practice deal with such a situation? There are two options.

1 Adopt the higher true market value of the building, as opposed to the lower value as a dental surgery. While this provides for a higher payout to a retiring partner, it increases the capital base for the practice and new partners.
2 Restrict the value of the property to that as a surgery, with a clause to the effect that if the property is sold within an agreed number of years, for a higher value as a residential property, the payout to the retired partner will be increased accordingly. This option keeps the capital base of the practice lower than the option above.

LIFE INSURANCE AND ENDOWMENTS

Lenders will often insist on dentists taking out life insurance cover so that a property loan can be repaid upon their death. While this is understandable when a single-handed dentist has a high level of personal borrowings, it can cause problems, and it is sometimes unnecessary in practices with a number of principals.

In addition, dentists offering NHS services often have a reasonably high level of life cover as part of the NHS Superannuation Scheme of which they are a member. This cover is often overlooked and additional cover taken out at the lender's insistence unnecessarily.

In practices where there are a number of principals the property deed usually provides for the continuing dentists to buy the deceased principal's share of the property upon his or her death. If that is the case, then their purchase of the property share will provide the funds for the repayment of any loan secured on it. This arrangement makes life insurance cover unnecessary, which often needs to be pointed out to lenders.

If life insurance is considered necessary it is essential that the details of the beneficiaries are correct for both the purpose of repayment of the loan, and for inheritance tax purposes.

Also if life insurance is considered necessary and the loan has been arranged on a capital-repayment basis, it would be advisable to take out an insurance policy where the level of cover reduces in line with the capital balance on the loan. This type of cover is often cheaper than a straight term cover.

Although not as popular in current times, endowments have often been used as a repayment vehicle on interest-only loans in the past. There have been significant problems with these policies and advice needs to be taken to ensure that they are suitable. Problems include:

➤ policies that are secured on the lives of ex-principals
➤ paying out shares of the values of continuing policies upon principals leaving
➤ policies not providing sufficient capital to repay the loan upon maturity
➤ differing values in the principals' policies due to differences in ages.

It is essential that dentists use IFAs with experience in the dental profession when arranging life policies, endowments, insurances and pensions. There are many IFAs who claim to have expertise but who sell inappropriate policies to dentists with devastating effects on their finances. Try to choose an adviser who charges fees, as they will not be governed by the commissions available on policies, and ask for and check references before appointing them.

CHAPTER 7

Buying and selling a practice

This chapter will look at the issues that arise upon the purchase or sale of a practice and will highlight the common pitfalls that may occur in the process. The detail below will look at the transaction from both the buyers' and the sellers' viewpoint and note the conflicts that may arise between the two. The impact the transaction will have upon the dentists' taxation position will only be outlined in this chapter, with further detail being included in Chapter 10 on taxation. We will start by looking at the purchase of a practice (or share of a practice) by an associate.

BUYING INTO YOUR FIRST PRACTICE

There comes a time in an associate's life when he or she will be asked to join a practice, either as a partner or as an expense-sharing principal. This promotion can often be a time for celebrations, but associates should ensure that this opportunity is really the one that they have been waiting for. Will they get their feet under the table and get to keep 100% of their income, or could this end up being a disastrous investment in a failing practice? In order to avoid the latter the associate will need consider the following issues.

What does the future hold for this practice?

Often as an associate you will be made an offer to become a principal at the practice where you have worked for a number of years. Assuming you wish to become a principal you will need to decide whether to accept this offer at your current practice or look at the opportunities elsewhere.

As a result of your time at the practice you will have become aware of the practice environment and working practices, and also have a detailed working knowledge of the state of your patients' teeth and treatments they have received to date. If you are happy with the financial package being offered to you, a partnership or principalship at your existing practice is the preferable route to take, as to join, or purchase, a practice without the knowledge above could be risky, with the possibility of staff issues or redundancies and dental remedial work taking up a lot of your time in your first few years in practice.

Therefore, when you are looking for your first associate post you should look ahead and aim to find a practice to work in that will provide a good working environment, challenging professional work and a short- to medium-term opportunity of being asked to become a principal.

The alternatives, should the offer of a partnership or principalship at the existing practice not be appropriate or available, would be to find another associateship with a view to a later partnership or principalship, purchase of a practice outright or to set up a squat practice (but these last two options may prove expensive).

Is the price right?

Often the retiring principal or the practice has obtained a valuation for the share of the practice being offered. The associate should ensure that the valuation has been prepared by a specialist valuer of dental surgeries, and that the state of the practice equipment and the mix of work that the practice provides have been taken into account.

It would be foolhardy to purchase a practice without a specialist valuation as this could lead to an overpayment.

Currently goodwill values are ranging from 70–100% of turnover for profitable practices, but specialist advisers (such as NASDA members) should be able to review the valuations against their current database and comment thereon.

Often associates are surprised at the amount that is being asked for the share of the practice by the vendor and perceive that they are being overcharged. A good exercise to do in this situation is to look at the cost of setting up a squat as an alternative. Once the cost of buying or renting a property, kitting it out with equipment, and living on reduced income, while a list builds up, is taken into account, the price of the share of the practice can appear quite reasonable. In addition, the associate buying into the practice where they currently work will know the dental needs of their existing patients, whereas there is the danger that the squat practice could attract patients that have neglected their dental health in the past.

How should I finance the purchase?

Most associates will not have the funds to buy into a practice outright and will need to raise funds from an external source to finance the purchase. As mentioned in the previous chapter there are a number of banks that have historically been keen to provide finance to dentists and offered discounted rates to those investing in practice; however, the recent credit crunch has resulted in an increase in the rates.

Advice needs to be taken as to the length of the loan period as there is no point in repaying a business loan (with interest eligible for tax relief) over a short period of time, when the borrower also has personal borrowings (e.g. a mortgage). In that instance it would be better for the borrower to take the maximum loan repayment period offered, and use the extra income this will free up to pay off personal borrowings.

The associate should consider whether an interest-only arrangement should be undertaken in the early years of the loan, as this will reduce the initial monthly cost at a time when cash flow may be tight due to investment in the practice.

Specialist advisers will usually have contacts with the main bankers and can assist to ensure that only the lowest interest rates are charged, and it is important that the banks' specialist lenders are approached as the high street bank managers are often not aware of the cut-price deals available to dentists.

Remember that in addition to the purchase price you will need to raise an amount of working capital, or agree an overdraft facility to finance the practice cash flow needs.

WHAT RECORDS SHOULD I INSPECT?

Usually, the practice manager will keep a record of the joint income and expenses and the contributions by the principals to the joint account, and the principals will usually keep records of personal income and expenses, along with lab bills, etc. incurred by the practice that will need to be prior charged to them. You will need to inspect these records, and examine, in particular, the monthly NHS schedules and Denplan (or similar) statements, in order to verify the income level of the practice. Given that the level of practice income is a major factor in calculating the purchase price of the practice there is sometimes a clause included in the sales agreement to the effect that any shortfall in the practice income in the first year following the purchase will result in a proportional refund of the sales price. This is especially so when the former principal becomes the associate and is likely to underperform!

A large number of practices use computerised accounting packages, such as Sage, which can provide detailed accounts that are not only useful to the practice for management purposes but also can provide a useful source of information to confirm the level of the practice expenditure.

Determine the level of gross income that each of the fee earners is generating currently and compare that with historical records to ensure the current performance is indicative of the usual practice income.

View the staff contracts of employment to identify whether the current level of pay is in line with that of the last year or so. Identify the long-term employees and be prepared to pay redundancy awards if any of those staff are not needed following the purchase of the practice. It would be usual to lose staff when taking over a practice, as the new management style may not suit all of the employees, so don't be surprised by staff resignations.

A very important point to check when purchasing an NHS practice is in whose names the contracts are registered, and whether the local PCO will be happy to transfer the contract to yourself or a company. If any of the contract is in the name of the associates it may be lost should they leave the practice; the value of the practice goodwill will be reduced as a consequence.

WHAT SHOULD I DO TO PROTECT MY INCOME?

Associates will usually not have large business liabilities and can often survive a period of time on a reduced income as a result of illness. Principals, however, cannot, as they will often have their share of the practice overheads to contribute to as well as a monthly bank loan to pay. A principal, therefore, will need to make the following provisions.

➤ **Locum cover:** to ensure that funds are available to pay a locum to undertake dental treatments in the principal's absence. This will ensure that the patients' needs are dealt with and an income is received by the practice so that the practice overheads and an income for the dentist can be provided for.

➤ **Practice expenses policy:** should a locum not be available an alternative arrangement would be to provide for the practice overheads to be paid. This type of policy would normally pay out a fixed amount based on the level of expenses in the latest set of practice accounts. It would not be usual for this type of policy to provide an income to the dentist in addition to the overheads.

➤ **Critical illness policy:** to provide a personal income in addition to the above. These policies will provide for a fixed level of monthly income for life (or until receipt of pension), the amount of which would usually be based on the after-tax level of drawings of the dentist.

➤ **Life cover:** to repay the practice bank loan upon death should the practice consider the short-term repayment of capital to the partner's executors a problem.

How will the purchase affect my tax bill?

The transition from associate to principal is treated as a cessation of the associate business and a commencement of the principal business, for tax purposes by HMRC. This can lead to cash-flow problems for those associates who have been in practice for some time and have an accounts year-end date other than 31 March. The reason for this is rather complicated and will not be detailed here; suffice to say that an additional amount of tax will be payable by those associates. However, there are a number of tax-planning opportunities to deal with this and specialist advice should be sought to reduce the amount payable.

If the practice that the associate is joining has an accounts year end other than 31 March there may be additional tax liabilities to pay upon a future retirement from that practice and advice should also be sought on this matter.

The fixtures, fittings and equipment and stock element of the purchase price of the practice will attract a deduction for income-tax purposes and assist in reducing the tax liability in the early years in practice. Unless there is an incorporation of the practice, tax relief on the goodwill element of the purchase price will only be available upon the eventual sale of that goodwill on retirement.

Is the practice right for me or should I consider the alternatives?

Before you commit to buy into the practice you need to look at the outlook for that practice and the effect any changes in legislation, etc. may have upon your future income. You need to ask yourself whether the practice has the potential to maintain its income and/or has opportunities to grow, in that it has the facilities available, and is within an area where a profitable practice could be established. The most profitable practices tend to be predominately private practices with multiple surgeries where economies of scale can be made. The least profitable practices are NHS single-surgery practices in areas of deprivation, as these practices do not offer the room to expand services nor the patient base to develop a private practice.

The associate needs to look at the age and income generation of the existing partners in order to ascertain whether multiple retirements will be likely in a short space of time, as you may have to find the funds to pay out retiring principals' practice shares before appropriate replacements can be found. The partnership agreement should be reviewed to identify the liabilities the associate may need to fund in such circumstances. It is better for the agreement to give continuing partners the option to buy out the outgoing partner's capital rather than including provisions which force them to buy it.

If a practice reduces the number of surgeries it operates upon the retirement of a principal, the level of overheads increases for the continuing partners. If those continuing partners are also required by the partnership agreement to pay the outgoing partner's goodwill, they will suffer a substantial financial loss.

Is the split of the sale proceeds right?

Usually, the price for the purchase of a practice will be split between property, goodwill, stock, fixtures, fittings and equipment. The vendor (the retiring dentist) would prefer the majority of the sale proceeds to be allocated to the property and goodwill as the CGT payable on those amounts will usually be less than the income tax payable on the sale of the stocks, fixtures, fittings and equipment. But the associate will normally gain greater allowances to set against his or her income tax if the sale proceeds are structured the other way round.

If the associate is considering buying the practice share through a limited company however, there are tax allowances available that will allow the goodwill expense to be set against the company corporation tax liability.

As with any business transaction, the valuation provides a figure that can be negotiated up or down, depending upon the willingness of the vendor to sell and the purchaser to buy, and the split of the sale proceeds can often be a negotiating point when reaching agreement on the final sale price.

It is important that all the items being purchased are listed in a detailed inventory, as this will prevent any confusion as to which items are to be included in the sale of the practice. Visit the practice to compare the list to the assets in situ prior to the completion of the sale.

Query the value given to the assets being purchased and ask for copies of any valuations provided by equipment suppliers. Second-hand dental equipment has very little value, other than replacement value.

Is the practice agreement up to date and adequate to cover the issues of dental practice?

It is very important that the practice has an up-to-date agreement that covers all aspects likely to cause disputes in the future. The main areas to consider are the arrangements upon a principal leaving a practice, due to death or retirement, and the problems associated with a principal being absent from the practice for a lengthy period of time due to illness, etc.

The issues highlighted above tend to arise in those practices where there is no agreement, or the agreement is out of date, and often result in a loss to the younger or continuing partners. All the principals need to provide for financial assistance in the event of sickness or death, in order that the continuing partners are not burdened with additional costs in that event.

The BDA provides pro-forma agreements that cover most of the issues that a dental practice ought to adopt in its agreement, such as how to deal with a deceased principal's widow or widower, or how to expel a partner who fails to abide by the clauses in the partnership agreement. Even though the BDA provides this assistance, the practice could still benefit by using a specialist legal firm to draft its partnership agreement, as they will be able to provide the most up-to-date provisions. Details of specialist legal firms can be found on the NASDA website.

Should I form a limited company to buy the practice?

There are substantial tax benefits to incorporation for some practices, but for others the benefits are small and the administration burden of incorporation too high to make the exercise viable. The tax benefits can be derived from restructuring the way that the practice profits are drawn, and given that an incorporated company can claim corporation tax relief on the amortisation of the goodwill each year, whereas an un-incorporated principal cannot, it is an area that needs to be examined as part of the purchase process.

As can be seen there are a number of issues that require advice from specialists in the field of dental finance and associates are strongly advised to approach them. The author has seen a number of unsuccessful practice purchases which have resulted from disregarding these issues.

A change in ownership of a practice is a good opportunity to assess the current practice suppliers and laboratories, and to invite new suppliers to quote for the business. The existing suppliers may improve their terms when faced with competition.

If the former principal is to be kept on as an associate it is important that this arrangement is short-lived, as the practice staff will still view the previous owner as the controller of the practice. It will be difficult to introduce new management initiatives if the previous owner is not seen to be in agreement by the staff.

SELLING THE PRACTICE

Currently, the more profitable sales of practices are those that are planned, where the dentist has considered succession planning at an early stage and has an associate within the practice who is ready to take over.

Historically, the more profitable sales were those to corporates, eager to expand the number of practices they operated. Recent indications are, however, that the corporates are no longer eager to buy practices at the prices that they used to, and they now usually further insist that the principals within the practice work for a fixed period after the sale and achieve increasing income targets, before the sales proceeds are paid in full to them.

If a suitable associate is not in place, and no corporate is interested in buying, at the time dentists wish to retire, they may need to put the practice on the open market for sale to all comers. In order to achieve a successful sale on the open market they will need to appoint a specialist agent to market the practice, and to produce a sales prospectus.

What to include in the sales prospectus

A sales prospectus needs to have sufficient detail in order to attract potential purchasers, without including detail that may be commercially sensitive and of value to nearby practices. All potential purchasers who are provided with a copy of the prospectus should be asked to sign a confidentiality agreement in respect of the detail contained therein.

The detail that needs including in the prospectus is as follows.

➤ **Disclaimer:** to explain that the information within the prospectus is selective and may be subject to updating, expansion, revision and amendment. It should explain that it does not purport to contain all the information that the potential purchaser may require. It should be made clear that the potential purchasers should conduct their own investigation and analysis of the practice and to seek their own professional advice on the legal, financial, taxation and other consequences of acquiring the practice.

➤ **Executive summary:** the executive summary should begin with a brief description of the practice, such as 'This is a one-off opportunity to buy a long-established mixed/private/NHS practice in a rural market town. This two-chair surgery offers expansion opportunities as there is room for further surgeries within the building.'

➤ The executive summary should also provide location details of the practice, and the distance and travel times to other local towns and cities. It would be usual to also include a brief history of the practice and the reason for the sale (i.e. retirement) in this section.

➤ **Practice details:** the practice details should include details of the NHS contract including the number of UDAs and the value attached to them, and the names of the dentists in whom the contracts are registered. Details of the number of Denplan (or similar) patients at the practice and the income from this source should also be disclosed here.

➤ Details of all the registered dental professionals should also be disclosed along with their experience and areas of expertise.

➤ Detail should also be provided of the practice accommodation and whether it is freehold or leasehold (and details of the rents payable if appropriate). It would be usual to provide details of the number and type of rooms on each floor at this stage.

➤ Details of the overall level of staff broken down, for example, as follows:
  • receptionist £13,455
  • dental nurse £12,370
  • dental nurse £17,680
  • cleaner £2,345
  • bookkeeper £5,040.

➤ Details of the practice opening hours and details of late surgeries, etc. would also be included in this section.

➤ **Financial information:** the financial details should include a summary of the last three years' gross revenue and profit and loss account. Often the profit and loss account is amended to exclude depreciation and all the principals' motoring and finance costs (mortgage interest, finance lease interest and any interest received on bank balances). The detailed accounts that provide the information for this summary should be included in the appendices.

➤ **Price guide:** a summary of the practice valuations should be included at this stage, giving a breakdown of the purchase price between the goodwill, property, fixtures and fittings and stock at valuation.

➤ **Offer process:** this section should deal with the timetable in respect of offers and details to whom the offers should be made. The offers should include the price the purchaser is offering, confirmation that the purchaser has the finance to buy or loan facilities available, and any conditions applying to that offer. There may be a holding deposit required upon the submission of the offer.

➤ **Appendices:** it would be usual to provide the following within the appendices of a sale prospectus:
  - accounts
  - NHS statements
  - Denplan statements
  - property valuation
  - photographs.

Selling an incorporated practice

There are two ways the sale of an incorporated practice can take place. It is important that dentists understand the differences between these two options as the tax liabilities, should the wrong one be chosen, can be substantial. The options are as follows.

➤ The sale of the shares in the company, i.e. the sale of the whole company with the practice included. In this case the individual selling the shares receives the sales proceeds.

➤ The sale by the company of the practice assets, i.e. the goodwill, fixtures and fittings and stock. In this case the company receives the sales proceeds.

The difference in the tax treatment can best be seen by way of an example, as follows.

- Mr Smith of Dental Smile Ltd has been offered £300,000 for his practice which he started when he incorporated the company five years ago.
- He has asked his accountant to compare the tax he will pay under each of the options above.

- For the purpose of this example both selling costs and capital gain personal allowances have been ignored.
- If Mr Smith sells the shares in his company he will be taxed at 10% as he will qualify for Entrepreneurs Relief, so his tax bill will be £30,000.
- If Dental Smile Ltd sells the assets of the practice for £300,000 it will pay tax at 21%, the current rate of corporation tax, a total of £63,000.
- There is a difference above of £33,000, before Mr Smith has even received any of the proceeds himself. If he needed to take the proceeds out of the company and pay them into his personal account he would suffer at least an additional 10% on the withdrawal, a further tax of £23,700.

Under the first option Mr Smith will retain £270,000 of the sales proceeds, whereas under the second option he would only retain £213,300, a difference in tax of £56,700!

Although the sale of the shares (i.e. the company) is the preferred option for the vendor, the purchase of the assets is the preferred route for most purchasers. The reasons for this are as follows.

➤ Capital allowances can be claimed on the purchase of the fixtures and fittings by the purchaser.
➤ Tax relief can be claimed on the purchase of goodwill (as long as it is purchased by a limited company).
➤ The purchaser does not know the history of the company and there may be potential liabilities that may arise after the sale that may relate to the period prior to the sale. For this reason, when companies are purchased there is an investigation undertaken by the purchaser's accountants, called due diligence, the object of which is to uncover any potential liabilities prior to the completion of the sale.

Given the difference in the tax cost a discount is often given to purchasers to accept a share sale.

However, there are a number of occasions where the sale of the company assets is the better option to take.

➤ Where the company has previously purchased the practice and has a cost to offset against the sales price. In the example above, if Dental Smile had purchased the practice five years ago for £250,000, it would only be taxed on the net gain of £50,000.
➤ Where the company is going to buy another practice, as it will be able to roll the gain on the sale against the cost of the new practice, effectively postponing the tax payable on the sale.
➤ Where the company has a number of practices or other assets under its

ownership the shareholder does not have the option to sell his shares, unless the business is restructured to transfer the practice being disposed of into a separate company. The costs of this may reduce the tax savings significantly.

As always, expert advice should be sought on a sale or purchase of a dental practice.

CHAPTER 8

Partnership, limited company or expense-sharing arrangement?

The majority of dentists practice in 'partnerships' of some description, although most of them have tried to arrange their affairs so that a partnership does not exist. The reason for this is to avoid the joint and several liabilities that come as a result of being a partner in a partnership. Unfortunately, even though a number of practices have appointed a solicitor to draft an expense-sharing arrangement to avoid the joint liability, they then hold themselves out as a partnership in their dealings with the public and suppliers. To avoid being treated as a partnership, principals should take legal advice as to how they should deal with third parties. A lot of the problems in dentist practice derive from the formation of 'partnerships', introduction of new principals, contributions of capital and expense-sharing.

If working with other dentists can present so many problems for them why do they do it? There are a number of answers.

➤ There are economies of scale that can be achieved by dentists working together, whether it is the ability to jointly fund a property purchase or sharing the telephone costs the savings can be significant.
➤ Dentists working together can split the management role and assist each other in running the practice.
➤ A larger practice is able to offer a wider service provision, as the dentists may have a number of differing disciplines to offer.
➤ A larger practice often will attract more associates and will assist in the process of succession.
➤ Dentists working together can produce enough work for other DCPs, such as hygienists.

➤ The combination of the above factors will make the practice more attractive for patients.

WHAT'S THE BEST WAY TO ORGANISE MY PRACTICE?

Dentists in practice can operate as sole practitioners, partnerships, in expense-sharing arrangements or limited companies. Very few practices, however, operate as a 'true' partnership and the most popular arrangements are usually sole practitioners or expense-sharing arrangements/partnerships. However, to take advantage of the tax savings available, there are an increasing number of limited companies being formed.

The reference to a 'true' partnership above was a reference to the way many professionals, such as accountants, solicitors and doctors run their practices and share their profits. While these other professions operate a profit share of the net income from the partnership, dentists, in the main, tend to keep their own income and only share the expenses within the practice.

Before we look at how most practices are organised we will look at the different types of dental practice that can be found.

Sole practitioners

There are still a number of dental practices operating as sole practitioners despite there being very few advantages in doing so. These sole practitioners tend to be found in smaller communities where the workload is insufficient to remunerate more than one dentist, or more typically where the dentist prefers his or her own company. A number of sole practitioners may at some time have had an unfortunate experience in partnership which has affected their outlook, or they may see a partnership as limiting their independence.

As all the economies of scale of a larger practice are not available to sole practitioners, their levels of profit tend to be less than those of multi-dentist organisations. Sole practitioners often will only have one fully equipped surgery from which they operate full-time, and as a consequence they will not have the opportunity to increase their earnings by providing the services of other professionals, such as hygienists.

There are also a small number of sole practitioner practices, usually predominately NHS practices, where the principal employs a number of associates, but does not have any intention of taking any of them on as partners. These practices can be quite profitable for the principal, but do not often provide any advancement for the associates, who as a result are fairly transient.

Partnerships

The major advantage of partnerships lies in the pooling of resources and the economies of scale which partnerships can achieve. Larger practices can offer a wider range of treatments and tend to attract more patients. As the costs of those practices are borne by a number of practitioners, the cost per principal is reduced, thus increasing their profits. Management responsibilities can be shared and practitioners can work with each other to lessen the pressures of running a business.

It can be confusing, sometimes, to ascertain whether the practice is operating as a partnership or as an expense-sharing joint venture, and often the practice does not know the answer to this itself. But, as mentioned above, where a practice holds itself out as a single business it can often be treated as a partnership for legal purposes, even if there is an agreement between the principals stating otherwise.

Partnership law is very complicated, and it is not the intention of this book to look into the legal position of the arrangements often made between dentists. Suffice to say that where a group of dentists work together, jointly employing staff, and operating within an agreement signed by them all, there is the real possibility that the practice could be deemed to be a partnership. This could have adverse effects upon the 'partners' in the event of a legal claim being made against one of them.

Interestingly, the most up-to-date legislation in respect of partners and partnerships is the Partnership Act 1890!

The characteristics of a partnership

Although the legislation governing partnerships is complicated, there are some common traits that may indicate that a partnership is in existence.

➤ The names of all the partners are on the partnership bank account and all partners are authorised to sign cheques.

➤ Either the names of all the partners are on the practice letterhead or the letterhead does not include any of the partners' names.

➤ There is a professional plate outside the surgery for every partner practising within the building.

➤ There is an agreement as to the number of hours each partner works, and the allocation of costs in respect of that work.

➤ That all the partners are a party to major decisions taken by the partnership.

➤ The partnership accounts show the partners' interest in the balance sheet by way of capital and current accounts.

➤ The partnership jointly contracts with employees and suppliers and holds itself out as a single entity.

Those practices that do not wish to be deemed to be partnerships will need to obtain legal advice to ensure they take the correct measures to remain joint venture or expense-sharing arrangements.

True partnerships

Most practices operate as expense-sharing arrangements, but there are a number of true partnerships in which the principals share profits in an agreed profit-sharing ratio with their income and expenses allocated accordingly. In these practices a single set of practice accounts is usually prepared, which show the partners' individual profit shares and their capital investment in the partnership.

These partnerships are not that common and are often restricted to married couples who share a surgery. The reason that partnerships are not popular is that in reality each dentist is working independently, keeping his or her own income, and has often contributed to the assets in his or her surgery with his or her own funds.

The partnership will submit a partnership tax return to HMRC each year showing how the taxable profits of the partnership have been allocated between the partners.

The partnership will be governed by a standard partnership agreement.

There are a number of practices (usually with non-specialist advisers), who consider themselves to be expense-sharing practices, but where their accountant has produced a set of partnership accounts and filed a partnership tax return each year. These practices could be at risk of being seen to be a partnership should a legal dispute arise!

Expense-sharing arrangements

Although to the outside world an expense-sharing practice looks the same as a partnership, it is treated differently for taxation and accounting purposes.

This is because each of the principals works independently from the other principals in the practice, and each often contributes to an agreed share of overheads and to the upkeep of his or her own surgery, and does not work under a partnership agreement.

Each principal may provide a different dental service from the others and may also be working longer or shorter hours, and as such will wish to keep the gross income that he or she generates.

Each principal may have a common investment in the property and contribute to the practice expenses (hence the 'expense-sharing' title) in line with his or her share of the property or on another agreed basis.

Most practices will have associates working within them and the net income produced by them will be allocated to the principals in line with the agreement to allocate expenses. HMRC will allow this sharing of income outside of a partnership for self-employed dental practitioners, but curiously enough they will not allow a similar arrangement between dental limited companies without them being deemed associated companies for corporation tax purposes. This is at odds with the VAT treatment where HMRC accepts that the arrangement is not subject to VAT for both self-employed and incorporated dental practitioners.

The practice accounts will often include a combined profit and loss account with an individual profit and loss account for each principal. Often there will be a combined balance sheet detailing the different investment in the assets that each principal has, this being reflected in their capital accounts.

Their current accounts will reflect their joint investment in the working capital of the practice.

Each principal will submit an individual tax return each year, and there is normally not a partnership return submitted. It should be noted, however, that there may be practices that HMRC will accept are not partnerships for tax purposes, but nevertheless would be deemed to be a partnership in a legal claim!

Partnership/practice and shareholder agreements

It is essential that dentists working together formalise their arrangement with a practice agreement, as a high proportion of the problems they will encounter in practice derive from 'partnership' issues. Such matters as how the practice capital is to be contributed, the organisation of the expense-sharing ratios, equalisation of current accounts and finance on principals' retirements and appointments are all matters which can cause great concern and confusion among dentists.

If there is no partnership agreement the partnership is a partnership at will and is governed by the Partnership Act 1890. Under this Act the only way a partner can be expelled is to bring about the dissolution of the partnership. In addition, a partnership at will automatically ends upon the death, retirement or bankruptcy of a partner. Any partner can choose to end a partnership at will, without giving notice to the other partners, and without giving a reason for doing so. This can put the practice's GDS or PDS contract at risk, especially if there is an acrimonious dispute.

WHAT DO I INCLUDE IN THE AGREEMENT?

The following list covers most areas that can cause problems, although other issues may need to be considered in order to deal with specific problems such as expense-sharing, incorporation and specific property issues.

➤ **Definitions:** the deed should begin with a list of the definitions of all matters to be covered by the deed. This will ensure that there are no misunderstandings or ambiguous clauses.

➤ **Practice name:** a lot of dental practices tend to practise using the surnames of the principals, with the name of the senior principal being the first name in the title. While this is simple, it does present a problem in that the stationery will need amending every time there is a change within the practice. Increasingly, there is a trend to give the practice a separate name or brand such as 'Smile' or 'Caring Dental' in an attempt to break away from the old image of dentistry. Whatever is decided it is important that it is agreed upon and included in the practice agreement. This part of the deed will also cover aspects such as the duration of the 'partnership' and the practice location.

➤ **Practice capital:** the practice assets, i.e. property and working capital, need to be defined in this section of the practice agreement, and each principal's contribution to those assets agreed. A minimum capital requirement should be agreed and procedures adopted to ensure that the minimum requirement is maintained. This section should also include details as to the method of valuation of goodwill, property and fixtures and fittings.

➤ **Profit sharing and drawings:** this section lays down the rules regarding profit or expense-sharing, the level of drawings that can be taken against those profits and the provisions for the repayment of excess amounts drawn. The basis of any expense-sharing arrangements would be included in this section. In addition, expenses that would be required to be funded by the practice and those to be funded by the principals, personally, may be listed here. To avoid having to change the agreement every time the profit-sharing arrangements are amended you can use a catch-all phrase such as 'or as the partners agree from time to time' thus enabling you to agree the ratios outside the scope of the deed.

➤ **Annual accounts:** this clause will cover issues such as the drafting of the practice accounts on an annual basis, and the provision of accounts following the retirement, death or expulsion of a principal. It will also detail the process by which the accounts become binding on the principals.

➤ **Extent of principals' authority:** without an agreement to the contrary, any principal can bind the 'partnership' without the consent of the other principals. The practice agreement should make it clear when this will be restricted, usually by including a monetary limit above which the principals would need to collectively agree upon.

➤ **Decision making:** this section would usually cover those aspects of the 'partnership' to be covered by unanimous or majority decision. Most 'partnership' decisions can be decided upon by a majority decision, but there will be one or two issues that a 'partnership' would require a unanimous decision, such as the appointment of a new principal. A common error in a number of 'partnership' agreements is that they require a unanimous agreement to expel a principal . . . turkeys voting for Christmas comes to mind.

➤ **Principals' duties:** this section will set down which principals are responsible for certain duties within the practice and facilitate for the non-compliance of those duties. This clause will set out that the principals will be just and faithful to each other in all transactions relating to the practice. This clause may also include restrictions on what the principals are able to do without the prior consent of the other principals. The clause may also provide for the rules regarding the principals' duty to keep up to date and to comply with the GDC CPD regulations.

➤ **Absence:** this clause will cover such items as the number of days of holiday leave, sabbaticals, maternity, paternity and adoption leave. The clause may also provide for compassionate leave and for the arrangements should one of the principals be required to undertake jury service. There may also be provisions included to deal non-authorised absences by the principals and the procedures to deal with one of them being suspended by their professional body or the PCT.

➤ As most dental practices operate on the principle of expense-sharing, provision needs to be made when one of the principals is unable to pay for his or her share of the expense. There are various times when a principal will be absent from a practice and unable to cover his or her share of the overheads, the most common times being sickness and maternity leave.

➤ It is important that the 'partnership' agreement covers such matters and dictates the action the principals need to take, as without any agreement the remaining principals may find their profit shares reduced by their absent principal's inability to pay his or her debts. These will subsequently have to be paid by the remaining principals.

➤ The agreement should ensure that each partner has:
  • either a locum insurance policy which will provide the funds for that principal to pay a locum dentist to treat his or her patients in his or her absence, hence the partner will continue to earn fees and provide for overheads
  • or, a practice expenses policy which will provide an insured amount to cover that principal's share of the practice expenses during illness or leave.

➤ The premiums on both of these policies will attract tax relief, but the amounts payable there under will be subject to tax.

➤ As mentioned earlier, an alternative to the above policies would be a permanent health policy, which will pay out a predetermined fixed amount, subject to income multipliers. But while premiums under these policies do not attract tax relief, the amounts subsequently payable thereunder are not taxable.

➤ The partners should regularly review the level of cover they each have, and take out extra cover should the expenses exceed the level of cover they have.

➤ A number of practices will have an agreement that they will cover for each other for short periods, thus reducing the amount of insurance cover they need, and ultimately the cost thereof.

➤ **Principals joining:** the procedure for new principals joining the practice and the amounts that they would need to pay in could be set down in this section. The purchase of goodwill from a retiring principal should be covered in this section and the next.

➤ **Principals leaving:** this section should cover the retirement, expulsion and death of principals and the rules regarding the payout of their capital. It is important here to include provisions or cross options to prevent the loss of Inheritance Tax Business Asset Relief on death of a principal. The value of your share of the surgery should be protected from inheritance tax if you die while still working as a partner. This is because Business Asset Relief covers the amount that might otherwise be taxed at 40%. However, if your partnership agreement contains a binding contract to buy your surgery share from your executors, there will be no relief and your family may inherit less than you might have expected. There is a simple way round this. Your agreement should contain a 'cross option' clause. This gives your executors the option to sell your share back to the partnership and it gives the partnership the option to buy your share. Either side can exercise their option, but there is no binding contract because if neither side wants the sale to go ahead then it does not have to. Full business property relief should be available in that case.

➤ If it is not covered above, the rules regarding the valuation of assets upon principals leaving are often included in this clause.

➤ **Resolution of disputes:** it is important to have an arbitration or mediation clause in the contract that provides for a resolution in the event of a deadlock in the practice. Without this the only way forward would be to resort to the courts.

The practice deed needs to be updated every time that there is a change in the principals or when there are adjustments to the NHS contract that may affect the timing of the payouts to the former principals.

It should be emphasised that the responsibility for the agreement should be with the practice, who should appoint a solicitor experienced in these matters. In addition the practice accountant should be asked to review the agreement prior to finalisation to ensure that there are no clauses that may present tax problems.

PARTNERSHIP OR PRACTICE CHANGES

Dentist practices are dynamic and change with some regularity, usually as a result of older practitioners retiring and associates 'buying in' to the practice premises and assets. However, there are some practices that increase the number of principals due to expansion of services and/or to reward their associates rather than lose them to a rival or squat practice.

It is usual for a new principal to be brought in on a full parity share, which is not the case in most other professions, but, with that said, the capital that the new principal contributes will often be a full share.

Often the retirement of the outgoing principal will have been planned for a number of years and an 'in-house' associate will be in place to take over from the retiring principal. In this instance the transaction will usually take place between those two parties with little impact on the rest of the practice.

There are cases, however, where a principal may wish to retire and there is not a replacement lined up, and it is in these instances that problems may occur. This is because the principal will want to be paid out from the practice but there is no one (other than the continuing principals) who can contribute to this payout. Similar problems can also arise upon the death of a principal, especially if there is not an agreement or insurance to cover such events.

As is usual in a dental practice, each principal will own the fixtures and fittings in his or her own surgery, as well as the goodwill, which will be valued on the level and type of fees he or she generates. Each principal works in his or her own surgery and, in the majority of cases, will be working full-time to meet the demands of their patients.

Given the above, it is important that any practice agreement does not oblige the continuing principals to buy the goodwill from the outgoing principal. The sale of the goodwill should remain the responsibility of the outgoing dentist or his or her representatives. The reason is that the continuing principals will not be able to gain any additional income from buying the former principal out, as they are already fully occupied in their own surgeries. It is only when a new dentist can be attracted to the practice, to work in the vacated surgery, that additional income can be obtained. The onus should be on the outgoing principal to attract the new dentist.

If the former principal cannot find a dentist to take over his or her surgery the continuing principals will suffer from the share of additional overheads that were previously paid by that principal. It would be unfair for them to also be required to pay him or her for the goodwill!

It would be usual to give the former principal up to a year to find a replacement to take over his or her goodwill, thereafter the continuing principals would usually pay for the fixtures and fittings in the outgoing principal's surgery, as they are tangible assets situated within the practice (and will still have a value irrespective of the level of work being undertaken within that surgery).

They will not contribute to the goodwill as if the surgery remains empty for a substantial period of time the value of that goodwill will reduce accordingly.

PROFIT-SHARING ARRANGEMENTS

Dental practices will often have much more specific and comprehensive profit-sharing arrangements than might usually be seen in other professional partnerships.

Most dental practices operate an expense-sharing arrangement when calculating the principals' profit shares. This is usually done by each principal keeping a separate record of their individual earnings and details of any expenses specific to them, usually laboratory fees and additional staffing costs in dealing with work in excess of that agreed by the principals. The principals are then allocated their individual income and expense along with an agreed share of the balance of the practice income and expenses.

There are various ways of apportioning the balance of the practice income and expenditure, the more usual being based on an equal share per principal. This method takes into account that each principal has an equipped surgery and the overheads of the practice are allocated on the assumption that each surgery will operate so many hours a week. If a principal works longer hours and incurs more practice overheads he or she will be charged for the additional expenses incurred. However, if a principal wants to reduce his or her workload on a temporary basis it would not be usual for their share of the practice overheads to be reduced. This is because his or her action would cause the other principals' costs to rise, and as they would not have the capacity to increase their own income, the principal would either have to bear the additional costs personally or pay an associate in order to fully utilise his or her available surgery time. Other agreements provide for permanent differences in working hours and the type and complexity of work performed by each principal.

In some instances the practice premises may not be owned by all the principals and a prior share or charge will be included within the accounts to take this into account.

The practice costs and joint income are usually transacted through a joint bank account, with contributions being made to that account from the individual principals, with their personal income usually being paid into their separate bank accounts. The contributions are usually calculated monthly by the practice manager or finance 'partner', and the balance transferred to or by the individual principals. It is important that the calculations of the balances paid to the principals take into account those items paid on their behalf by the practice, for instance superannuation and taxation, as to overlook those payments may cause the principals' current accounts to become unbalanced and require monies to be repaid to the practice at the year end.

It is important that the principals can agree collectively on the 'quality of life' issue, in that they have the same approach to work and leisure time and conflicts do not arise in this respect. There are an increasing number of dentists reducing their working week in an attempt to achieve a better quality of life;

some are doing this by finding replacement dentists to utilise their surgery time, while others are reducing the opening hours of their surgeries. A new generation of dentist is emerging who are not too concerned with maximising the level of practice profits at all costs, but are more interested in earning a comfortable living while having the time to enjoy the fruits of their labour. Most accountants spend their lives advising clients as to ways to improve their levels of profit and often find that their clients have other and perhaps less tangible preferences in mind.

The success of a dental practice should not be judged purely on the overall financial results, but on the satisfaction of the individual dentists within the practice. The dental profession allows each dentist within a practice to decide his or her own pace of working. This is possible as most practices operate on an expense-sharing basis where each dentist keeps the gross income he or she generates. So, as long as each dentist contributes to his or her share of the overheads they are free to work to their own timetable.

LIMITED COMPANIES

There has been a sharp increase in the number of practices that have incorporated in the last year or so, the main reason being to take advantage of the tax savings that can be made from doing so. Prior to July 2006 it was not possible for dental practices to incorporate to gain the tax advantages given to so many other businesses and it was only with the amendment order to the Dentists Act that the opportunity became available.

Given the level of dentists' profits, the incorporation of a practice can only provide tax benefits to one- or two-principal practices, as the level of profits from three principals upwards will often exceed the £300,000 limit for the lower level of corporation tax. However, it is not uncommon in larger practices for all the expense sharers to incorporate individually. Care has to be taken in those circumstances to ensure any such arrangement will not be subject to the associated companies rules.

The incorporation of practices with high levels of NHS earnings had been largely avoided until 2009, as there was uncertainty as to how the superannuation deductions that are taken from the practice income would be treated in the company accounts. But guidance issued by HMRC in respect of the treatment of superannuation in medical companies has been adopted by dental accountants, with the directors' superannuation deductions being charged to directors' loan accounts in the company accounts. The deduction of superannuation from the other performers at the practice can be treated as an expense in the company accounts.

Another problem with incorporation of NHS practices is that a number of PCOs have been treating any variation in a contract as a reason to cancel or renegotiate the contract. A variation can occur when a practice requests the transfer of the contract from the names of the partners to that of the incorporated practice. This approach has meant that some practices have been denied the tax-saving opportunities of incorporation as a result.

However, some practices have incorporated and retained their contract by incorporating the practice, but leaving the contract in the name of the performer, and subcontracting the work under the contract to their company, similar to the way they would utilise the services of an associate dentist.

Some PCOs have, however, allowed practices to incorporate and transfer their existing NHS contract to their company. Many practices have done this to benefit from the tax savings, but others have done this to protect their NHS contract, as the company can retain the contract irrespective of any future changes in the shareholders. In fact the 'corporates' insist on the practices they are buying incorporating and transferring their NHS contract to a company, prior to the completion of the transfer of the business.

As mentioned above, prior to July 2006 it was not possible for dentists to incorporate their practices, as the running of a dental practice through a limited company was forbidden, except for a very small number of companies (the corporates) that were in existence prior to the rules preventing incorporation which were introduced in 1955.

The Dentist Act 1984 (Amendment) Order 2005 repealed section 42 of that Act, which prevented incorporation and allowed for the first time individual dental practices to form limited companies. Prior to this the only incorporated bodies that could operate dental practices were those companies which had had that status since 1955. Those companies, known in the profession as the 'corporates', had been able to expand and run multiple practices by taking advantages of the financing opportunities and the limited liability that incorporation can provide. The corporates have grown into very large organisations that provide dental services nationwide. The amendment order was introduced to bring more competition to the profession.

Although the change in the law has brought new opportunities for dental practice, there are still restrictions to ensure that the quality of dental services does not suffer as a result. The rules state that at least 50% of the directors of a dental limited company should be dental professionals registered on the list of DCPs kept by the GDC. In addition, the use of the words dental, dental practice, dental surgeon, dentist and dentistry is restricted, and companies using any of those words need to apply to the Professional Standards Directorate at the GDC for permission to use them.

Although incorporation provides limited liability for dentists in practice, the majority of practitioners already have this to some extent in the cover that they have under their professional indemnity policies. Practitioners in partnerships can further reduce their exposure to liability by signing up to a comprehensive partnership agreement. A dentist could benefit from additional limited liability, as a result of incorporation, if he or she is running a number of surgeries in separate locations, as there would be a higher exposure to risk involved with this set-up.

There are, however, a number of tax advantages to incorporation and where these apply to dentists the opportunities to reduce tax can be quite significant. There are three distinct ways in which savings are currently being made.

The first way to achieve savings through incorporation is by changing the way that remuneration is taken from the practice. By restricting the director's salary to the Secondary Limit for National Insurance purposes (currently £95.00 to £109.99 a week) the dentist does not pay any PAYE on the salary but is still entitled to contributory benefit entitlements. Any additional funds above this amount which the dentist needs would be taken from the company by way of dividends. The savings that can be made from this action are usually in the region of £4,000 to £5,000 a year depending upon the level of income the dentist is generating.

The second saving that can currently be made is the practice of paying income by way of dividends to spouses and family members to reward them for their investment in the practice. If they are basic-rate or non-tax payers, significant reductions in higher rate tax liabilities can be made. Although the government has withdrawn its plans for now to introduce 'Income Splitting' legislation which would have stopped this, it is likely that this method of reducing tax liabilities may be stopped in the next few years.

The third saving, which can prove quite significant, comes as a result of the director's loan account that is created upon the sale or transfer of the practice to the limited company. The transfer will result in the goodwill, fixtures and fittings and stock being taken over by the company, and unless the company has applied to its bankers for funding it will not have the money to pay for these amounts. As a consequence the amounts will be credited to a director's loan account. It is by drawing down this loan account, rather than taking income from the company that the tax savings are made. If the dentist restricts the taxable income taken from the company to approximately £43,000 by taking a combination of salary and dividend, and tops up the extra funds needed by drawing down his or her director's loan account, he or she can remain as a lower rate taxpayer for a number of years. How long he or she can remain as a lower rate taxpayer will depend upon the size of the director's loan account and the individual's need to draw income from the practice. Further details of the tax savings that can be made can be seen in Appendix 3: Example of tax savings on incorporation.

For a dentist nearing retirement the above may provide an opportunity for significant savings, in that the current market value of the goodwill may be in excess of what its value will be in a year or two's time. Therefore, the dentist can get a higher price for it by an early incorporation, and although he or she will pay CGT on that higher amount, it will probably be at only 10%, and the higher amount in the director's loan account may prevent the dentist from paying higher rate tax of 40% again in his or her career. If the value of the goodwill does fall, the company will receive loss relief at 22% on the subsequent sale it may make to a third party.

The capital gain on the sale or transfer of the practice goodwill to the company could possibly be reduced by Entrepreneurs Relief and tax of only 10% may be paid on the amount. (Further details of this relief can be found in Chapter 10 covering taxation.)

Depending upon the date that the goodwill was first purchased or generated by the dentist there may be an annual taxable write-off allowed against the company profits. This deduction is not allowed to sole traders or partnerships.

The incorporation of dental practices can bring benefits other than tax savings. Currently associates, when asked into partnerships, complete that transition in one year. The company structure, however, allows for transfers of shares (and percentage of ownership) over a number of years. This can be of benefit to both the principals and the associates.

Long-serving staff could be encouraged to buy shares in the company and receive dividends related to profit growth each year. Care needs to be taken, however, not to fall foul of anti-avoidance legislation which was brought in to prevent the payment of employees by way of dividends.

Incorporation can also provide tax-saving opportunities upon the ultimate sale of the practice. This is dependent upon whether the company has received a tax allowance against the write-off of goodwill, and there may be the beneficial option to sell the company (i.e. the owner to sell the shares), or for the company to sell the practice. The tax benefits of these options depend upon the number of years that the practice has been in existence.

A disadvantage to incorporation is that the practice accounts (although abbreviated) need to be filed at Companies House each year and additional administration is needed for dividend paperwork and annual returns, etc. The rules regarding the withdrawal of funds from the company are more onerous than the procedures of drawing funds from a sole trader or partnership. In addition both income tax and corporation tax returns would need completing at the end of each year.

CHAPTER 9

Associates, hygienists and staff matters

There are a number of financial issues that arise frequently, regarding the mix of professionals who work within a dental practice, and in this chapter we will look at those issues and suggest ways to avoid the problems that may occur as a result of them. But first it would be useful to provide an explanation of the distinction between associates and principals.

THE DISTINCTION BETWEEN ASSOCIATES AND PRINCIPALS

Self-employed dental practitioners in practice can be divided into two groups, principals and associates. As discussed earlier in the book the principals are, in the main, the owners of the practice and provide the facilities for the associates to supply their services to the practice. The principals will employ the practice staff and will have provided the capital to fund the practice. They take a bigger commercial risk in that they have to manage the practice to ensure that the fee income it receives is sufficient to pay for the practice overheads and provide a profit for themselves. How efficiently the principal runs the practice can have a big effect upon his or her level of income.

The associate, conversely, will have very little to do with the management of the practice, and will often work within an allotted surgery dealing with patients that have been allocated to him or her by the principal. Associates' level of income is dependent upon the amount and type of work they receive from the principal, and their ability to increase their income themselves is very limited.

The principal will receive all the practice income and will pay the associate an agreed amount from those gross proceeds. Details of a typical payment to an associate can be found later in this chapter.

EMPLOYMENT STATUS: EMPLOYED OR SELF-EMPLOYED?

Within a dental practice there will often be a mix of DCPs, some of whom will be employed by the practice, while others will be providing their services on a self-employed basis. The distinction between the two in some cases is not clear-cut, and often causes confusion, but it is a matter that dentists must get right as the tax and National Insurance liabilities of getting it wrong are significant.

HMRC make it quite clear that it is the employers' responsibility to correctly determine the employment status of their workers – that is, whether they're employed by the practice or self-employed. This will depend upon the terms and conditions of the working relationship with the practice.

It is important to get the employment status right as it affects the way tax and NICs are calculated and whether or not the practice will have to operate a PAYE scheme to collect the tax and National Insurance on their earnings.

If the practice doesn't get it right, not only could they end up having to pay the extra tax and NICs but interest and penalties on those amounts also.

So when a practice takes a worker on, they are responsible for determining the employment status of that worker; this applies for all workers, whether they're full-time, part-time, permanent, temporary or casual.

Employment status is a matter of fact, based on key terms and conditions of the working relationship between the practice and the worker, and in most cases those terms and conditions will be reflected in the contract with the worker. But even if a contract says a worker is self-employed, if the facts indicate otherwise the worker may be an employee.

Note that a worker can:

➤ be both employed and self-employed at the same time – for example, working as an employee during the day and running their own business in the evenings

➤ change employment status from contract to contract – the fact they were employed on their last contract (whether with the practice or another employer) doesn't mean anything if the facts of their next contract point to them being self-employed.

So how does the practice determine a worker's employment status? In most cases, the employment status is quite straightforward. As a general rule, a worker is:

➤ employed if they work for the practice and don't have the risks of running a business

➤ self-employed if they're in business on their own account and are responsible for the success or failure of their business.

The sections below contain a series of further pointers issued by HMRC that should help a practice determine a worker's employment status; there is also an online Employment Status Indicator (ESI) tool on HMRC's website.

An individual is likely to be employed by the practice if most of the following statements apply to them.

➤ The practice can tell them what work to do, as well as how, where and when to do it.
➤ They have to do their work themselves.
➤ The practice can move the worker from task to task.
➤ They're contracted to work a set number of hours.
➤ They get a regular wage or salary, even if there is no work available.
➤ They have benefits such as paid leave or a pension as part of their contract.
➤ The practice pays them overtime pay or bonus payments.
➤ They manage anyone else who works for the practice.

If *any* of the following statements applies, the worker is likely to be self-employed.

➤ They can hire someone else to do the work the practice has given them, or take on helpers at their own expense.
➤ They can decide where to provide their services, as well as when and how to do the work the practice has given them.
➤ The practice pays them an agreed fixed price – it doesn't depend on how long the job takes to finish.
➤ They can make a loss or a profit.

Even if none of the statements in the previous list applies, the worker is still likely to be self-employed if *most* of the following apply to them.

➤ They use their own money to buy business assets, pay for running costs, etc.
➤ They're responsible for putting right any unsatisfactory work, at their own expense and in their own time.
➤ They provide the main tools and equipment needed to do their work.

There are two main ways that HMRC can help the practice make sure they have the employment status of a worker right.

The ESI is an online interactive tool that asks a series of questions about the working relationship between the practice and the worker. It is the quickest way of getting HMRC's view on whether a worker is employed or self-employed.

HMRC will accept the tool's outcome as binding, as long as the answers accurately reflect the terms and conditions under which the worker provides their services. The practice must also retain a printout of:

➤ the ESI result screen
➤ the Enquiry Details screen showing the replies to the questions asked.

The practice can also request a written opinion on a worker's employment status by contacting the Status Inspector in the local Tax Office. Provided the practice accurately explains all the relevant facts to them, HMRC will accept the inspector's opinion as legally binding.

If the worker is an employee of the practice, the practice must use the PAYE system to deduct and pay HMRC any tax and NICs due on the employee's earnings.

If the worker is the practice's first ever employee, the practice will also have to register as an employer so that HMRC can set up a PAYE scheme.

If the worker is self-employed, the practice doesn't need to operate PAYE on their earnings. Self-employed individuals are responsible for calculating and paying their own tax and NICs on any payments you make to them.

The two DCPs that the issue of employment status affects most are associates and hygienists. Associates are dealt with later in this chapter, so we will only look at the hygienists' employment status at this stage.

The BDA considers that, as members of the dental team, working to a dentist's prescription, hygienists do not normally meet the standard requirements for classification as self-employed for either tax or National Insurance purposes.

The BDA, therefore, advises that all hygienists should be employed. Even where a hygienist has worked for many years on a self-employed basis, the Inland Revenue may in individual cases change their status because of the inevitable degree of control and direction involved in the dentist–hygienist relationship. There have been examples of Inland Revenue investigations where the notional self-employed status of the hygienists has been rejected, and the dentist as the newly deemed employer has been made responsible for considerable shortfalls in tax and NICs. Employment tribunals have also found that 'self-employed' dental hygienists are in fact employees and practice owners have had to pay compensation for unfair dismissal.

Many dental hygienists wish to be engaged under a contract for services rather than a contract of services, however; that is, they prefer to be considered as self-employed rather that as employees. And local Inland Revenue offices will recognise self-employed status in some cases.

As a result the BDA does offer a draft of a contract to be used where there is a self-employed arrangement between the hygienist and the practice. However, it qualifies its advice and recommends the practice obtains legal advice to ensure that it is appropriate to their circumstances.

ASSOCIATES AND HOW THEY ARE PAID

The comparison of principals and associates, above, showed that associates are dentists who work on a profit-sharing basis within a dental practice, but do not have a share in responsibility of running the practice, nor in the ownership of practice property and equipment. This is made possible as the principal grants a licence to the associate to see patients (on the same basis as the principal) on the principal's premises, for a share of the associate's fees. There are a number of reasons why a principal or practice owner may take on an associate. The more usual are as follows.

➤ **Succession:** the majority of principals in practice started work in the surgery they currently operate from as an associate, and after a period of time were asked to buy out one of the retiring principals. This is the usual route that principals take and they often start looking for an associate a few years prior to their retirement date. The alternatives are to try to sell the practice as a going concern or to cease the practice, but both of these options bring with them a number of problems which can be overcome by a sale to an associate within the practice.

➤ **To reduce a heavy workload:** often associates are taken on to assist the principal as the workload has become too much for the principal to deal with on their own. This was historically common under the old NHS contract in England and Wales where a practice could expand by taking on more NHS patients. This is no longer possible now without prior approval from the PCO.

➤ **To increase the practice profit:** a dentist's profit is maximised when his or her surgeries are working at full capacity and the most profitable practices are those with a large number of associates utilising all the available surgery time.

➤ **To provide more services:** often a practice will take on an associate to expand the services that the practice can provide. An associate with, say, additional skills in sedation or implants could attract new patients to a practice.

It is usual for associates to have deducted from their earnings an amount for the costs attributable to the surgery they use plus an amount for overheads. The deduction is often calculated as a percentage of the gross income earned by the associate, less a deduction for laboratory fees and other direct costs, such as hygienists.

Until recently the usual agreement was for the associate to be paid 50% of their gross earnings less the laboratory bills that could be attributed to them. In recent years, however, there has been a move from the above approach, to one where principals have varied the proportion of income they deduct from the associate as the associate's gross income increases.

A significant change in the way that associates receive payment has arisen as a result of the new NHS contract which was introduced in England and Wales in April 2006. The contract provides for payment of fees to the practice based on the number of UDAs the practice has completed, and as a result of this a number of principals have rewritten their associate agreements so that the associate is similarly remunerated in line with the number of UDAs that they have completed.

As the practice can be subject to a claw-back of the monies it receives under its NHS contract should it fail to achieve the agreed level of UDAs, an increasing number of practices now also provide for a claw-back for underachievement by the associate.

Although the advice to principals is that they should concentrate on premium work to maximise their profits and leave less profitable work to the more junior staff, this does not necessarily apply to associates. Many a principal has been tempted to do this with their associates, whereby any premium treatments are steered to the principal and the less profitable work, such as check-ups, are left to the associate. While this ensures the maximum income for the principal, it also results in an underpaid associate who receives no job satisfaction, the result of which is that the principal will not retain the associates for very long. Given that associates also provide for succession, it is not in the principal's best interest to treat associates so badly.

The BDA has issued a code of practice for associates and practice owners. The code of practice recommends that the principal provides the associate with a position which will provide job satisfaction and a reasonable level of income, and in return the associate will provide quality work and patient care.

The BDA code of conduct provides that the associate should be given:
➤ the opportunity to earn a reasonable income
➤ a level of work to challenge their clinical skills
➤ the support of nurses, hygienists and administration staff
➤ access to quality materials and choice of dental laboratory
➤ access to an adequately equipped surgery
➤ copies of NHS and private income statements and a detailed breakdown of his or her remuneration statements
➤ reasonable holiday periods and maternity and sick pay arrangements
➤ a signed agreement detailing the above.

The code of conduct also provides that the principal can expect the associate to:
➤ provide a high level of clinical care
➤ work as part of the practice team
➤ keep full and accurate accounts of his or her work
➤ comply with the signed agreement.

Dentists who are members of the BDA can obtain a copy of the code of conduct from the BDA website.

While principals should take heed of the rules above, they should also ensure that they are getting a good return on their associates, given the investment that they have made in surgery equipment and providing staff, etc.

A very basic way of checking the profitability of the associate is to provide a simple profit and loss account at the year end. This account will include details of the associate's gross earnings, less the laboratory and hygienists' fees charged against those fees, and less the payments made to the associate. This account will show the contribution that the associate has made to the practice overheads and is particularly useful for comparison between a number of associates working in the same practice.

Another method which is slightly more complicated is to look at the profitability of the associate in terms of the contribution they are generating per hour from their surgery, by allocating the overheads of the practice to the number of available surgery hours available in the year. This will provide a good comparison with the level of work that the principal generates per hour.

It is useful to carry out the above calculations to identify those associates who contribute more to the surgery and should be remunerated accordingly.

Associates are usually treated as self-employed for income tax purposes as a result of the contract that they signed with their principal. The contract will provide for the payment to them of a proportion of the income they generate, and they will not be due any of the advantages that employment may bring them. They will be responsible for the correction of any faulty work that they make and will shoulder any commercial risk themselves. They will not get paid unless they generate fees.

Associates' accounts do not require a lot of work as the major expenses they incur are paid on their behalf by the practice, and will be shown on the schedule of pay they receive each month.

Not all of the associate's expenses will be paid for by the practice and care should be taken to ensure that amounts paid personally by them are notified to their accountants to be included in their accounts and tax deductions claimed accordingly.

The practice will pay the associate's laboratory fees and additional costs they incur such as hygienist and nurses wages, but it is usual for the associate to pay their own dental defence or indemnity insurance and locum insurance (if appropriate). The associate may also be able to justify claims for motor expenses, especially for domiciliary visits and courses, mobile phone costs, and computer or Internet expenses incurred while preparing patient records and obtaining clinical updates. Other deductions may be appropriate for standard expenses such as postage and stationery, bank charges, repairs, etc.

It would not be usual to prepare a balance sheet for an associate as they have very little investment in assets, or exposure to liabilities, and often bank their earnings in a personal account to save themselves bank charges.

An example of an associate's profit and loss account has been included in Figure 2.2 in Chapter 2.

The associate will usually be paid once a month and will be supplied with a schedule detailing the gross income that he or she has generated from NHS and private treatments. The schedule will include deductions for laboratory fees and other agreed deductions, as well as the superannuation that has been withheld by the PCO. The agreed percentage will be taken from the total and the balance paid to the associate.

Figure 9.1 shows a typical associate's payslip.

THE ASSOCIATE AGREEMENT

It is good practice for the principal to have a signed contract with his associate to cover any disputes that may arise. The BDA can provide draft copies of an associate contract to its members. The contract should cover the following:

➤ names of the parties to the contract
➤ start date of the agreement, and end date, if a fixed-period contract has been agreed
➤ the facilities being provided: staff, equipment, premises, patients
➤ a statement that the agreement is a licence for the associate to practise dentistry at the premises
➤ a statement that the associate will be provided with patients but will not be obliged to see them so that clinical freedom is protected
➤ responsibility for breakdowns of equipment
➤ hours that the facilities will be available to the associate
➤ holidays and CPD days that will be allowed
➤ responsibility for bad debts, i.e. are they suffered by the principal or the associate?

		£	£
Income	NHS		7 825
	Private treatments		4 265
			12 090
Less:	Laboratory fees	1 235	
	Bad debts	275	
			1 510
Income after expenses			10 580
50% agreed			5 290
Less: superannuation			210
Net pay for June			5 080

FIGURE 9.1 A typical associate's payslip

➤ how the associate's licence will be paid for, i.e. on a percentage basis or a fixed amount per UDA
➤ responsibility for obtaining locums
➤ what to do regarding maternity or adoption and parental leave notice periods
➤ in an NHS arrangement, a requirement to comply with the NHS regulations and, in England and Wales, to attain a set UDA target
➤ assignment of NHS patients after the agreement is terminated
➤ restrictive practice clause upon leaving a practice
➤ ownership of goodwill
➤ arbitration or mediation
➤ defective work; who should pay for the replacement, free of charge, for NHS and private treatments that fail
➤ post agreement; how long after the end of the agreement should the associate still be responsible for restitution.

The reason for the restrictive practice clause is to prevent the associate, having built up a reputation, leaving and establishing a competitive practice nearby, which could result in a loss of goodwill and patients to the practice. However, the courts will rule such a clause unenforceable should the restrictions be deemed to be onerous, either in the distance from the practice, or the period over which the restriction will apply.

Although it is usual for the NHS contract to be between the PCO and the principal, there are some instances where the contract is directly between the associate and the PCO. In those instances the contract between the associate and the principal will need to take account of the direct nature of the NHS contract. It is not in the principal's interest to have the contract directly between the associate and the PCO and the principal should strive to get the contract rewritten to the practice, as while it is in the associate's name there is no value in that contract to the practice. In fact, while it is in the associate's name there is a real danger of the practice profits reducing significantly as a result of the movement of the contract.

In a recent case when an associate, who held an NHS contract, left a practice, the PCO did not renew the contract with the practice. As a result the practice lost a significant amount of money but also had no work with which to attract a new associate.

The contract between the practice and the associate should allow for the payment to the associate, when entitled, of maternity, paternity or sickness benefits under the NHS contract, in full. The contract should also provide for a payment date within a few days of when the practice receives the gross monthly earnings. If the associate is being paid based on the number of UDAs they are performing, they should be given details regularly of the number of UDAs achieved in order that they can monitor their position. The associate should be given a fixed value per UDA he or she performs.

Whether the agreement is or is not based on the number of UDAs performed, there should be a clause to allow the principal to deduct from the associate his or her share of any claw-back for underperformance of UDAs.

Private treatments can be contracted for on a percentage share basis.

The agreement between the practice and the associate needs to provide for a basis of payment should the practice be sold and the NHS contracts terminated.

It is important, if the associate incorporates, to have the contract rewritten in the name of the limited company.

EMPLOYED DENTAL PROFESSIONALS

Both the principal in the un-incorporated practice and the associate will normally operate as self-employed individuals, but there are occasions where dentists provide their services as employees (there are approximately 34,000 dentists registered with the GDC of which 9,000 are estimated to be in employment). The number of employed dental practitioners working within the profession is increasing due to the following reasons.

➤ In order to achieve their targets to provide NHS dentistry, an increasing number of PCOs and health boards have opened NHS access centres and are employing dentists to provide this service. A large number of these dentists have been sourced from overseas as an increasing number of UK-based dentists move away from providing core NHS services.

➤ Dentists who practise through limited companies are required by the GDC to be directors of their own companies. They often take a salary and are therefore employees of those companies.

➤ Dentists working under the VDP scheme are employed at the practice they are training at.

➤ There are an increasing number of initiatives where PCOs have taken over NHS practices and retained the principals as employees in order to preserve the practice as an NHS outlet.

Employed dentists will pay their tax and NICs through their employers' payroll system. They will pay NHS superannuation by deduction from their salary, which will represent all or part of their superannuable earnings (*see* Chapter 11 for further information on the NHS Superannuation Scheme).

Employed dentists may need to consider completing a claim for expenses for their tax return. This may involve business mileage, professional subscriptions, courses and technical updates. However, many employers would reimburse most of the necessary expenses incurred. Dentists should be aware of the HMRC

tests in respect of expenses deductions, which are as follows.
➤ The expense must be one that is incurred by all holders of that employment.
➤ The expense must be wholly, exclusively and necessarily incurred.
➤ The expense must be incurred in the performance of the duties of the employment.
➤ The expense must be incurred and paid.

An employed dentist, who is also self-employed, needs to exercise care with regard to any overlap of expenses to ensure that expenses are claimed against the appropriate related income source.

If employed dentists are also self-employed, they may be overpaying National Insurance as a result of paying class 1, class 2 and class 4 contributions. Many accountants overlook this, and as a claim has to be made, dentists often lose out on amounts due to them. A reclaim in most cases is appropriate and/or a deferment can be put in place to prevent overpayments in future years.

The other employed professionals usually found in practice are hygienists, dental technicians, therapists and dental nurses.

Hygienists currently do not have a framework for the tasks that they can perform, but they used to have a list of permitted duties, which were laid down in the Dental Auxiliaries Regulations (which have now been repealed). They were as follows.
➤ Cleaning and polishing teeth.
➤ Scaling teeth. Scaling may be carried out by a dental hygienist under local infiltration analgesia administered by the dental hygienist under the direct personal supervision of a registered dentist who is on the premises at the time, or any local or regional block analgesia administered by a dentist.
➤ The application to the teeth of such prophylactic materials as the GDC may from time to time determine. In the past the Council has determined that dental hygienists may use solutions, gels and sealants.
➤ Placing a temporary dressing in a tooth if a filling falls out while other dental treatment is being carried out by the hygienist. A written prescription is not required provided the patient is advised to see the dentist as soon as possible and the hygienist informs the patient's dentist as soon as reasonably practical after the treatment. The dental hygienist may only place a temporary dressing if appropriate training has been received.

If trained, a hygienist may additionally undertake the following.
➤ The emergency replacement of crowns with a temporary cement.
➤ The removal of excess cement by instruments which may include rotary instruments.

➤ The taking of impressions.
➤ The administration of inferior dental nerve-block anaesthesia, under direct personal supervision (the dentist must be on the premises).
➤ The administration of local infiltration anaesthesia without the need for direct personal supervision.
➤ The administration of local infiltration anaesthesia without the need for direct personal supervision.
➤ The treatment of patients under conscious sedation or general anaesthesia provided a dentist remains in the room throughout the treatment.

A dental hygienist may provide treatment only under the direction of a registered dentist and:
➤ may undertake oral health education
➤ may carry out interim treatment between dental examinations of the patient by the dentist at 0 and 12 months, provided that the treatment intervals have been specified in the written prescription
➤ may undertake domiciliary visits
➤ may work only with a third person present on the practice premises or when domiciliary visits are undertaken (this need not be another practice staff member)
➤ may not undertake any duties not specified in the Regulations
➤ may apply tooth whiteners and Dentomycin when prescribed by a dentist
➤ may take radiographs if trained according to the Ionising Radiations Regulations 1988
➤ may not treat patients under conscious sedation
➤ must be registered with the GDC and renew their registration before 31 December each year
➤ if administering local infiltration analgesia and qualified before July 1991, must possess a certificate from a School of Dental Hygiene attesting that the necessary training has been undertaken
➤ may now practise independently, receive money directly from patients or employ or engage dentists to examine and prescribe treatment.

As mentioned above, dentists should maximise their earnings by ensuring that they are always involved in premium work and leaving the more basic work to others in the practice. The work usually undertaken by hygienists can be performed by dentists, but they would be unable to charge their usual fee to do it. It makes sense, therefore, for the dentist to concentrate on higher margin work and to pay a hygienist to deal with scale and polishes, etc.

Larger practices tend to employ hygienists as they can offer them a more full-time position, while a number of smaller practices may utilise the services of a hygienist on an ad hoc or part-time basis.

Dental therapists (sometimes also known as oral health practitioners) are DCPs and work as part of the dental team. A registered dentist must examine the patient and indicate clearly in writing the course of treatment that the dental therapist needs to carry out.

Like the hygienist, the dental therapist has an important role in promoting dental health. They will treat adults and children. Since July 2002, dental therapists have been able to work in all sectors of dentistry including general dental practice.

A dental therapist can carry out a range of procedures, including:

➤ intra and extra oral assessment
➤ scaling and polishing
➤ applying materials to teeth such as fluoride and fissure sealants
➤ taking dental radiographs
➤ providing dental health education on a one-to-one basis or in a group situation
➤ undertaking routine restorations in both deciduous and permanent teeth, on adults and children
➤ using all materials except pre-cast or pinned placements
➤ extracting deciduous teeth under local infiltration analgesia.

Provided that they have completed appropriate training, dental therapists can perform such extended duties as the following:

➤ undertaking the pulp therapy treatment of deciduous teeth
➤ placing pre-formed crowns on deciduous teeth
➤ administering inferior dental nerve-block analgesia under the supervision of a dentist
➤ providing emergency temporary replacement of crowns and fillings
➤ taking impressions
➤ treating patients under conscious sedation provided the dentist remains in the surgery throughout the treatment.

The dental therapist may treat a wide range of patients with high treatment needs, from those who:

➤ are dentally anxious
➤ are medically compromised
➤ are physically disabled
➤ have learning disabilities
➤ have high levels of untreated decay
➤ are unable to access regular dental care in the GDS.

The dentist is always responsible for the treatment carried out by the therapist. But as a registered DCP, the therapist is also responsible before the GDC for standards of conduct and patient care.

In addition to the above staff, the dental practice will normally employ dental nurses and administration and support staff. In 2008, Dodd & Co Chartered Accountants undertook a pay survey of these DCP, and Table 9.1 lists their findings:

TABLE 9.1 Average dental professionals' pay levels (hourly rate) 2008

Trained dental nurse	£7.91
Trainee dental nurse	£6.30
Employed hygienist	£21.46
Self-employed hygienist	£27.68
Dental therapist	£22.50
Receptionist	£7.32
Practice manager	£12.20
Bookkeeper	£8.30
Cleaners	£5.27
Oral health educator	£9.00

The level of pay can vary around the country, given the difference in the cost of living and the availability of staff in certain areas. The BDA keeps a similar list of average pay levels and updates the same each year.

OTHER EMPLOYMENT ISSUES

Although a written contract between an associate and the practice is highly recommended, it is not a legal requirement, whereas an employment contract with all employees of the practice is. Members of the BDA can access assistance on the drafting of employment contracts with reference to matters specific to dental practice from the BDA website; non-members should consult a specialist lawyer.

The essential elements of an employment contract are:
➤ the name and address of the employer
➤ the name and address of the employee
➤ terms and conditions of the employment
➤ detailed job description and summary of duties
➤ the practice absence or sickness procedures
➤ the number of working hours
➤ the rate of pay
➤ amount of holidays and special leave

➤ the length of the probation period
➤ notice period required
➤ the performance management structure
➤ the practice discipline procedures
➤ the practice grievance procedures
➤ the practice confidentiality policy
➤ the practice equal opportunities policy.

The practice has three months to supply a copy of the employment contract to the member of staff, but good practice would be to provide it on the first day of employment as a prerequisite to the practice's induction procedure.

With the new regulations issued to registered DCPs by the GDC, regarding the need for CPD, the issue of staff training needs to be addressed by practices. The GDC recommends that all dentists and DCPs carry out verifiable CPD in three core recommended subjects. The recommended core subjects and suggested minimum number of verifiable hours per CPD cycle that dentists and DCPs should spend on them are:
➤ medical emergencies (at least 10 hours per CPD cycle)
➤ disinfection and decontamination (at least five hours per CPD cycle)
➤ radiography and radiation protection (at least five hours per CPD cycle).

They also recommend that all dentists and DCPs do CPD in medical emergencies every year.

In addition, the GDC recommends that dentists and DCPs working in a clinical environment carry out CPD (verifiable or general) to make sure they are up to date in:
➤ legal and ethical issues
➤ handling complaints.

The GDC is also recommending that all dentists and DCPs use a personal development plan so that patients and dentists and DCPs themselves benefit as much as possible from their CPD.

A condition of retention on the Dentists or DCP Register is compliance with the CPD requirements over a five-year period (a CPD cycle).

During a CPD cycle dentists are required to undertake 250 hours of CPD with 75 hours being verifiable, and DCPs are required to undertake 150 hours of CPD with 50 hours being verifiable.

Dentists and DCPs must maintain their own CPD records and an annual statement of the CPD hours completed must be submitted each year.

Failure to comply with the requirements may lead to removal from the Dentists or DCP Register.

At the end of a CPD cycle dentists or DCPs will be asked to confirm their compliance with the CPD requirements. They need to return a declaration of the hours of CPD that they have completed over the last five years.

There are a number of other employment issues that the dentist in practice needs to be aware of, but which will not be dealt with in this book. Further reading is advised in respect of:

➤ staff recruitment policies
➤ non-DCPs staff training
➤ staff records
➤ dismissal procedures
➤ statutory maternity, paternity and adoption leave rights
➤ health and safety
➤ operating a PAYE scheme
➤ tax on staff benefits in kind.

Many banks now offer a legal helpline to employers as part of their service. It is recommended that practitioners utilise these services or pay a retainer to a specialist firm of employment advisers, as it is easy to fall foul of the law and litigation in this area is increasing.

CHAPTER 10

Taxation

The purpose of this chapter is to highlight those areas of taxation which are of special interest to dentists, and to look at the opportunities there are to reduce the amount payable on the income generated from the practice. The following paragraphs provide details about the taxes and allowances that are likely to affect dentists in practice, and the information includes the rates current in the tax year 2009/10.

INCOME TAX

Income tax in the UK was introduced initially to provide the funding to fight the Napoleonic Wars, and although the rates and types of taxes have changed many times since, the collection of tax is still a popular pastime for the government of the day.

Income tax is raised on individuals, is a personal tax and is levied as a percentage of the total income, after allowances. It is the tax that dentists in practice will pay on their practice profits, unless they have incorporated (see later notes on corporation tax). The rate at which the tax is levied and the allowances available are listed in Table 10.1. Table 10.2 shows other current tax bands and income or savings income tax rates.

TABLE 10.1 Tax rates and allowances available 2009/10

Allowances that reduce taxable income

Personal allowance:	Under 65	£6 475
	65 to 74	£9 490
	75 and over	£9 640

(continued)

Allowances that reduce tax

Married couples allowance:	Under 65	N/A
	65 to 74	N/A
	75 and over	£696.50

With regard to Table 10.1, note the following.
➤ Married couples allowance is only available where one of the spouses was 65 or over on 5 April 2000.
➤ Ages are at the end of the tax year. Ages for higher rates of married couples allowance relate to the elder of husband and wife.
➤ The higher rates of personal allowances for older people are reduced by £1 for every £2 of income exceeding £22,900 until the basic allowance of £6,475 is reached. Similar limits apply to the married couples allowance (basic allowance is £267.00), but only the husband's income is taken into account.
➤ From April 2010 the personal allowance will be restricted for individuals whose income exceeds £100,000, by £1 for each £2 of income exceeding £100,000 until it is reduced to nil.
➤ Child Tax Credit and Working Tax Credit are available in certain circumstances, depending upon income.

TABLE 10.2 Tax bands and income or savings income tax rates

Income tax bands	
Basic rate band	up to £37 400
Higher rate band	in excess of £37 400
Earned income tax rates	
Basic rate	20%
Higher rate	40%
Savings income tax rates	
Dividends	10%
Interest	20%*

* A 10% rate of up to £2,440 will apply to certain individuals with low earned income.

In 2010/11 the following changes will affect higher earning individuals:
➤ There will be a higher rate of 50% for taxable income above £150,000. Dividends are taxed as the 'top slice' of income. Where total income is above £150,000, the tax rate on dividends falling into the new higher rate will be 42.5%.
➤ The personal allowance will be restricted for individuals with 'net income'

of over £100,000. For every £2 of 'net income' above £100,000 the allowance will be restricted by £1 until it is reduced to nil.

For example, if the basic allowance for 2010/11 is set at £7,000:
➤ individuals earning over £107,000 will receive half the personal allowance (£3,500)
➤ individuals earning over £114,000 will receive no personal allowance.

For this purpose, 'net income' means income subject to income tax.

As a result of these changes dentists who increase their level of income from £100,000 to £114,000 will effectively suffer a tax charge of 60% on the additional £14,000 of profits.

This is because the £14,000 will attract tax at a rate of 40% as usual, but the loss of personal allowances means that £7,000 of income that had previously been covered by those personal allowances will now also be taxed at the 40% rate. The total tax will be £8,400, which is 60% of £14,000. When the superannuation payable of up to 8.5% is added to the tax, this is a band of income that NHS dentists, in particular, should try to avoid.

Given the way that tax is collected, i.e. the collection of the balance due and the payment on account of next year, the cash cost of earning those extra profits is even higher than the 60%, as can be seen below.
➤ Tax due on £14,000 extra profits for the year to 31 March 2011 will be £8,400 and will be payable on 31 January 2012.
➤ On that day the first on-account payment for 2011/12 will also be due (of half the balance above) of £4,200.
➤ On 31 July 2012 a second on-account payment will be payable of £4,200. A total cash tax bill of £16,800 will be paid on earnings of £14,000 (120% tax!).
➤ The tax on-account payments of £8,400 in total will be offset against the income earned in the next year 2011/12.

CORPORATION TAX

Corporation tax is levied on the profits of incorporated businesses, i.e. limited companies, and the rates shown in Table 10.3 were current in the year from 1 March 2009.

TABLE 10.3 Corporation tax rates

First £300 000 of profits	21%
Next £1 200 000	29.75%
Balance over £1 500 000	28%

VALUE ADDED TAX

VAT is levied on a business's turnover subject to VAT, after allowing a deduction for the VAT on the expense incurred in creating that turnover. The taxable turnover limits are as follows.

➤ Registration is required if turnover over the last 12 months or next 30 days is likely to exceed £68,000.

➤ Deregistration is possible if the turnover in the coming year will fall below £66,000.

The current rates of VAT are shown in Table 10.4.

TABLE 10.4 VAT rates from 1 December 2008

Standard rate	15%*
VAT fraction	3/23

* The standard VAT rate was reduced from 17.5% to 15% for supplies made from 1 December 2008. This reduced rate will be in place until 31 December 2009.

Many of the services provided by dentists are exempt from VAT. The general criteria for the exemption are whether the primary purpose of the service is the protection, maintenance or restoration of the health of the patient. This means that most dental services delivered through the NHS or the private sector will be VAT-exempt activities.

However, as many practices look to expand their income by providing more cosmetic dental services there is a danger that the services that they provide will become subject to VAT. Clearly, those practices will need to ensure that they understand which of their services could be potentially standard rated.

Even though an increasing number of practices are providing tooth whitening, Botox and other non-surgical cosmetic treatments, it is not likely that many of them will exceed the turnover threshold. This means that they do not need to charge VAT on their fees.

Even those practices supplying cosmetic dentistry in excess of the turnover limits may not need to charge VAT on their services if they consider that those services are necessary for the protection, maintenance or restoration of a patient's health. This situation may occur when a patient is depressed about their appearance and it is thought that their depression may be lessened as a result of cosmetic dentistry to improve their appearance. Obviously, this is an area where there is a lot of scope for disputes with HMRC, but to date there has not been an instance where a dentist's clinical opinion has been questioned.

As a result of dentists mainly providing exempt services for VAT purposes there is little scope for them to reclaim VAT on any of their expenditure.

There have been 'tax schemes' in the past where rules were circumvented in order to achieve VAT savings, but there are currently no opportunities available for the majority of dentists in practice.

NATIONAL INSURANCE

Current NIC rates are shown in Table 10.5.

TABLE 10.5 National Insurance contributions 2009/10

	Weekly earnings	Employer	Employee
Class 1 – Employment income	Up to £94.99 (lower earnings limit)	NIL	NIL
	£95.00 to £109.99 (secondary limit)	NIL	NIL*
	£110.00 to £844.00 (upper limit)	12.8%	11%
	£844.01 and above	12.8%	1%
Men 65 and over and women 60 and over		12.8%	NIL
Class 1A NIC – On benefits in kind		12.8%	NIL
Class 2 – Self-employed		£2.40 per week	
Small earnings exception limit		£5075 per annum	
Class 3 – Voluntary		£12.05 per week	
Class 4 – Self-employed	On profits £5715 to £43875	8%	
	On profits above £43875	1%	

*Employees in this wage band are entitled to contributory benefit entitlements.

STAMP DUTY AND STAMP DUTY LAND TAX

The rates of stamp duty and stamp duty land tax are shown in Table 10.6.

TABLE 10.6 Stamp duty and stamp duty land tax 2009/10

Zero rate threshold: residential property	
From 3 September 2008 to 31 December 2009	£175000
From 1 January 2010	£125000
From 1 January 2010 (disadvantaged areas)	£150000
Zero rate threshold: leases of less than 21 years	
£125000	

(continued)

Zero rate threshold: non-residential property

Rent of less than £1 000 per annum	£150 000

Higher rate thresholds

Above zero rate threshold to £250 000	1% of total
£250 001 to £500 000	3% of total
Over £500 000	4% of total

Stamp duty on share transactions

0.5% of total	

PENSION CONTRIBUTIONS

The maximum pension contributions available for tax relief are the greater of:
➤ £3,600
➤ 100% of the net relevant earnings for the year (subject to an annual maximum of £245,000 in 2009/10).

Contributions are paid net of basic rate tax. Relief has to be claimed for the tax year of payment. A tax charge may arise if the value of the pension at retirement exceeds the lifetime limit. The lifetime limit is £1,750,000 in 2009/10.

HMRC AUTHORISED MILEAGE RATES

Authorised mileage rates are given in Table 10.7.

TABLE 10.7 Mileage rates

Rates for 2009/10	Tax free rate per mile
All cars – first 10 000 miles	40p per mile
All cars – all additional miles	25p per mile
Motorcycles	24p per mile
Pedal cycles	20p per mile

Fuel rates for company cars

These rates per mile apply where employers require employees to repay fuel costs for private travel or when employees are reimbursed for business travel in company cars.

TABLE 10.8 Fuel rates for company cars from 1 January 2009

Size of engine	Petrol	Diesel	LPG
0–1400 cc	10p	11p	7p
1401–2000 cc	12p	11p	9p
2001 cc and over	17p	14p	12p

Note: hybrid cars are treated as petrol cars for this purpose.

INHERITANCE TAX

Inheritance tax rates are given in Tables 10.9 and 10.10.

TABLE 10.9 Inheritance tax rates 2009/10

Nil rate band*	£325 000
Rate of tax on excess	40%
Annual exemption per donor	£3 000
Annual gifts per donee	£250

* If an individual's nil rate band is not fully utilised on death, the nil rate band available on the death of his or her spouse, at a later date, is increased. The maximum joint nil rate band for married couples and civil partners is, therefore, £650,000 in 2009/10.

TABLE 10.10 Reduced tax charge on gifts within seven years of death

Years before death	0–3	3–4	4–5	5–6	6–7
% of death charge	100%	80%	60%	40%	20%

CAPITAL GAINS TAX

Current rates of CGT are shown in Table 10.11.

TABLE 10.11 Capital gains tax 2009/10

Tax rate	18%
Annual exemption	
• individuals	£10 100
• settlements	£5 050
Chattels exemption (proceeds)	£6 000

Entrepreneur's relief

Entrepreneur's relief applies to qualifying disposals of businesses, shares in personal companies and assets used in a personal partnership or company. Qualifying conditions exist. The effect of the relief is to reduce the tax rate on gains to 10%. A lifetime total of £1 million of gains can qualify for relief.

CAPITAL ALLOWANCES

Table 10.12 presents current allowances on plant and machinery. Table 10.13 shows allowances for motor cars acquired from April 2009.

TABLE 10.12 Capital allowances on plant and machinery

Writing down allowance rate	20%
Annual investment allowance: 100% rate*	£50 000
First-year allowances**	40%
Fixtures integral to a building	10%
Long-life assets	10%
Industrial/agricultural buildings	2%
Enterprise zone buildings	100%
Energy-efficient equipment	100%
Motor cars acquired before April 2009***	20%
Low-emission cars – limit for 100% allowance	110 g/km

* Annual investment allowance excludes expenditure on motor cars. The allowance applies to expenditure from 6 April 2009. Where an accounting period starts before this date, or is less than 12 months in length, the £50,000 maximum is restricted proportionately.

** The 40% first-year allowance in 2009/10 applies to new expenditure above the annual investment allowance amount. Certain assets such as motor cars are excluded.

*** There is a £3,000 cap on allowances for motor cars acquired before April 2009.

TABLE 10.13 Motor cars acquired from April 2009 (1 April for companies, 6 April in other cases)

The rate of allowances will depend on the car's carbon dioxide emissions:

Emission band	Rate
160 g/km or over	10%
110 g/km to 159 g/km	20%
Under 110 g/km	100%

As regards Table 10.13, the following applies.
- ➤ Cars will be 'pooled' with other cars in the same carbon dioxide emissions band.
- ➤ Balancing allowances will not be available on disposal.
- ➤ Where there is no approved carbon dioxide figure, the car will go into the 20% pool.

It will often be found that when a practice undertakes a surgery development, that within the building contract there will be a number of items which can fall under the headings of 'plant and machinery' or 'fixtures and fittings' and as such be eligible for claims for capital allowances. Included under this heading are likely to be such items as fitted furniture, sanitary and washing facilities, dentist chair and associated plumbing and wiring.

As can be seen from Table 10.12 the capital allowance regime allows an annual investment allowance of £50,000, writing down allowance of 20%, and an allowance on integral fixtures and plant of 10%.

In order to claim these allowances it will be necessary to obtain from the builder or the architect a breakdown of the costs between plant, fixtures and repairs/remedial works, so that the correct allowances can be applied to the work.

INCOME TAX COMPUTATIONS

Dentists are little different from the majority of businesses in the way they are taxed, but the computations of the tax liabilities, and in particular the allocation of the taxable profit between the principals, is rather more complex than that of other trading partnerships of similar size. This can be seen from the example in Figure 10.1.

In order to calculate the taxable profit, adjustments are made to the profit as shown in the practice accounts in Figure 10.1. Expenditure that HMRC will not allow needs to be added back, such as depreciation, accountancy costs for personal tax issues and other items of expenditure such as entertaining expenses. But further deductions can be claimed against the profit, such as capital allowances (as listed in Table 10.12). In addition, items which are not taxable or investment income, which is taxed elsewhere, are deducted from the profit at this point.

The capital allowances that are claimed are split between:
➤ those in respect of the total practice assets
➤ those relating to the individual principal's assets.

In this way the latter can be allocated to the principals who own those specific assets.

Finally, a deduction can be made for those expenses incurred personally by the principals themselves, which are allowable as an expense against the taxable income.

Once the taxable profit, known as Schedule D Case I/II Profit, has been calculated it is then allocated to each of the principals, as can be seen in Figure 10.2. The most common approach used in the allocation of the taxable profit to the principals is to use the overall percentage split of the accounts profits, after taking into account any prior shares or charges allocated to the principals.

To complete the tax computation the principal's own capital allowances and his or her personal expenses are deducted from the allocation of the profit. The

	£	£
Schedule D Case I/II Assessment		
Smile Dental Partnership		
Basis Period: Year ended 31 March 2009		
Profit before tax per accounts		405 124
Add:		
Depreciation	16 486	
Accountancy	300	
General expenses	84	
		16 870
		421 994
Less:		
Partnership capital allowances	17 833	
Interest received	265	
PAYE online filing	250	
		(18 348)
		403 646
Less:		
Personal capital allowances Cars	577	
Other	650	
Personal expenses	10 056	
		(11 283)
Schedule D Case I/II Profit		392 363

FIGURE 10.1 Calculation of tax liability

practice investment income and any superannuation deductions are noted for inclusion on the relevant sections on the tax return.

ALLOWABLE EXPENDITURE

While preparing the tax computations for a dental practice an accountant should refer to the partnership agreement to ascertain the treatment of such expenditure as is:

➤ paid by the practice and charged against the partnership profit
➤ paid personally by the individual partner.

Smile Dental Partnership

Profit allocation for the year ended 31 March 2009

		Total	East	Brown	West
Profit allocation as below		403 646	162 904	123 765	116 977
		403 646	162 904	123 765	116 977
Less	Personal Expenses	(10 056)	(5 264)	(2 402)	(2 390)
Less	Capital allowances				
	– Personal Others	(650)	(332)	(44)	(274)
	Cars	(577)	(551)	(26)	0
Assessable 2008/09		392 363	156 757	121 293	114 313

	Total	East	Brown	West
Net Bank interest	263.85	87.95	87.95	87.95
	0.00			
Tax credit	65.96	21.99	21.99	21.98
	329.81	109.94	109.94	109.93
Superannuation		0.00	477.72	0.00

Allocation of balance

Partners share per accounts	× Adjusted profit (403 646)
405 124	

	Total	East	Brown	West
Balance per partner	403 646	162 904	123 765	116 977

FIGURE 10.2 Allocation of taxable practice profit

There are often expenses, such as locum fees and sickness insurance premiums, and other items of a personal nature, paid out of the partnership accounts, where it is agreed that these expenses are to be the liability of the individual partner. In such circumstances these items will be posted to that partner's drawings and the details included, if appropriate, in a personal expense claim to be completed later by that partner. The fact that the expense was paid from the partnership account does not necessarily mean that the expense will be treated as a partnership expense for tax purposes.

The accountant will also need to identify those items included within the accounts which are not allowable for tax purposes and to ensure the same are added back in the computation. Details of the more common expenses that are not allowable as an expense against taxable income were included in Chapter 2.

The accountant also needs to identify those expenses which are partly allowable (e.g. motor expenses incurred for business travel) and ensure a proportionate deduction is made in the tax computation.

The following expenses are commonly found in dental accounts and may require special treatment for tax purposes.

Permanent health insurance

Most dentists will pay premiums on insurance policies designed to provide income during periods of sickness. These policies are invariably marketed as locum insurance, whether or not that is strictly speaking the case.

A genuine locum policy is one where a direct refund is made, during or following a period of sickness, of costs directly incurred in payments to locum dentists, whereas a permanent health policy provides for a lump-sum payment which the recipient can use at his or her discretion.

There is often confusion regarding the tax treatment of locum insurance policies and permanent health insurance policies, and further confusion is often caused by the dentist's lack of knowledge regarding which policies he or she has. The policy document needs to be examined in those cases.

As mentioned in Chapter 2, the locum policy attracts tax relief on its premiums, but with tax being due on the receipt of any claims made on the policy. As the expenses which the proceeds will pay for will mostly be tax allowable, there is a tax-neutral situation with this policy. However, these policies are not of much use if it is difficult to find a locum dentist to cover for the claimant during a period of sickness.

Whereas the permanent health policy does not attract tax relief on its premiums, nor attract a tax charge upon the receipt of proceeds, it is not dependent upon expenses actually being incurred. The expenses paid from the proceeds of these policies will still attract tax relief, if appropriate.

Legal and professional fees

It is usual to find expense in dentists' accounts in respect of solicitors and other professionals who have provided advice on various matters. However, this expense is often disallowable for income tax purposes. If the advice is in respect of expense of a capital nature, it is not allowable for income tax purposes and must be added back in the tax computations. It is common, for instance, for practices to obtain legal advice in respect of the preparation of partnership agreements and supplementary deeds; the costs of obtaining this advice are not allowable. Similarly, where fees are payable in connection with capital property transactions and partnership disputes, again this should be written back. In some cases, such charges could represent a deduction in a future capital gain computation, so it is essential a full record is maintained.

Legal fees, however, are allowed when incurred in dealing with revenue items, such as the collection of bad debts, so it is essential that the detail of what the fees were incurred for is made available when preparing the tax computations.

Bank interest and charges

A number of practices choose to finance the practice working capital by way of an overdraft, and incur bank interest as a result. One would normally expect this expense to be allowable without dispute and in many cases this will be so.

Where, however, the partners' current accounts are overdrawn as a consequence of drawing over and above the level of partnership profits, the interest on any overdraft needed to finance that position may be disallowed for tax purposes.

Bank charges incurred as a result of transactions on the bank account will be allowable in the income tax computations; however, bank charges incurred as administration fees in arranging loans may be disallowed, if they are of a capital nature.

The interest on a loan used to purchase or develop a surgery (or part of) will be allowable as a deduction against the income generated from that surgery. If the loan and the interest thereon are in the name of the practice it must be shown in the practice accounts as an expense. If the loan is in the individual partner's name, relief can be claimed as a deduction in the tax computation.

Interest will not be allowed on a loan taken out in excess of the cost of the surgery, to the extent of the interest on the excessive part of the loan.

Overdrawn current accounts

As mentioned above, where the principals draw more than their profits from the practice, HMRC may restrict the tax relief on the interest charges on borrowings to support that position.

However, non-cash items such as depreciation should not be taken into account in determining the level of the overdrawn current accounts. Therefore, the accumulated depreciation in the fixed asset note should be added back in order to determine whether the account in question was overdrawn.

Similarly, if there are any other non-cash provisions in the accounts these will need to be added back in a similar manner.

Domestic mortgage interest relief

Many dentists will use their private houses partly for practice purposes, for example, from providing facilities for out-of-hours services to undertaking paperwork and research. But unless there is significant use of the home for business purposes it is difficult to justify a claim for an element of the domestic mortgage interest to be allowed for tax purposes. It is more usual to claim a more modest 'use of home' or 'study allowance' to compensate the dentist for a proportion of the household expenses that could be attributable to the practice work performed in the home.

Where a dentist has raised finance on his or her house by way of extending a personal mortgage to pay capital into the practice, the interest on that proportion of the loan will be allowable in calculating the dentist's tax liability.

Interestingly, a large number of dentists draw their income gross from the practice and deposit amounts to save for their tax liability in an offset mortgage account. This has the benefit of reducing the average mortgage balance and consequently the interest charge thereon. But it also ensures that the tax savings are effectively obtaining a rate of return equating to the mortgage interest charge.

Entertaining expenses

Where dentists have incurred expenses in entertaining business associates, unless there is an element of staff entertaining involved, that expenditure must be added back in the tax computations.

Staff uniforms and clothing

Many practices provide their administrative staff with items of clothing or a uniform. Practices should be aware that where clothing is provided which can be used for private purposes, this represents a benefit in kind and is taxable upon the staff member concerned.

The only exception is where the uniforms provided cannot be reasonably used for any other purpose. To fulfil this requirement, the item of clothing should bear, say, the name of the practice or a distinctive logo, which should be woven into the items of apparel. The use of adhesive stickers or badges is insufficient.

Staff entertaining and benefits

There are a number of initiatives where the employer can provide benefits to staff and receive tax relief thereon, but there are limits on the amounts that can be expended and if these are exceeded the staff may be charged income tax on the benefit.

An example of this is the allowance for staff Christmas parties and outings during the year, which is currently £150 per person attending those events. The rules allow the staff to bring their partners, who will also qualify for their own allowance of £150. But if this limit is exceeded the member of staff will need to pay tax on the total amount paid in the year.

A benefit that can be provided to staff that is currently very popular with dentists and their employees is the Cycle to Work scheme, whereby the employer can provide their staff with a free or subsidised bicycle, with which they can travel to and from work. Dentists themselves, if employees of their own incorporated practice, can also benefit from this scheme, which can provide bicycles up to the value of £1,000, with no taxable benefit thereon. Further details of this scheme can be found on HMRC's website (www.hmrc.gov.uk).

CHARGEABLE INCOME

The computations above showed that there are a number of items of income that are not assessable or chargeable within the tax computations of dental practices, and it is necessary that these be deducted in arriving at the taxable profits.

Bank and building society interest

If a practice holds funds in banks or building society accounts, the interest on those accounts will be taken out of the computation. The income thus deducted will be recalculated on a tax-year basis (i.e. 6 April to 5 April), allocated in profit-sharing ratios between the partners, and shown in their own income tax returns.

Permanent health insurance benefits

If benefits from these policies are paid into the practice account, they should be ignored for tax computation purposes. This is different from the position on genuine locum policies; see above.

Schedule E income

Some practices receive income from outside appointments (often positions with the PCO) which may be subject to Schedule E tax. If this income represents the personal income of the principal performing the duty it is correct that it suffers tax, and it should be posted to that partner's current account as capital introduced and disclosed as income on his or her personal tax return.

If, however, it is intended that the income should be that of the practice, then a NT (no tax) code ought to be applied for to stop the deduction of tax at source, and the income included in the practice tax computation.

It should also be noted that in addition to Schedule E tax, there may also be deducted from that income Class 1 National Insurance, and, in some cases, superannuation. These should be charged to the current accounts of the principals concerned. The National Insurance will, if deferment has not been obtained, be refunded if all the contributions paid exceed the annual threshold. This is an area where non-specialist accountants fail with alarming regularity, and it is common for a specialist accountant, upon gaining a new client, to put together a backdated claim for overpaid NICs going back over a number of years.

Rent receivable

A number of practices will sublet part of their premises to another business and include the rent received within the practice accounts. This amount will be deducted from the practice tax computations, and a share of that income included on the income from land and property, on each principal's income tax return.

PERSONAL EXPENSE CLAIMS

Where dentists in practice have agreements in place to fund certain expenses outside of the practice, a personal expense claim will need to be drafted for each principal in order for him or her to be able to claim tax relief on those expenses.

As the expenses will not be included in the partnership accounts (other than those posted to the dentist's drawings), it is up to the dentist to provide the details of the amounts paid personally.

The specialist adviser should have an average expenses database to use as a benchmark to ensure all relevant expenditure has been claimed, and to also ensure that the amounts are not that excessive as to attract HMRC's interest and result in an enquiry.

One of the reasons that the practice may have an agreement to prevent personal expenses from being paid from practice funds could be to ensure that the practice cash flow cannot be affected by, for example, the principals' differing motoring expenses. Another benefit of keeping personal expenses outside of the practice could be to avoid any possible issues with the effect those expenses could have on the principals' current accounts.

Where the expenses are paid personally a personal expense claim should be drafted for inclusion in the practice tax computations, to ensure tax relief is obtained on that expense.

In most cases the dentist's personal expense claims will be prepared on an individual basis by their accountant. This is because some dentists prefer that their colleagues do not know what their individual expenses are, and such claims, being personal to each principal, may be considerably different even within the same practice.

The typical expenses that may be found on a personal expense claim are included in Figure 10.3 and detailed as follows.

➤ **Practice use of the home:** where there is significant use of the dentist's home for practice purposes a claim for the expenses incurred should be made. The claim can be made a number of different ways, and the sensible approach would be to take a proportion of the overall costs of running the property, apportioned with reference to the number of rooms used for practice purposes. However, it is not very common for dentists to have a significant business activity at the family home and this approach in most cases would not be appropriate.

➤ But there are a number of practices, mostly single-handed, where the surgery and the private residence are within the same building. If separate services are not provided for the business some apportionment of costs will be required.

➤ **Study allowance:** where there is not significant use of the dentist's home for business purposes, but the dentist does spend some time working from home, a claim for study allowance would normally be made. The allowance is based on a lump-sum estimate of the additional cost to the dentist of using the house for that purpose, and should be insignificant enough for it not to be a contentious issue should HMRC enquire into the dentist's affairs.

➤ **Locum fees, etc.:** where a partner has had a period of sickness or maternity/paternity leave they may have taken on a locum dentist or associate to service their patients in their absence. The cost of the locum or associate is a personal expense of that dentist and should be included on the claim.

Expenses			£
Car 1			2 648
	private use	90%	(2 383)
Home telephone			375
	private use	75%	(281)
Mobile telephone			110
	private use	10%	(11)
Subscriptions			4 674
Books and courses			395
Sundries			21
Study allowance			780
Spouse's salary			520
Journals			48
Capital allowances			252
Expenses claimed			7 148

FIGURE 10.3 Specimen personal expense claim

➤ **Accountancy fees:** in some cases partners will pay personal fees to their accountants for dealing with their own personal tax affairs. Such a fee can be included in a personal expense claim, but any fees relating to personal tax returns must be excluded. The fee for dealing with the expense claim can, however, be included.

➤ **Private telephone bills:** it is difficult to claim a significant amount of the home telephone landline for business purposes, given that primarily the line is for personal use, and the rental included in the cost will relate to that personal use and consequently be disallowable.

➤ The costs of business calls can be identified from the detailed bills provided and, given the way that phone costs are structured towards rental and fixed costs, the amount will often be minimal.

➤ For those do not have landlines anymore and use their mobile phone solely, where it is used for business purposes a proportion of the cost can be claimed.

➤ **Computers and broadband:** most dentists will have a computer at home with a broadband connection and will make a claim for the business element of the cost incurred in its operation. The dentist will need to identify the business or personal use of the same and try to apportion the cost accordingly. HMRC are aware of the recreational element in such items and would expect to see an add-back of costs in respect of personal use.

➤ **Courses and conferences:** the cost of attending courses will be allowable as an expense as long as the course is to update existing skills. If the course was one where the dentists will be training to acquire new skills there will be no allowance made. The distinction between updating and acquiring a new skill can be difficult to make, especially as the pace of technological change increases, and new ways to do old tasks emerge.

➤ In some cases courses are run at overseas holiday resorts. In these instances the cost of the travel and accommodation, etc. will need to be apportioned in line with the time spent on extracurricular activities, and further reduced if any members of the dentist's family attended.

➤ Personal development may take place within the surgery, and to assist with this, dentists will often purchase a camera or video recorder to monitor the work they and their trainees are doing. If this equipment remains within the practice it will qualify for a personal capital allowances claim, but where it is taken to the partner's home an add-back of part of the cost may be necessary.

➤ **Motor expenses:** the average dentist in practice will not use his or her car a lot for business purposes, but will probably take business trips as follows:
  • to the bank, accountant or solicitor and other professional advisers
  • to the dental laboratory to check the work being done

- to courses and training events
- to branch surgeries, if appropriate
- on domiciliary visits
- to trade shows
- to suppliers to pick up materials, if appropriate
- to local hardware stores, etc. in regards to maintenance of the property.

➤ It is generally understood that journeys between home and surgery are not allowable for tax purposes, other than those outside the normal hours or course of business.

➤ In order to obtain relief for the motor expenses incurred while on business the dentist is strongly advised to keep a log of those miles and of the total mileage of the car in the same period. That log would be used to arrive at a proportion of the total motor expenses that could be claimed as a business expense.

➤ The expenses that can be claimed would be all those usually associated with running a car, such as licence and insurance, repairs, petrol and oil, cleaning, etc. and the costs of financing the purchase. Similarly, if the car is leased, the costs associated with the hire can also be claimed.

➤ Without the mileage log to register the proportion of the expenses claimed it is difficult to justify any claim!

➤ It is the calculation for the restriction of expense for private use which often presents a problem when preparing an expense claim. While there are a handful of dentists who still feel that they can justify a high percentage business use of their car, the majority have accepted that a lower claim is more reasonable. There are still some dentists that can justify up to 80% business use, but these are more likely to be rural dentists with branch surgeries. The majority of claims for business use will be for less than 10–15% of the total costs of running the vehicle.

➤ **Spouses' salaries:** historically dentists have been able to make claims for employing their spouse to undertake duties for the practice and obtain tax relief on those claims. Although improvements in technology have reduced the number of tasks that the spouse can legitimately perform there may still be some scope for continued claims.

➤ The payment of a salary to a spouse is a legitimate expense to claim if the spouse does provide services to the practice. However, the payment of a spouse's wage in the accounts can often attract the attention of HMRC, so the amount needs to be justified.

➤ The duties a spouse would usually undertake for a practice include:
- telephone answering when providing on-call facilities, although the common use of mobile phones has negated the need for this in most cases
- secretarial duties

- chauffeuring services
- advice to patients if the spouse is qualified in dentistry or nursing
- general counselling
- appointment scheduling and reception
- chaperone duties.

➤ The level of salary paid should equate to that which would be paid to an independent person carrying out the same tasks. As the number of tasks is small and the work tends to be of a part-time nature, the salary paid will usually fall below the level that PAYE applies.

➤ If a small salary can be justified, further thought should be given as to whether a pension, based on that level of salary, should also be paid.

➤ While the payment of the salary is, primarily, to compensate the spouse for the work undertaken, there are tax advantages for the dentist as well. But those tax advantages may well diminish if the spouse has also got an income subject to higher rates. In those instances it may not be appropriate for a salary to be paid.

➤ The salary that is claimed as an expense will need to have been actually paid over and evidence of the payment must be kept. It is recommended that a payment from the dentist's account to a separate account maintained by the spouse be made. If the duties performed are of a regular nature a standing order could be set up to provide, say, a monthly payment of salary.

HMRC ENQUIRIES

Where an enquiry is undertaken by HMRC into the accounts of a practice, it is likely that the expenses of the partners will be reviewed as part of that process, and in particular they will look at the following expenses:

➤ motor expenses
➤ house expenses
➤ spouses' salaries and pensions
➤ telephone costs.

These tend to be expenses which, while they are wholly or partly allowable in principle, are frequently subject to negotiation in respect of the element of private use.

Under self-assessment the tax return is filed with very little review from HMRC, and if an enquiry is opened in a later year which uncovers a cavalier approach to the claiming of expenses, the result can be that the tax returns of earlier years are opened and subject to reassessment. When the lost tax, interest and penalties are added together for up to six years the costs can be quite significant. It is essential to be aware that the submission of unrealistic claims

could spark off an in-depth enquiry. Dentists should ensure that:
➤ all claims submitted are clearly justified
➤ the expenditure has *actually been paid out* for practice purposes
➤ receipts are provided in support of all claims
➤ where restrictions for private use are applicable, claims are both justified
  and regularly reviewed
➤ estimated expenditure is excluded as far as possible.

Experience shows that in most dental practices, the scope for in-depth enquiries
by HMRC are likely to be limited to two factors:
➤ the non-declaration of income
➤ the over-claiming of expenses.

For NHS practices the scope for under-declaration of income is limited to the
receipt of the patient charges, as the receipt of the NHS contract amounts will be
direct to the practice bank account. The specialist accountant, however, would
normally reconcile the patient charges received to those deducted by the PCT
and investigate any significant difference. Any shortfall would be added on to
the practice fees in the accounts.

Practices with payment plan contracts will have the monthly fees paid direct
to the practice bank account, and the additional charges for laboratory fees, etc.
would usually be demanded from the patients as they leave the surgery. There is
an opportunity in this instance for the errant dentist or staff member to divert
those sundry funds from the practice account.

Those practices which operate on a fee per item basis will have the most
scope for under-declaration of their income, but as an increasing number of
patients are using their credit and debit cards to pay their fees the amount of
cash that can be taken will be relatively small.

The benchmarking process can be used to highlight practices that are underperforming, and those practices should try to identify where the reduction in
practice profits is coming from.

It is important that a detailed cash reconciliation is performed on a daily
basis, in order that discrepancies can be rectified. Without detailed cash records
it is difficult to defend the practice from an assessment raised as a result of an
enquiry.

The usual method adopted by HMRC when checking for under-declaration
of income by dentists is to look at the dentists' diary system. Appointments in
the diary are chosen, and the receipts that would be due as a result of the treatment provided are then identified in the books and records. Problems arise
when the receipts cannot be found!

Dentists should take out insurance to cover the accountancy fees that may
be incurred as a result of an HMRC enquiry into the accounts. The insurance

cover will allow the accountant to take a harder line with HMRC, as the practice will not have to pay if a lot of time is taken to come to an agreement on the matter.

WHAT'S THE BEST RETIREMENT DATE?

Since the introduction of self-assessment there has not been a date within a tax year which would provide an optimum tax saving upon retirement. So dentists should retire on a date most suited to them, although from a tax administration point of view, the end of a tax year would be the most convenient, especially if their practice had a March year end. The reason is that retirement on any date after March will result in the necessity to file an income tax return for the following year.

There is a complication, however, that affects those dentists retiring from practices with other than March year ends. Additional tax will be payable by those dentists in their retirement year as a result of the closing year rules basis of assessment. The rules are quite complex and I do not intend to explain them fully in this book. Suffice to say that where these rules do apply, more than 12 months' profits will be taxed in the final year in practice. There is no way to avoid the rules by retiring on a specific date within that final year. HMRC allows a credit against the extra tax liability by way of a claim for 'overlap relief', although the longer the dentist has been in practice the less the value of that credit will be.

When a retirement date falls part way through the practice year should a separate set of accounts be prepared?

This is not required for tax purposes and, unless the parties are desperate to finalise affairs, it is cheaper to wait for the normal practice year end, and prepare a single set of accounts and divide the profits on an agreed basis.

Given that each dentist will have a record of his or her own income and expenses, it will only be the practice income and expense that will need to be apportioned, and in most cases this can be done equitably on a time-apportioned basis. Other methods may be applied if thought equitable.

For those dentists providing NHS services there is the added complication of superannuation upon retirement. The superannuation contributions in each year to March are confirmed by the practice on the annual reconciliation form in July, and finalised in the autumn of that year. Therefore, it is likely that a dentist will be retired for a period of months before their superannuation records are updated and their final pension can be finalised. In the interim they will be paid a provisional pension amount.

STAFF ENTERTAINING AND BENEFITS

There are very few 'tax-free' perks that dentists can give to their staff without HMRC taking a very keen interest and seeking to impose tax and NIC liabilities. For example, if a practice wants to provide their staff with free meal vouchers, the value of the meal voucher must not exceed 15p per day, otherwise tax and NIC liabilities will arise. Ebenezer Scrooge springs to mind! However, even HMRC has a heart when it comes to Christmas, as they are far more generous when looking at the staff Christmas party. This is because the 15p limit is swept away and a 'tax-free' exemption of £150 per person is allowed. As you might have guessed, there are a number of conditions that need to be met, but these should not be a problem, as they will apply in most situations:

➤ the party must be open to all staff
➤ in calculating whether the cost of the party has exceeded the £150 per person exemption, all other related costs such as taxis, overnight accommodation and also VAT need to be taken into consideration. If spouses or partners are attending, they also have a £150 exemption.

There is a small trap for the unwary, because the £150 exemption applies to the total *annual* cost per person of all staff social functions during the year, so practices need to take account of other functions, such as the office summer barbecue. Dentists need to be careful if they party regularly! Finally, if the practice 'parties' regularly and the total cost exceeds £150, the whole amount is then taxable on the staff, not just the excess over £150.

As an alternative to a Christmas party, some businesses give a bottle of wine or a turkey to their staff at Christmas. In the past, the Revenue would normally seek to impose a tax liability on such gifts. However, they have now adopted a more pragmatic approach and will allow this, providing the gift does not exceed, typically, £25 per employee. Unfortunately, a case of wine or a food hamper is likely to be viewed as being too generous in the eyes of the Revenue. Likewise, vouchers (e.g. M&S or Debenhams) would not qualify as tax-free gifts, even if their value fell within the £25 limit.

Where a practice does exceed the limits, or provides their staff with vouchers, it needs to deal with the tax payable on those gifts, or the staff will receive a tax bill from HMRC. The most popular way of dealing with the tax implications is for the practice to enter into a PAYE Settlement Agreement with HMRC, whereby the business essentially pays the tax and NICs on behalf of their employees. Businesses can also claim tax relief on the cost of gifts to customers and key contacts. However, in order to qualify for tax relief:

➤ the cost of the gift must not exceed £50 per recipient
➤ the gift must carry a conspicuous advertisement of the practice
➤ the gift must not be food, drink, tobacco or tokens or vouchers exchangeable for goods.

So while the bottle of malt whisky will easily fall within the £50 limit, it does not satisfy the latter of the above conditions and will not therefore qualify for tax relief. Typical qualifying gifts will be calendars, pens and diaries, providing they carry the name of the business.

Showing your appreciation of your staff's efforts by means of gifts and benefits is good for morale, but you need to take care to do this in the most tax-efficient way.

If staff are paid a cash bonus this must be put through the payroll and the appropriate tax and National Insurance must be deducted.

Generally, if you provide gifts to your staff such as a bottle of wine, chocolates, flowers, etc. there are no tax implications providing that the gift is considered to be 'trivial' by HMRC. There is no specific value that constitutes a 'trivial' gift, but it is thought to be up to approximately £30 to £40 per member of staff.

If a practice provides their staff with a uniform, it must include a permanent employer logo or badge otherwise it may become taxable. Alternatively, the practice can agree with its employees that the uniforms are merely provided on loan. A written agreement is advisable for this.

If a practice provides food and drink to its staff over a lunchtime meeting, this may be taxable. For the lunch to be provided tax free, it must be available to all members of staff so practices should make sure everyone receives a meeting invitation, or at the very least that the leftover food is shared by everyone else.

To promote healthier lifestyles and to reduce environmental pollution, the government has introduced a scheme to allow employers to loan cycles to employees as a tax-free benefit.

The Cycle to Work scheme enables employers to purchase a cycle and loan it to an employee for a period of time (normally 12 months) during which there will be a tax exemption. After the 12-month loan period, the employee has the option of purchasing the cycle from the employer at its market value, said to be around 5% of the original cost. The employee will then acquire a cycle at a snip since it has a second-hand value as well as all the advantages of having had just one owner.

The employer may loan the cycle to the employee completely rent free. Or, it may be that the employer wishes to recover the cost of providing the cycle and associated safety equipment by charging a rent. In this case, the employee is making a salary sacrifice, which reduces earnings as well as the associated National Insurance paid by the employer, but provides a valuable benefit.

For example, the employer could purchase a cycle for £600 and charge a monthly rent of £30. This would only cost a basic rate taxpayer £20.10 or a higher rate taxpayer £17.70 because the money would be coming out of their gross earnings. The employer would therefore collect £360 in rent over the 12 months and then the employee could purchase the cycle for £30 (market value = 5% of the original cost).

In addition to paying less National Insurance, the employer would get capital allowances on the cost of the cycle. The total net cost to the employer of providing the cycle would be £130 (or £100 if the business was not incorporated). The total net cost to the employee would be £270 for a basic rate taxpayer and £240 for a higher rate taxpayer. As you can see, this is significantly less than the original cost of the cycle.

If no rent is charged at all and therefore no salary is sacrificed by the employee, the total net cost to the employer would be £450 (or £335 if the business was not incorporated) and the employee would just pay the £30 to purchase the cycle after 12 months. The savings in this scenario are not as significant when no rent is charged as there is no tax or National Insurance saving on the salary sacrificed.

For the tax exemption to apply there are a number of conditions.

➤ Ownership of the equipment must not be transferred to the employee during the loan period.

➤ Employees must use the equipment mainly for qualifying journeys (in this case, 'mainly' means that more than 50% of time using the cycle and safety equipment must involve a qualifying journey) and for journeys made between the employee's home and workplace, or for journeys between one workplace and another.

➤ The Cycle to Work scheme must be made available generally to employees of the employer concerned and not confined to directors or offered to them on more favourable terms.

Employers can pay up to 20p per mile tax free to employees who use their own cycles for business travel. Journeys between home and work are not business travel for this purpose.

Any employee considering joining a Cycle to Work scheme will need to consider whether they would prefer to use their own cycle and be able to claim up to the 20p per mile tax free for any business miles they travel, as opposed to having a cycle loaned to them by their employer.

Employees cannot claim the 20p per mile tax-free mileage allowance for business travel if they use a cycle loaned to them by their employer.

Employers can also purchase a 'pool' cycle which must be kept at the practice for all employees to use only for qualifying business journeys. No benefit in kind will arise in this situation. Employees can make deliveries, collections, etc. without any tax or National Insurance implications. The cycle must be made available to all employees. This purchase too is advantageous to the employer because capital allowances over several years will reduce the amount paid in tax.

A practice can provide childcare vouchers to each member of staff worth up to £55 per week completely tax free. The practice can gift the vouchers instead of salary. The practice saves the employer's National Insurance and the staff save the tax and employee's National Insurance. Everyone's a winner! Vouchers may be used for nurseries, etc. as well as for some out-of-school activities.

A practice may provide each member of staff with a mobile phone tax free. This is usually done by reducing their salary by the appropriate amount, then providing the phone to them free. This will save the associated tax and National Insurance costs.

A practice could also provide its staff with a computer or Blackberry. HMRC will not tax the staff providing that they are used mainly for business purposes with any private use being insignificant. This does not apply to mobile phones which can be provided tax free even when there is no business use.

If a practice provides a car to an employee, the employee will have to pay tax on this benefit. This benefit charge is calculated based on the list price of the car and the carbon dioxide emissions. Therefore, an expensive, high-emitting car such as a Range Rover Sport will have a much higher tax charge than a less expensive, low-emitting car such as a Ford Fiesta.

A further tax charge arises where the practice pays for the employee's private fuel. Again this is linked to the emissions. The benefit charge is taxed as additional earnings on the employee so they will pay tax at 0%, 20% or 40% depending on their other income.

The business is also charged Class 1A National Insurance on the benefit at 12.8%.

An example follows.

Ford Fiesta 1.4 Zetec – list price £10,705, carbon dioxide emissions 147 g/km
Annual car benefit charge = £10,705 × 17% (percentage defined by emissions)
= £1,820
Annual fuel benefit charge (if applicable) = £16,900 (fixed) × 17% = £2,873

Range Rover Sport 4.2 V8 HSE – list price £57,855, carbon dioxide emissions 374 g/km
Annual car benefit charge = £57,855 × 35% = £20,249
Annual fuel benefit charge (if applicable) = £16,900 (fixed) × 35% = £5,915

As you can see, the list price and emissions have a huge impact on the benefit charge. The Range Rover Sport annual benefit charge is more than 10 times that of the Ford Fiesta.

From the employer's point of view, cars are eligible for capital allowances at a rate of 20% (for cars with emissions up to 160 g/km) or 10% (for cars with emissions over 160 g/km) reducing balance each year. They do not qualify for annual investment allowance (given at 100%) so it takes a number of years to claim tax relief on the entire cost.

If a business provides a van to an employee, the benefit that will be taxed is a flat £3,000 with an additional £500 charge if the business pays for any private fuel.

However, there is no benefit charge whatsoever if the van is used solely for business purposes. 'Business' purposes can, for vans only, include home to work travel and even the very occasional incidental private journey as long as it is not significant. A van can therefore be provided to an employee completely tax free if there is no private use.

From the employer's view, vans are much more attractive than cars as they qualify for annual investment allowance. Providing the employer has not already used their £50,000 annual investment allowance elsewhere, 100% tax relief will be available in the year of purchase.

Obviously, a van is much more favourable than a car for tax purposes. Most of the time you can tell by looking at a vehicle whether it is a car or a van, but some vehicles are not quite as obvious. Vehicles such as 4x4s, pickups, double-cab pickups, etc. all cause confusion. The main 'rule' is that a van is designed mainly for the conveyance of goods and a car is designed mainly for the conveyance of people.

4x4s with rear seats and rear windows are generally considered to be cars; however, 4x4s with no rear seats or rear windows are generally accepted as vans. Pickups are classed as vans, as are double cab pickups providing they have a payload of at least 1,000 kg.

Double cab pickups have became quite an attractive vehicle to provide to staff as they have two rows of seats, but most of them are still classed as vans. The employer can therefore claim a generous tax deduction and providing the vehicle is not used privately, there will be no benefit charge whatsoever.

CHAPTER 11

Retirement and superannuation

This chapter will mainly look at how the NHSPS works, how an eventual pension can be improved and other retirement matters relevant for dentists.

THE NHS SCHEME

The present NHSPS dates back to the formation of the NHS in 1948 and is available to all dentists and other healthcare professionals working within the NHS. It is generally considered to be a very good scheme.

This section looks at how the NHSPS applies specifically to dentists. Only those areas relevant to dentists will be covered so those readers who wish to obtain more complete details should apply to the NHS Pensions Agency, Hesketh House, 200–202 Broadway, Fleetwood, Lancs. FY7 8LG or full details can be obtained from the National Health Service Pensions Agency website, www.nhspa.gov.uk.

The NHS Superannuation Scheme for a number of years consisted of two separate schemes, one for the employed and one for the self-employed, but from 1 April 2008 two new schemes were introduced, again one for the employed and one for the self-employed. As the older schemes still remain current, dentists are affected by all four of these schemes and they are summarised below.

Prior to 1 April 2008

The NHSPS is the only occupational pension scheme available to the self-employed, with contributions partly funded by a 'principal' (i.e. the DoH).

➤ The officer scheme covers employees of the NHS, for example, hospital consultants and dentists practicing in PCT-run practices. This scheme is a final salary scheme with an accrual rate of eightieths for pension. This means that the pension is calculated based on an eightieth of the annual salary each year. The plan being if an employee works for 40 years they will effectively retire on a pension worth half of their final salary. The pension also provides for a half-rate survivors pension and a separate lump sum of three times the initial pension, with a normal pension age of 60. Given that this scheme is solely for employees of the NHS no further detail will be included in this book.

➤ The practitioner scheme covers dentists providing NHS dentistry in practice. The basic feature of this scheme is that the eventual pension and lump-sum entitlement are calculated on a formula using the accumulated earnings of the dentist concerned during their period as an NHS dentist.

➤ This scheme calculates the members' pension based on their earnings throughout their career. These are revalued to maintain a current value and are known as career average revalued earnings (CARE). The CARE calculations have been updated following the revision of the scheme in April 2008. The amount of earnings that could be included in the calculation were restricted to a pre-set limit each year, called the Maximum Allowable Remuneration, which for 2007/08 was set at £115,800. (This limit was scrapped following the changes in April 2008, although all earnings prior to that date remain capped.)

➤ The CARE are accumulated over the dentist's career in a separate notional account and increased by a dynamising factor each year. The dynamising factor was, until April 2008, calculated based on the average increase in practitioner earnings each year. The pension was eventually calculated as 1.4% of the CARE, with the lump sum being 4.2% (i.e. being three times the pension). This scheme also provides for a half-rate survivor's pension and a normal pension age of 60.

Post 1 April 2008

From 1 April 2008 the New NHSPS was introduced for both employed and self-employed dentists, and new entrants to the NHS automatically join this scheme. Existing members are given the option of joining the new scheme or staying with the existing pension scheme (slightly amended).

The new scheme brings with it a number of changes with one of the most significant relating to the pension deduction, which is changing from a flat rate to an earnings-related sum (see later notes below).

➤ The new officer scheme again covers employees of the NHS, for example, hospital consultants and dentists practising in PCT-run practices. This scheme is a final salary scheme with an accrual rate of sixtieths for pension. This means that the pension is calculated based on a sixtieth of the annual salary each year. The plan being if an employee works for 30 years they will effectively retire on a pension worth half of their final salary (subject to an actuarial deduction; see later notes). The pension also provides for a 37.5% survivor's pension and a separate lump sum of 2.25 times the initial pension, with a normal pension age of 65. Again given that this scheme is solely for employees of the NHS no further detail will be included in this book.

➤ The new practitioner scheme covers dentists providing NHS dentistry in practice. The basic features of the new scheme are the same as the old scheme, but the differences can be seen in Table 11.1 (extracted from the NHSPS guide).

Table 11.1 provides details for NHS staff, practitioners and practice and approved employer staff. The NHS staff category covers most employees working for the NHS. The practitioners' category applies to NHS medical, dental and ophthalmic practitioners, including assistants and some locum practitioners. This includes practitioners included on an NHS trust performers list. The practice and approved employer staff category applies to general practice and direction body staff or staff working for other approved employers connected to the NHS.

Opting out

Since 1988, when legislation demanded that it become a voluntary scheme, membership of the NHS scheme has not been compulsory. Dentists can, if they so wish, decline to join the scheme at the outset or, having joined, opt out at some future time.

The dentist in normal circumstances would be extremely unwise to exercise this option as the benefits that the scheme provides are highly unlikely to be matched by any private funded pension.

Levels of contributions

Up until April 2008 the usual annual superannuation contribution for dentists was 20% (an employer contribution of 14% and an employee contribution of 6%). The 6% was deducted monthly from the monies due to the dentist under the NHS contract. The further amount of 14% was theoretically contributed by the DoH as the 'employer', although this has no material effect on the eventual benefit.

Since April 2008 the flat rate scheme above has been replaced by an earnings-related scheme in respect of the employee contribution; the employer contribution of 14%, however, remains unchanged (except in Scotland, where an actuarial valuation of the scheme has resulted in the employer's contribution being reduced to 13.5%, with effect from 1 April 2009). The earnings-related sums will apply to all dentists (i.e. those on both the old and the new scheme), and the earning levels have been divided into four different bands, each with a differing percentage to determine the size of the deduction made.

TABLE 11.1 Differences between the schemes (extracted from NHSPS guide)

Feature or benefit	NHS staff		Practitioners		Practice and approved employer staff	
	1995 section	2008 section	1995 section	2008 section	1995 section	2008 section
Scheme section						
Member contributions	5–8.5% depending on rate of pensionable pay		5–8.5% depending on rate of pensionable earnings		5–8.5% depending on rate of pensionable pay	
Pension	A pension worth 1/80th of final year's pensionable pay per year of membership	A pension worth 1/60th of reckonable pay per year of membership	A pension based on 1.4% of uprated earnings per year	A pension based on 1.87% of uprated earnings per year	A pension worth 1/80th of final year's pensionable pay per year of membership	A pension worth 1/60th of reckonable pay per year of membership
Retirement lump sum	3 × pension. Option to exchange part of pension for more cash	Option to exchange part of pension for cash at retirement, up to 25% of capital value. Some members may have a compulsory amount of lump sum.	3 × pension. Option to exchange part of pension for more cash	Option to exchange part of pension for cash at retirement, up to 25% of capital value. Some members may have a compulsory amount of lump sum.	3 × pension. Option to exchange part of pension for more cash	Option to exchange part of pension for cash at retirement, up to 25% of capital value. Some members may have a compulsory amount of lump sum.
Normal retirement	60	65	60	65	60	65
Pensionable pay	Normal pay and certain regular allowances		Pensionable earnings from NHS work		Normal pay and certain regular allowances	
Uprated earnings	Not relevant		The final value if pensionable earnings after adding all year's earnings and applying revaluation factors		Not relevant	
Death in membership lump sum	2 × reckonable pay (actual reckonable pay for part-time workers)		2 × average annual pensionable earnings		2 × reckonable pay (actual reckonable pay for part-time workers)	

TABLE 11.2 Bands for 2009/10

Annual pensionable pay	Contribution rate
(full-time equivalent)	
Up to £20 709	5.0%
£20 710 to £68 392	6.5%
£68 393 to £107 846	7.5%
£107 847 plus	8.5%

Note the following in regards to levels of contributions.

➤ The Dental Services Division will arrange for the appropriate rate of contributions to be applied to GDPs each year.

➤ Once a rate has been set it is applied to all of the dentist's pensionable pay. For example, a dentist's total pensionable income is £130,000, comprised of practice-based income of £120,000, and income of £10,000 from a PCO appointment. The dentist would pay 8.5% on the total income of £130,000.

➤ If a salaried dentist receives a normal annual pay award it should not change the rate he or she is on, as the bands are adjusted annually in line with pay awards.

➤ The rules in respect of rates of contributions apply to members of both the 1995 and the 2008 NHSPS.

➤ A dentist's aggregated pensionable earnings are scaled to a full year (i.e. annualised) for the purposes of setting a rate if he commenced his NHS earnings after 1 April 2009.

➤ A part-time dentist's actual pensionable pay is not converted to a whole time equivalent value for the purposes of setting a rate.

➤ For a dentist who is in receipt of maternity or paternity pay in 2009/10, the full deemed pensionable pay (i.e. the unreduced pay) must be used to set the rate.

➤ The added years pensionable pay cap, if relevant, was £123,600 in 2009/10.

Dentists with superannuable earnings of up to £20,709 are in the lowest band and will pay employee contributions at a rate of 5% of their earnings. Those earning over £107,847 will be in the top band and pay employee contributions at a rate of 8.5% of their earnings. The increases in the contribution rates from the flat rate of 6%, unfortunately, will not result in higher pensions for the dentists. The rates have been increased in an attempt to reduce the perceived shortfall in funding the NHSPS. For high-earning dentists, the impact of these additional contributions (i.e. increases of up to 2.5% of their superannuable earnings) could be quite significant and they may result in a downward review of their drawings.

The superannuable earnings are calculated as 43.9% of the gross contract received from the NHS (although some elements of the payment may not be superannuable). The 56.1% deduction is a standard reduction to take into account the dentist's expenses in practice. How this 56.1% deduction compares to the actual expenses of a dentist can be seen in the benchmarking statistics available from the specialist accountancy practices. The contribution year for superannuation runs to 31 March each year.

The rates are levied on the level of income of the practice's UDA contract in England and Wales, and on the previous year's superannuable earnings in Scotland and Northern Ireland. Following the completion of the Annual Superannuation Reconciliation Report (see later notes) an adjustment will be made to the contributions records if the levied rates do not match the actual earnings levels of the performers.

Multi-dentist practices

NHS contracts are undertaken by dental practices either by way of a performer and/or a provider-based contract; the perfomer contract will be in the name of an individual dentist or performer, whereas the provider contract can cover a whole practice and will include the names of a number of performers.

The performer or practice receives a monthly schedule which details the amount of superannuation deducted from the monthly NHS payment due. The principal at a practice will notify the PCT of the split of the overall provider or practice contract between the performers at the practice, and the superannuation deductions that are to be made on those performers' behalf each month will be allocated according to that split.

Each year the dentist responsible for either a performer or a provider contract will be asked to complete an Annual Superannuation Reconciliation Report to confirm that the amounts allocated to each dentist or performer on that contract are correct.

Listed on this report are the figures for the baseline payment contract amount, the patient charges and other deductions, i.e. the total net value of the annual contract value payments, being the net pensionable earnings, made in the financial year.

The report asks that the dentist confirms those figures, and also asks for confirmation of the breakdown of those figures between the performer dentists as notified to the PCT earlier in that year. It also asks for details of actual payments, within 43.9% of the contract value, if different from those on the form.

The dentist is also required to identify those who are partners in, or directors of, the contract and to enter the amount of seniority payments, maternity leave payments, paternity leave payments, adoption leave payments or sickness leave payments paid under the contract.

The information therein will form the basis of the SD86C that will be sent in the autumn to each performer. The SD86C form summarises the detail that has been added to the dentist's pension records for that year.

Appendix 19, Superannuation annual reconciliation report, provides further information regarding the details included on the report (*see* www.radcliffe-oxford.com/financefordentists).

Guidance on completing the annual declaration for 2008/09 has changed. Each year contractors in the GDS and PDS in England and Wales must declare their performers' pensionable pay for the preceding year. This year contractors are required to declare the net superannuable earnings from April 2008 to March 2009. The emphasis is now on earnings accrued during the year, rather than payments made as in previous years.

For 2006/07 and 2007/08 contractors were asked not to include the March payment as this was paid in April. The payment for March 2009, however, should be included in the 2008/2009 statement. This leaves the question: where will the superannuation for March 2008 be accounted for? The advice received from the NHS's Business Services Authority Dental Services Division is that the pensionable pay and contributions for March 2008 will be included on the statement, by way of a separate adjustment that they will effect. The statement, known as the SD86C, which will be issued in December 2008/January 2009, for 2008/09 will therefore cover 13 months. The figure will be notified to the NHS Pensions Agency at the same time as the 2008/09 remuneration and contributions. A footnote will be added to all SD86Cs advising that the statement includes the March 2008 figures.

It is important that the SD86C is agreed with all the dentists in the practice as the submission of this report forms the basis of the pensions record for that year, and consequently the amount of pension the dentists will receive.

Tax relief on contributions

Tax relief will be allowed on pension premiums *paid* in a year up to the extent of the amount of earnings in that year.

To ensure tax relief is granted it is essential that the superannuation is detailed in the accounts, and posted to the partners' current accounts where appropriate, or treated as part of the costs of the associates that provided their services during the year. Given that the superannuation is deducted from the income before it is received from the PCO, a number of non-specialist accountants erroneously omit the detail of the superannuation in the accounts they prepare. The deductions in respect of the associates' superannuation should be notified to them by the principal, and copies of NHS schedules provided for their accountants to confirm the figures.

Tax relief will then be claimed on the contributions by inclusion of the amounts on the dentists' personal tax return, and not as a deduction in the accounts.

The dynamising factor

In most occupational pension schemes the calculation of the eventual pension is made using a formula based upon salary earned in the final year or years of service.

This system cannot apply to dentists who do not earn a salary in the accepted sense of the word, and who may often reduce their commitment nearer to their retirement date. To base their pension purely on earnings from earlier years would not produce an equitable solution as their value would diminish over time.

To solve this problem, there was devised some years ago a system known as 'dynamising' or uprating, which is intended to ensure that a dentist's career earnings are properly protected against inflation during his or her career and have not lost real value by pensionable age. By this means, the superannuable remuneration earned by the dentist in each individual year is uprated, in order to convert the amount of income in the year it was earned to its equivalent value at the date of retirement. The dynamising factor up until April 2008 was based on the annual increase in dentists' earnings.

Following the introduction of the new schemes in April 2008 all pensionable earnings are revalued by a dynamising factor determined by movements in the Retail Price Index (i.e. inflation levels) plus 1.5%. This will stop pensions rising too fast if there is an unexpected rise in dentists' earnings. It has been agreed that the dynamising factor can never be less than 1% in order to prevent a reduction in the level of pensionable earnings in times of deflation.

Summary of the benefits of the scheme

There are numerous benefits which arise from membership of the NHSPS as follows.

➤ A pension of either 1.4% (for the old scheme) or 1.87% (for the new scheme) of the total uprated career earnings of the dentist concerned.
➤ The pension is indexed-linked by a factor announced each year, linked to the Retail Price Index.
➤ Under the old scheme, a lump-sum retiring allowance of 4.2% of the total uprated career earnings is payable, free of tax.
➤ A lump-sum retiring allowance is now not automatically payable under the new scheme. However, it is possible to obtain a tax-free cash sum upon retirement by way of trading £1 of annual pension for £12 of tax-free cash sum. For example, for a reduction of £500 from the annual pension, a tax-free lump sum of £6,000 in cash can be obtained upon retirement. It

is possible for members of the old scheme to increase their tax-free lump sum from the 4.2% above, by way of trading annual pension for a larger lump sum in a similar way. The tax-free lump sum is capped at 25% of the capital value of the pension fund; this has been calculated by HMRC by multiplying the reduced pension by 20 and adding the total retirement lump sum. In the majority of cases the maximum lump sum works out as approximately 5.36 times the 1995 section pension, and 4.28 times the 2008 section pension.

➤ The death benefits of both schemes are detailed in Table 11.3.
➤ Under the new scheme there have been key changes relating to marital status and entitlement. In the past, it was only the spouse who could benefit from a proportion of the pension on the death of a dentist. Now it can be the partner or future post-retirement spouses who could get the pension for the rest of their life.
➤ Children's benefit is payable upon the death of the dentist to dependent children up to the age of 23.
➤ A death-in-service lump sum is payable at the rate of twice the annual pensionable pay.
➤ An ill-health retirement benefit is paid if a dentist is obliged to cease work through illness, subject to a minimum period of service.

Estimates of potential pension benefits can be obtained prior to retirement from the NHS Pensions Agency in Fleetwood.

PURCHASING ADDITIONAL BENEFITS
One feature of the NHSPS is that members have the opportunity of buying an additional pension (AP) where, provided the circumstances are right, their eventual total service appears unlikely to provide them with a full pension.

This section looks at the means of enhancing those eventual retirement benefits through schemes available through the NHSPS.

The standard retirement age of those dentists under the old scheme is 60, with membership limited to the age of 70. The new scheme increases these figures to 65 for retirement, and 75 (or an overall limit of 45 years) for membership.

ADDED YEARS AND ADDITIONAL PENSION
The earliest date that a dentist can retire on a full pension is aged 60. Total superannuable service cannot exceed 45 years, of which, not more than 40 may accrue by the normal retirement date, which was 60 under the old scheme, and is 65 under the new scheme.

As most dentists qualify in their mid-twenties, it is not possible for more than about 35 years of pensionable service to be completed by the age of 60. In some cases it may be less, and if nothing is done to enhance this entitlement, the dentist will be unable to obtain a full pension on retirement. For this reason there was a scheme (up to April 2008) known as added years which gave the dentist the opportunity of buying additional years to allow him or her to build up a full career entitlement.

The purchase of these added years was subject to two limitations, as follows.

➤ Total service, both worked and purchased, must have not exceeded 40 years at age 60, or 45 at age 65.

➤ The maximum contribution to the scheme by the dentist could not exceed 15% of the NHS superannuable income. This figure included the standard 6%, so that the maximum allowable payment for added years could not exceed 9% of NHS superannuable income. The limits for pension contributions since April 2008 have been increased to 100% of pensionable income (up to a maximum of £245,000 in 2009/10).

Following the change in the schemes in April 2008 the added years' option was withdrawn and dentists had up to 31 March 2008 to notify the NHSPS that they wished to start paying added years by their next birthday. The scheme has been closed to members since that date, and there has been a new simplified scheme introduced which will now apply to members of both the old and the new schemes.

AP is the new simplified scheme which allows members to purchase an additional annual pension of up to £5,000 per annum, in increments of £250. AP is a flexible way of increasing your Scheme pension. It allows the dentist to choose to buy extra annual pension, in today's terms, and see clearly how much the purchase will cost.

Under this option the dentist elects to buy a set amount of annual pension for an agreed amount of contributions that they can choose to pay either as a lump sum or as a regular payment for an agreed period of time. The minimum amount of AP they can buy is £250 and the maximum amount is £5,000. AP is revalued in line with inflation both before and after retirement.

They can choose whether the AP is just for themselves or also provides benefits for their dependants in the event of their death.

Incidentally, the new scheme does not prevent those already purchasing added years from joining.

The option of purchasing AP should always be discussed with an IFA with a specialist knowledge of the NHSPS .

TABLE 11.3 Death benefits under both NHSPSs (extracted from NHSPS guide)

1995 Section

Benefit	Death in membership (with at least 2 years membership)	Death after retirement	Death with deferred pension	Death within 12 months of leaving membership if benefits remain in Scheme
Lump sum	2 × annual pensionable pay or average uprated earnings for Practitioners ***	The lesser of 5 × pension less pension already paid or 2 × pay less any retirement lump sum	3 × pension payable if member had retired on date of death	3 × annual pension the member would have received had they retired on the date of death
Widow's pension	1/2 of your notional upper tier ill-health retirement pension	1/2 of your pension in payment	1/2 of your pension at the date of death	1/2 of your notional upper tier ill-health retirement pension at date of leaving
	Short-term pension payable at rate of your pensionable pay for the first 6 months	Short-term pension payable at rate of member's pension paid for first 3 months or 6 months if there is at least one dependent child	No short-term pension	No short-term pension
Widower's/Civil partner's/nominated partner's pension	1/2 of your notional upper tier ill-health retirement pension, based only on membership from 6 April 1988*	1/2 of your pension in payment, based only on membership from 6 April 1988*	1/2 of your pension in payment, based only on membership from 6 April 1988*	1/2 of your notional upper tier ill-health retirement pension at date of leaving based only on membership from 6 April 1988*
	Short-term pension payable at rate of your pensionable pay for the first 6 months	Short-term pension payable at rate of member's pension paid for first 3 months or 6 months if there is at least one dependent child	No short-term pension	No short-term pension

(continued)

| Children's pension** | 1/2 of your notional upper tier ill-health retirement pension for 1 child
1/2 shared equally if 2 or more | 1/4 of your pension for 1 child
1/2 shared equally if 2 or more | 1/4 of your pension for 1 child
1/2 shared equally if 2 or more | 1/2 of your notional upper tier ill-health retirement pension for 1 child
1/2 shared equally if 2 or more |

1998 Section

Benefit	Death in membership (with at least 2 years membership)	Death after retirement	Death with deferred pension	Death within 12 months of leaving membership if benefits remain in Scheme
Lump sum	2 × annual pensionable pay or average uprated earnings for Practitioners ***	The lesser of 5 × pension less pension already paid or 2 × pay less any retirement lump sum	3 × pension payable if member had retired on date of death	3 × annual pension the member would have received had they retired on the date of death
Adult dependant's pension	37.5% of your notional upper tier ill-health retirement pension Short-term pension payable at rate of your pensionable pay for the first 6 months	37.5% of your pension in payment* Short-term pension payable at rate of member's pension paid for first 3 months or 6 months if there is at least one dependent child	37.5% of your pension at the date of death* No short-term pension	37.5% of your notional upper tier ill-health retirement pension at date of leaving No short-term pension
Children's pension**	18.75% of your notional upper tier ill-health retirement pension for 1 child 37.5% shared equally if 2 or more	18.75% of your pension for 1 child 37.5% shared equally if 2 or more	18.75% of your pension for 1 child 37.5% shared equally if 2 or more	18.75% of your notional upper tier ill-health retirement pension for 1 child 37.5% shared equally if 2 or more

* These benefits may be higher if you have purchased Additional Survivor Penson cover for your dependants.

** Higher rates may be payable if there is no survivors pension payable.

*** A death gratuity lump sum is payable for members with less than 2 years membership.

MONEY PURCHASE ADDITIONAL VOLUNTARY CONTRIBUTIONS (MPAVCs)

There is available, through the NHS, a scheme of MPAVCs with Standard Life. Given the benefits that the NHS scheme provides, advice needs to be taken before investing in MPAVCs as the return on the investment is not likely to equate to that of the AP scheme. However, there are a number of situations where this scheme may be of interest to a dentist.

➤ Where a dentist wants to retire at an earlier age allowed under the NHS scheme the option of MPAVCs could provide a pension at that earlier age.
➤ Where a dentist has had a career break from the NHS, the NHS pension may be reduced as a result. MPAVCs can provide for an AP.
➤ Where a dentist has taken on a larger amount of private dentistry they may want to maximise their pension by paying MPAVCs.

In addition to MPAVCs the dentist may invest in private pensions outside of the NHS scheme, and given the amount that un-incorporated dentists pay in tax there are clear benefits to investing in pensions. The tax savings at 40% can be significant, and for those earning in excess of £100,000 there are possible savings of 60% to be made (see earlier notes regarding income tax in Chapter 10).

In Chapter 6 we looked at the benefits of the tax savings that can be obtained by transferring the practice premises to a SIPP, where there were no borrowings secured on the property. It is unlikely that a lot of dentists will be in that position and will be unable to effect such a transfer until the levels of borrowings are reduced significantly. In those cases the payment of contributions to a SIPP over a number of years, in order to build up a fund to purchase the practice premises from the dentist, could be the aim.

Although there are significant tax advantages to paying pension contributions there are two reasons for a dentist not to do so.

➤ Where the dentist already has significant pension funds that are likely to produce a substantial pension on retirement that may be subject to higher rates of tax post retirement. In this case the tax benefit of paying the contribution will be offset against the tax charge on the eventual pension, and, depending upon the number of years the dentist survives, may result in a net tax charge.
➤ Where the dentist is not settled in their plans for the future. If an emigration is likely or possible in the future it would not be in the dentist's interest to have their capital tied up in funds which they are unable to access until the age of 55. In those cases the provision for retirement should be done by way of deposit-based savings, which could be accessed if needed, or invested in a pension as a lump sum if they decided to remain in the UK.

DEATH AND SICKNESS BENEFITS

The NHSPS effectively insures the dentist against loss of earnings through death or sickness. If a dentist dies while a member of the scheme a lump-sum gratuity is paid to the spouse and children's pensions become payable (see Table 11.3).

The death gratuity is an insurance cover for which the dentist is covered during his or her period in the NHSPS. This is a tax-free lump sum equal to twice the annual pensionable pay. This is paid direct to the dentist's spouse or otherwise direct to his or her estate.

Upon the death of a dentist a continuing pension will be paid to the widow or widower or qualifying partner. These benefits become due six months after the dentist's death. For those six months, a short-term pension equal to the actual rate of the dentist's pensionable remuneration at the date of death is payable.

Where an NHSPS member is obliged to retire on grounds of ill health, an enhanced pensionable lump sum will be payable in most cases. Where a dentist retires on health grounds, full credit is given for the added years or AP being purchased, although these will not have been fully paid up.

LEAVING THE SCHEME

Where a dentist leaves the pension scheme, for whatever reason, with less than two years' service, a refund of contributions can be claimed unless the dentist is over the age of 60. This should be avoided because the pension scheme membership benefits are lost and the refund suffers income tax and National Insurance.

If the service has lasted over two years, then a refund cannot be taken but accrued benefits can be left in the scheme or transferred out. Careful consideration should be given to all these options, and specialist advice should be sought.

VOLUNTARY EARLY RETIREMENT

Since 1995 it has been possible for dentists to opt for voluntary early retirement after their fiftieth birthday (fifty-fifth birthday for those dentists joining the scheme after April 2008), and at the same time attract a pension and lump-sum benefit. Before 1995 those benefits would have been held in abeyance until the dentist reached the age of 60.

The new scheme and the existing scheme will run in tandem, with dentists under the old scheme being able to retire five years earlier than those that joined the scheme after April 2008.

Where an early retirement is taken, the pension and the lump sum accrued to the date of retirement will be reduced actuarially to take into account payments commencing before the normal retirement age of 60 (65 for those who joined post April 2008).

Tables 11.4 and 11.5 show how much the dentist's pension and lump sum are reduced by if they choose to retire early. If they retire between the ages shown, the benefits payable will vary proportionately.

TABLE 11.4 1995 Scheme

Age	59	58	57	56	55	54	53	52	51	50
Pension	6%	11%	16%	20%	24%	28%	31%	35%	38%	40%
Lump sum	4%	7%	10%	13%	16%	19%	22%	24%	27%	29%

TABLE 11.5 2008 Scheme

Age	64	63	62	61	60	59	58	57	56	55
Pension	6%	12%	17%	22%	26%	31%	34%	38%	41%	44%

THE EARNINGS CAP

Up until April 2008, those dentists who joined the NHSPS after July 1989 had the amount of superannuable earnings, upon which their pension was to be based, capped. The consequence of this was to limit the amount of pension they were able to eventually receive.

The cap was applied on an annual basis and restricted the amount of earnings that were added to the CARE calculation each year to a maximum amount set by the NHS. The earnings cap for 2007/08 was £112,800.

In April 2008, the earnings cap was removed, except in the case of added years.

Although the cap has been removed with effect from 1 April 2008 service up to that date which is currently capped will remain so.

Useful publications, journals and websites

While this book can look at topical issues and highlight several areas which are of special interest to dentists, it cannot look at every single issue in detail, and given the passage of time some of the detail in this book will quickly become out of date.

Developments in dental finance tend to take place regularly and it is important to keep up to date with these changes. Therefore, it would be advisable to subscribe to one or more of the specialist dental journals which are regularly published.

Periodicals

➤ *The British Dental Journal*, published by the BDA. This magazine focuses predominately on dental procedures but does deal with management and finance issues occasionally.
➤ *Dentistry/Private Dentistry*, published by FMC. These magazines regularly have articles on finance and management issues.
➤ *The Dentist*, published by George Warner Publications. This magazine has regular articles on finance and management issues.

Digest

➤ *Acting for Dentists*, published by CCH Wolters Kluwer. This digest is published to give accountants in practice a brief insight into dental finance, and will be of interest to those who wish to further expand upon their financial knowledge.

Books

➤ *Dentists: An Industry Accounting and Auditing Guide*, published by CCH Wolters Kluwer. This book has been published to give accountants in practice a detailed insight into dental finance, and will be of interest to those who wish to further expand upon their financial knowledge.

Internet newsletters and e-zines

➤ *Breathe Business E-zine*, published by Breathe Business Group, a business coaching organisation specifically advising dentists; see website details below.
➤ *The Confidence Club E-zine*, published by Chris Barrow, who is also a business coach specifically advising dentists; see website details below.

Both of the above e-zines provide useful tips on managing and marketing a dental practice.

Websites

The following websites can provide a lot of the detail necessary to maintain a detailed knowledge of dental finance.

➤ *NHS Business Services Authority Dental Services*. This website provides all the details needed to claim for all payments due under the General Dental Services Statement of Financial Entitlements, and can be found at: www. nhsbsa.nhs.uk/dental.
➤ *The British Dental Association*. This website provides a lot of useful information for dentists in practice which members of the association can access at: www.bda.org.
➤ *The Department of Health Dentistry and Dental Services Team*. This website works to support the NHS, the dental care professions and other stakeholders to maximise oral health, improve NHS dental services and promote high-quality dentistry. The latest dental policy publications, guidance documents, events and news can be found on this site at: www. dh.gov.uk/en/Healthcare/Primarycare/Dental/index.htm.
➤ *The NHS Dental Commissioning and Contract Monitoring Department*. This website provides details of the rules under which PCTs evaluate dentistry services, and can be found at: www.primarycarecontracting.nhs.uk/163. php.
➤ *Department of Health Chief Dental Officer*. This section of the website provides details of the latest dental policy publications, guidance documents and consultations and can be found at: www.dh.gov.uk/en/ Aboutus/Chiefprofessionalofficers/Chiefdentalofficer/index.htm.
➤ *The Breathe Business Group*. This website provides details of the services

this group provides to dentists in practice and can be found at: www.nowbreathe.co.uk.

➤ *Chris Barrow.* This site provides details of the services which Chris Barrow provides to dentists in practice and can be found at: www.coachbarrow.com.

Specimen Dental Partnership Accounts

This Appendix sets out a form of accounts similar to that which is generally used by accounting firms specialising in dental accounting.

The accounts are for a five-principal expense-sharing practice, with three associates and two VDPs. The practice is a mixed practice, in that neither the NHS nor private income exceeds 80% of the total practice income. The principals jointly hold a freehold property and hold a lease on some adjacent property.

The appendix is mainly intended to set out a recommended form of accounts and for that reason no figures are illustrated.

TABLE A Proforma Dental Practice Accounts

A's Dental Practice
Income and Expenditure Account for the year to 31 March 200x

		200x		200y	
		£	£	£	£
Income	(see below)				
NHS fees		0		0	
Private fees		0		0	
			0		0
Other income	(see below)		0		0
Total income			0		0
Expenses	(see below)				
Practice expenses		0		0	
Employment costs		0		0	
Establishment costs		0		0	
Repairs and maintenance		0		0	
General administrative expenses		0		0	
Financial charges		0		0	
Depreciation charges		0		0	
			0		0
Interest payable	(see below)		0		0
Net income			0		0

Allocation of practice profits

	Mr A	Mr B	Mr C	Mr D	Mr E
NHS fee income	0	0	0	0	0
Private & insured fees	0	0	0	0	0
Other income	0	0	0	0	0
	0	0	0	0	0
Less:					
Laboratory fees	0	0	0	0	0
Wages and salaries	0	0	0	0	0
Hygienists' costs	0	0	0	0	0
Subscriptions	0	0	0	0	0
Motor expenses	0	0	0	0	0
Interest payable	0	0	0	0	0
	0	0	0	0	0
Balance of practice costs	0	0	0	0	0
Net income	0	0	0	0	0

A's Dental Practice
Income and Expenditure Account for the year to 31 March 200x

	200x £	200y £
NHS fees		
Dental Practice Board – Principal	0	0
Dental Practice Board – Associate	0	0
	0	0
Private fees		
Private and insured fees – Principal	0	0
Private and insured fees – Associate	0	0
	0	0
Other income		
Vocational Training Grant	0	0
Rates reimbursement	0	0
Bank interest receivable	0	0
VDP reimbursement	0	0
	0	0
Practice expenses		
Materials	0	0
Laboratory fees	0	0
Payments to associates	0	0
Hygienists' costs	0	0
	0	0
Employment costs		
Wages and salaries	0	0
Recruitment costs	0	0
Staff training	0	0
VDP salary	0	0
	0	0
Establishment costs		
Rates and water	0	0
Light, heat and power	0	0
Use of home as office	0	0
Clinical waste	0	0
	0	0
Repairs and maintenance		
Repairs and maintenance	0	0
Equipment repairs and renewals	0	0
	0	0

A's Dental Practice
Income and Expenditure Account for the year to 31 March 200x

	200x	200y
	£	£
General administrative expenses		
Telephone	0	0
Printing, postage and stationery	0	0
Subscriptions	0	0
Equipment leasing	0	0
Sundry expenses	0	0
Insurance	0	0
Motor expenses	0	0
Advertising	0	0
Accountancy	0	0
Legal and professional fees	0	0
	0	0
Finance charges		
Bank charges	0	0
Credit card charges	0	0
	0	0
Depreciation charges		
Depreciation of plant and machinery	0	0
Depreciation of fixtures and fittings	0	0
Depreciation of motor vehicles	0	0
Depreciation of office equipment	0	0
	0	0
Interest payable	0	0
Bank loan interest	0	0
Hire purchase interest	0	0
Interest on overdrawn balance	0	0
	0	0

A's Dental Practice
Mr A's Income and Expenditure Account for the year to 31 March 200x

		200x		200y	
		£	£	£	£
Income	(see below)				
NHS fees		0		0	
Private fees		0		0	
			0		0
Other income	(see below)		0		0
Total income			0		0
Expenses	(see below)				
Practice expenses		0		0	
Employment costs		0		0	
Establishment costs		0		0	
Repairs and maintenance		0		0	
General administrative expenses		0		0	
Financial charges		0		0	
Depreciation charges		0		0	
			0		0
Interest payable	(see below)		0		0
Net income			0		0

A's Dental Practice
Mr B's Income and Expenditure Account for the year to 31 March 200x

		200x		200y	
		£	£	£	£
Income	(see below)				
NHS fees		0		0	
Private fees		0		0	
			0		0
Other income	(see below)		0		0
Total income			0		0
Expenses	(see below)				
Practice expenses		0		0	
Employment costs		0		0	
Establishment costs		0		0	
Repairs and maintenance		0		0	
General administrative expenses		0		0	
Financial charges		0		0	
Depreciation charges		0		0	
			0		0
Interest payable	(see below)		0		0
Net income			0		0

A's Dental Practice

Mr C's Income and Expenditure Account for the year to 31 March 200x

		200x		200y	
		£	£	£	£
Income	(see below)				
NHS fees		0		0	
Private fees		0		0	
			0		0
Other income	(see below)		0		0
Total income			0		0
Expenses	(see below)				
Practice expenses		0		0	
Employment costs		0		0	
Establishment costs		0		0	
Repairs and maintenance		0		0	
General administrative expenses		0		0	
Financial charges		0		0	
Depreciation charges		0		0	
			0		0
Interest payable	(see below)		0		0
Net income			0		0

A's Dental Practice
Mr D's Income and Expenditure Account for the year to 31 March 200x

		200x		200y	
		£	£	£	£
Income	(see below)				
NHS fees		0		0	
Private fees		0		0	
			0		0
Other income	(see below)		0		0
Total income			0		0
Expenses	(see below)				
Practice expenses		0		0	
Employment costs		0		0	
Establishment costs		0		0	
Repairs and maintenance		0		0	
General administrative expenses		0		0	
Financial charges		0		0	
Depreciation charges		0		0	
			0		0
Interest payable	(see below)		0		0
Net income			0		0

A's Dental Practice
Mr E's Income and Expenditure Account for the year to 31 March 200x

		200x		200y	
		£	£	£	£
Income	(see below)				
NHS fees		0		0	
Private fees		0		0	
			0		0
Other income	(see below)		0		0
Total income			0		0
Expenses	(see below)				
Practice expenses		0		0	
Employment costs		0		0	
Establishment costs		0		0	
Repairs and maintenance		0		0	
General administrative expenses		0		0	
Financial charges		0		0	
Depreciation charges		0		0	
			0		0
Interest payable	(see below)		0		0
Net income			0		0

A's Dental Practice
Balance Sheet as at 31 March 200x

	Note	200x £	£	200y £	£
Fixed assets					
Tangible assets	2		0		0
Current assets					
Stocks	4	0		0	
Debtors	5	0		0	
Cash at bank and in hand		0		0	
		0		0	
Current liabilities	6	0		0	
Net current liabilities			0		0
Net assets			0		0
Financed by					
Capital accounts	3		0		0
Current accounts	3		0		0
			0		0

A's Dental Practice
Notes to the accounts for the year ended 31 March 200x

1 ACCOUNTING POLICIES

Basis of Preparation
The accounts have been prepared under the historical cost convention.

Turnover
Turnover represents the invoiced value of fees, net of VAT where applicable, except in respect of service contracts where turnover is recognised when the right to consideration is obtained.

Depreciation
Depreciation is provided on tangible fixed assets so as to write off the cost or valuation, less any estimated residual value, over their expected useful economic life as follows:

Plant and machinery	15% reducing balance
Fixtures and fittings	15% reducing balance
Motor vehicles	25% reducing balance
Computer equipment	15% reducing balance

Stock
Stock is valued at the lower of cost and net realisable value, after due regard for obsolete and slow moving stocks. Net realisable value is based on selling price less anticipated costs to completion and selling costs.

Hire purchase and finance lease contracts
Assets held under finance leases, which are leases where substantially all the risks and rewards of ownership of the asset have passed to the business, are capitalised in the balance sheet and are depreciated over their useful lives. The capital elements of future obligations under the leases are included as liabilities in the balance sheet.The interest element of the rental obligation is charged to the profit and loss account over the period of the lease and represents a constant proportion of the balance of capital repayments outstanding.

Assets acquired under instalment finance agreements are treated as tangible fixed assets and depreciation is provided accordingly. The capital element of future finance payments is included within creditors. Finance charges are allocated to accounting periods over the length of the contract.

A's Dental Practice

Notes to the accounts for the year ended 31 March 200x

2 Tangible fixed assets	Goodwill purchased	Freehold property	Improvements to leasehold property	Equipment
	£	£	£	£
Cost				
As at 1 April 200y	0	0	0	0
Additions	0	0	0	0
As at 31 March 200x	0	0	0	0
Depreciation				
As at 1 April 200y	0	0	0	0
Charge for the year	0	0	0	0
As at 31 March 200x	0	0	0	0
Net book value				
As at 31 March 200x	0	0	0	0
As at 31 March 200y	0	0	0	0

	Fixtures and fittings	Motor vehicles	Office equipment	Total
	£	£	£	£
Cost				
As at 1 April 200y	0	0	0	0
Additions	0	0	0	0
As at 31 March 200x	0	0	0	0
Depreciation				
As at 1 April 200y	0	0	0	0
Charge for the year	0	0	0	0
As at 31 March 200x	0	0	0	0
Net book value				
As at 31 March 200x	0	0	0	0
As at 31 March 200y	0	0	0	0

A's Dental Practice
Notes to the accounts for the year ended 31 March 200x

3 Capital and current accounts

Capital account

	Mr A	Mr B	Mr C	Mr D	Mr E	Total
Freehold property	0	0	0	0	0	0
	0	0	0	0	0	0
Less: long-term loan	0	0	0	0	0	0
Net Equity	0	0	0	0	0	0

Current account

	Mr A	Mr B	Mr C	Mr D	Mr E	Total
As at 1 April 200y	0	0	0	0	0	0
Capital introduced	0	0	0	0	0	0
Profit	0	0	0	0	0	0
	0	0	0	0	0	0
Drawings	0	0	0	0	0	0
Superannuation	0	0	0	0	0	0
Taxation	0	0	0	0	0	0
	0	0	0	0	0	0
As at 31 March 200x	0	0	0	0	0	0

A's Dental Practice
Notes to the accounts for the year ended 31 March 200x

4 Stocks and work in progress	200x	200y
	£	£
Stocks	0	0

5 Debtors		
Trade debtors	0	0

6 Current liabilities		
Bank loans	0	0
Trade creditors	0	0
Obligations under hire purchase and finance leases	0	0
	0	0

7 Drawings analysis

	Mr A	Mr B	Mr C	Mr D	Mr E	Total
April	0	0	0	0	0	0
May	0	0	0	0	0	0
June	0	0	0	0	0	0
July	0	0	0	0	0	0
August	0	0	0	0	0	0
September	0	0	0	0	0	0
October	0	0	0	0	0	0
November	0	0	0	0	0	0
December	0	0	0	0	0	0
January	0	0	0	0	0	0
February	0	0	0	0	0	0
March	0	0	0	0	0	0
Other drawings	0	0	0	0	0	0
Private expenses	0	0	0	0	0	0
Insurances	0	0	0	0	0	0
	0	0	0	0	0	0

A's Dental Practice

Notes to the accounts for the year ended 31 March 200x

8 Analysis of associates' contributions

	Mr P	Mr Q	Mr R
	£	£	£
Dental Practice Board	0	0	0
Private and insured fees	0	0	0
	0	0	0
Less:			
Laboratory fees	0	0	0
Hygienists' costs	0	0	0
	0	0	0
Contribution to practice overheads	0	0	0

Example of tax savings on incorporation

Mr Dentist
Tax Liability
Five year summary

Assumptions
Tax/NIC Rates Remain as 2009/10
Incorporate end of March 2009
Year end is March

Option One – Remain as a sole trader

	Year 1	Year 2	Year 3	Year 4	Year 5	Total
Personal tax	33 669	33 669	33 669	33 669	33 669	168 344

Option Two – Incorporation

	Year 1	Year 2	Year 3	Year 4	Year 5	Total
Capital Gains tax	25 682					25 682
Corporation tax	20 743	20 743	20 743	20 743	20 743	103 715
Personal tax	–	–	–	–	–	–
Total tax	46 425	20 743	20 743	20 743	20 743	129 397
Tax savings on incorporation	**12 756**	**12 926**	**12 926**	**12 926**	**12 926**	**38 947**

Retained profits in the company

	Year 1	Year 2	Year 3	Year 4	Year 5	Total
Goodwill owing to Director	275 000	–	–	–	–	275 000
Profits	100 000	100 000	100 000	100 000	100 000	500 000
Less: corporation tax (above)	(20 743)	(20 743)	(20 743)	(20 743)	(20 743)	(103 715)
Money drawn	(92 013)	(66 331)	(66 331)	(66 331)	(66 331)	(357 337)
Remaining in company	262 244	12 926	12 926	12 926	12 926	313 948

(see notes following page)

1. Gross income per the accounts, say £398,550 @ 69% = £275,000 goodwill.

2. Annual earnings per the accounts £100,000.

3. Drawings calculated at £66,331 being the maximum that could be taken by a self-employed person earning £100,000 before tax.

4. Further savings could be made by paying dividends to a spouse.

5. After five years £38,947 tax saved, a further £48,042 could be saved before the director's loan runs out.

6. Cash could be invested in pensions further reducing the tax payable by the company.

7. Further savings may be possible as there may be allowable deductions for goodwill, depending when it was bought or created.

8. Further savings can be made by reducing the level of drawings taken from the business.

CAPITAL GAINS TAX

Goodwill	275 000
Entreprenerial relief (4/9)	(122 222)
Taxable gain	152 778
Less: annual exemption	(10 100)
Chargeable	142 678
Charged at 18%	**25 682**
Effective rate	**9.34%**

DRAWINGS FROM COMPANY

	Year 1	Year 2	Year 3	Year 4	Year 5	Total
Salary	5715	5715	5715	5715	5715	28575
Net Dividends	34344	34344	34344	34344	34344	171720
Draw-down on loan account (see below)	72265	26272	26272	26272	26272	177353
Additional dividends					–	–
Tax on goodwill/additional dividends	(25682)					– 25682
Total drawings	**66331**	**66331**	**66331**	**66331**	**66331**	**351966**

Director's loan account

Goodwill due from company	275000					
Year 1	(72265)					
Year 2	(26272)					
Year 3	(26272)					
Year 4	(26272)					
Year 5	(26272)					
	97647					

Mr Dentist
Year ended 31 March 2010

Sole trader

Earnings										100 000
Income tax:	1	×	6 475	=	6 475	@	0%	=		0
	1	×	37 400	=	37 400	@	20%	=		7 480
					56 125	@	40%	=		22 450
					100 000					29 930
Class 2 NIC	1	×	52	×	2.40			=		125
Class 4 NIC	1	×	5 715			@	0%	=		0
	1	×	38 160			@	8%	=		3 053
	1	×	56 125			@	1%	=		561
			100 000							3 614
Total tax and NIC liability										£33 669

Company

Profits						100 000
Employer's NIC						0
Employee's NIC						0
Income tax on salary of		£5 715				0
Corporation tax:	Profits	100 000				
	Less: Salaries	(5 715)				
	Less: Employers NIC	0				
	Taxable profits	94 285				
		94 285	@	22%	=	20 743
		0	@	32.50%	=	0
		0	@	30%	=	0
Total tax and NIC liability						£20 743
						£12 926

Mr Dentist
Year ended 31 March 2011

Sole trader

Earnings									100 000
Income tax:	1	×	6 475	=	6 475	@	0%	=	0
	1	×	37 400	=	37 400	@	20%	=	7 480
					56 125	@	40%	=	22 450
					100 000				29 930
Class 2 NIC	1	×	52	×	2.40			=	125
Class 4 NIC	1	×	5 715			@	0%	=	0
	1	×	38 160			@	8%	=	3 053
	1	×	56 125			@	1%	=	561
			100 000						3 614
Total tax and NIC liability									£33 669

Company

Profits						100 000
Employer's NIC						0
Employee's NIC						0
Income tax on salary of	£5 715					0
Corporation tax:	Profits	100 000				
	Less: Salaries	(5 715)				
	Less: Employers NIC	0				
	Taxable profits	94 285				
		94 285	@	22%	=	20 743
		0	@	32.50%	=	0
		0	@	30%	=	0
Total tax and NIC liability						£20 743
						£12 926

Mr Dentist
Year ended 31 March 2012

Sole trader

Earnings								100 000
Income tax:	1 ×	6 475	=	6 475	@	0%	=	0
	1 ×	37 400	=	37 400	@	20%	=	7 480
				56 125	@	40%	=	22 450
				100 000				29 930
Class 2 NIC	1 ×	52 ×	2.40				=	125
Class 4 NIC	1 ×	5 715			@	0%	=	0
	1 ×	38 160			@	8%	=	3 053
	1 ×	56 125			@	1%	=	561
		100 000						3 614
Total tax and NIC liability								£33 669

Company

Profits						100 000
Employer's NIC						0
Employee's NIC						0
Income tax on salary of	£5 715					0
Corporation tax:	Profits	100 000				
	Less: Salaries	(5 715)				
	Less: Employers NIC	0				
	Taxable profits	94 285				
		94 285	@	22%	=	20 743
		0	@	32.50%	=	0
		0	@	30%	=	0
Total tax and NIC liability						£20 743
						£12 926

Mr Dentist
Year ended 31 March 2013

Sole trader

Earnings								100 000
Income tax:	1 ×	6 475	=	6 475	@	0%	=	0
	1 ×	37 400	=	37 400	@	20%	=	7 480
				56 125	@	40%	=	22 450
				100 000				29 930
Class 2 NIC	1 ×	52	×	2.40			=	125
Class 4 NIC	1 ×	5 715			@	0%	=	0
	1 ×	38 160			@	8%	=	3 053
	1 ×	56 125			@	1%	=	561
		100 000						3 614
Total tax and NIC liability								£33 669

Company

Profits						100 000
Employer's NIC						0
Employee's NIC						0
Income tax on salary of		£5 715				0
Corporation tax:	Profits	100 000				
	Less: Salaries	(5 715)				
	Less: Employers NIC	0				
	Taxable profits	94 285				
		94 285	@	22%	=	20 743
		0	@	32.50%	=	0
		0	@	30%	=	0
Total tax and NIC liability						£20 743
						£12 926

Mr Dentist
Year ended 31 March 2014

Sole trader

Earnings									100 000
Income tax:	1 ×	6 475	=	6 475	@	0%	=		0
	1 ×	37 400	=	37 400	@	20%	=		7 480
				56 125	@	40%	=		22 450
				100 000					29 930
Class 2 NIC	1 ×	52	×	2.40			=		125
Class 4 NIC	1 ×	5 715			@	0%	=		0
	1 ×	38 160			@	8%	=		3 053
	1 ×	56 125			@	1%	=		561
		100 000							3 614
Total tax and NIC liability									£33 669

Company

Profits				100 000
Employer's NIC				0
Employee's NIC				0
Income tax on salary of	£5 715			0
Corporation tax:	Profits	100 000		
	Less: Salaries	(5 715)		
	Less: Employers NIC	0		
	Taxable profits	94 285		
		94 285 @	22% =	20 743
		0 @	32.50% =	0
		0 @	30% =	0
Total tax and NIC liability				£20 743
				£12 926

Index